The
HOUSE
of
BEAUTY

The
HOUSE
of
BEAUTY

Lessons from the
Image Industry

ARABELLE
SICARDI

W. W. Norton & Company

Independent Publishers Since 1923

Copyright © 2025 by Arabelle Sicardi

All rights reserved
Printed in the United States of America
First Edition

"House of Self" from *Mysteries of Small Houses: Poems* by Alice Notley, copyright © 1998 by Alice Notley. Used by permission of Penguin Books, an imprint of Penguin Publishing Group, a division of Penguin Random House LLC. All rights reserved.

Excerpt(s) from *Waiting for God* by Simone Weil, translated by Emma Craufurd, translation copyright 1951, renewed © 1979 by G. P. Putnam's Sons. Used by permission of G. P. Putnam's Sons, an imprint of Penguin Publishing Group, a division of Penguin Random House LLC. All rights reserved.

"Leaving the House" from *Dream of the Divided Field: Poems* by Yanyi, copyright © 2022 by Yanyi. Used by permission of The Wylie Agency LLC and by permission of One World, an imprint of Random House, a division of Penguin Random House LLC. All rights reserved.

For information about permission to reproduce selections from this book, write to Permissions, W. W. Norton & Company, Inc., 500 Fifth Avenue, New York, NY 10110

For information about special discounts for bulk purchases, please contact W. W. Norton Special Sales at specialsales@wwnorton.com or 800-233-4830

Manufacturing by Lakeside Book Company
Book design by The Cosmic Lion
Production manager: Lauren Abbate

ISBN 978-0-393-53162-6

W. W. Norton & Company, Inc., 500 Fifth Avenue, New York, NY 10110
www.wwnorton.com

W. W. Norton & Company Ltd., 15 Carlisle Street, London W1D 3BS

10 9 8 7 6 5 4 3 2 1

*it's quiet, & destructive: won't let you have
anything
No house in beauty or power
Just myself
I am*

—ALICE NOTLEY

CONTENTS

Introduction   1

Choose Your Own Disaster   10
Le Monstre   50
An Empire of Hair   85
Nailing the Landing   111
In Case of Emergency   136
How Beauty Survives a Plague   167
Near Death Is the Father of Beauty   188
The House of Beauty Is Burning   213

Heart Chest   223
Acknowledgments   241
Notes   247

The
HOUSE
of
BEAUTY

Introduction

When I tell you that beauty is a monster, I need you to know it is my favorite kind. As a young kid, I tied the idea of beauty into the depths of queer desire, and I knew that to find other girls beautiful seemed too dangerous to admit but too obvious to ignore. We are drawn to what frightens us, and sometimes to make ourselves safe from it we crawl into it, try to love it, try to become it—to go from the hunted to the hunter. I learned about beauty because finding something beautiful scared me and made me curious about the power beauty holds. For years, when a beautiful person even looked at me, I felt that the force of the desire I had to be them or love them was enough to make me want to dissolve into fog or turn to stone. Who doesn't want *that* power? Who isn't frightened by it?

Years into my obsession with beauty—the industry and the theory of it—and I have given the monster my whole life just to keep it around. Beauty connects me to the people I love. When the politics of the world burn me out, beauty rituals help keep me alive. It is a detour in desperate times, a place of refuge in a firefight. To say: "Wait, look at this good thing!" And to remember the possibility that bad things can still be otherwise.

Some years ago, I quit my high-profile job as the beauty editor for BuzzFeed, that colossal web giant that attracts over 200 million unique visitors a month. As a pop culture hub, the site traffics in beauty norms and standards, and sitting as its beauty editor often led to my own internal conflict. The resignation itself was very public; a post I had written criticizing Dove's recent campaign that forced women to categorize themselves as "average" or "beautiful" had been deleted by the editor-in-chief against the company's own editorial guidelines. I hadn't considered it a huge deal at first, even though the women editors on staff above me had approved the post, but then I realized that my post was a litmus test as to what critical thought I was permitted to express in my role. To have my voice silenced when I was the editor in charge of my topic was to say my work was not to be trusted, and if it could not be trusted, I had no business being there at all.

It was not that my approach was out of left field: I have made a name being critical of the beauty industry at large and was doing so before I was hired—it was part of why I was hired. I wrote about domestic violence, whitewashing, and chronic illness and how they are intertwined with beauty long before I was offered the job. I knew you could be critical of the beauty industry and still work within it.

But it was the erasure of conflict that I couldn't shake. My resignation was a result of what happens when advertisers sustain your full-time job. The fashion industry has critics, and it can afford that because taste is subjective, specific, and those

INTRODUCTION

brands do not pay the bills. But beauty is not fashion. There is a reason that beauty advertising lives on every other page of a magazine. The average reader cannot afford a Gucci trench coat, but splurge for a nice lipstick? That will do. Beauty is more democratic with its demands, which makes avoiding them far more futile. As the last beauty intern at *Teen Vogue*, I learned this many times over, and I learned it again when Gawker—and then the *New York Times*—reported on my deleted BuzzFeed post before I was aware of it being gone at all.

It is hard to live under the specter of what bodies are supposed to be. It gets even more complicated when you are getting paid to articulate those rules—when your job is to give voice to the rules at the same time that you have to make it seem like you're pushing against them. But whether you're for or against them, the rules are always there, and you're still living off what power you've sown. You can say there are monsters, but you can't say exactly who. When you do, you may turn around to see that you are standing by yourself in a room full of mirrors, wondering if you had ever been talking to anyone other than yourself at all. The dilemma's conceit might change, but the fundamental problems never do. I was learning how to better navigate them in a collapsing media landscape I had worked my entire life to be part of.

Now, of course, political beliefs surrounding bodies, belonging, and identity are central to the dangers people face in their daily lives. The power of beauty shapes how our bodies can move through the world. Ideas of beauty shape the laws that rule us and the ways they are enforced. Concepts of "otherness" drive government policy and party lines, street harassment violence and police brutality. Our looks have been weaponized against us, and the violence they often inspire has become a ticking time bomb that goes off every single day without fail, over and over again, and people are killed because of it—stolen from life and transformed into statistical tragedies, lucky to be reported on.

The French sociologist Pierre Bourdieu wrote that "the very lifestyle of the holders of power contributes to the power that makes it possible, because its true conditions of possibility remain unrecognized." This collection of essays is about the myriad ways that aesthetics and politics intertwine, shaping not only our definitions of ourselves and our relationship with others, but also the economy, our countries, our ethics, our technology, and our future. I explore how beauty fosters the conditions that have made resistance to abuse of power possible. It highlights communities of beauty lovers that create spaces where direct action and community organizing thrive. It is, as best I could write it, both sides of the knife.

This is not a rehabilitation of the beauty industry using feminist ideas. If you are hoping for a book to promise you that if we only innovate enough products, we will solve all our problems, or to try a juice cleanse and vibe it out—this is not the right book for you. Or perhaps it is *exactly* the right book. Let this book be an undoing—an incendiary device thrown at your notions that systemic injustices can be solved in our shopping carts. Because the burden of failures in this world will not be solved by the power of positive thinking, purchasing power, or calling our senators. Understanding the possibilities of beauty as a method of power

INTRODUCTION

requires much more from us, and from our relationships with each other. We need a better view of what it's capable of to survive it.

The motive that drove me to spend years of my life writing this wasn't the need to be right. I wanted to see if the misery beauty causes so many people has a floor—if the power it wields is something to hack and reformat. I wanted to get bigger than the hurt, the betrayal, the suspicion, the pressure, the shame it often summons. If I could get bigger, then I could trace its shape and find the roots like a gardener weeding in the sun. I live with a need to understand the harm being done to perfect strangers, to myself, to the people that I love, all in the name of beauty. And I am haunted by the compulsion to try to figure out how to prevent it from happening over and over again. This book is a container to share what I learned in the process, even if it has meant learning ways that I, too, caused harm.

The idea of beauty practices as self-care was first suggested by the medical field for high-stress professionals and then adopted by the civil rights movement to address the violence of white supremacy and a surveillance state. The Black Panthers created programming around health and wellness that included clinics and holistic practice to counteract these experiences in the late 1960s. The Black writer and organizer Audre Lorde then wrote in 1988 a declaration on the act of self-care from a Black perspective: "Caring for myself is not self-indulgence, it is self-preservation, and that is an act of political warfare." That ethos morphed over the years to the chant "Treat yourself," and it is whispered into the advertising we're inundated with at the checkout counter when we buy Epsom salts and face masks. It has been defanged from political commentary and stamped with a barcode. This book aims to peel the barcode off.

One of the founding moments of this book was the reaction of revulsion I experienced from that now-old beauty campaign challenging women to choose from two doorways to walk through, "average" or "beautiful," with pitying music accompanying anyone who walked through the first door. It posited that the only "good" way to feel as a woman was to feel beautiful, to feel anything but is to be a failure, someone lacking measure of worth. We deserve so many more options on how to experience ourselves, and transparency around the hypocrisy of a brand framing this social experiment when it also spends millions of dollars promoting skin bleach to women on the other side of the world. Not only did it set up a troubling dichotomy of cultural worth, but it framed beauty as the only worthwhile reward, while pretending it didn't prescribe the definition of beauty across the world—and then it created pressure against any critique pointing out what it was doing. In the end, it was a perfect campaign and situation to illustrate the complexities of the beauty industry at large. Walking away from a binary definition of beauty was an act of self-preservation: I would not lie about what beauty does to people to stay comfortable in my job.

Beauty is an industry that accommodates both the idea of agency regarding our bodies and the politics and expectations that bring us harm. It accommodates many choices as to how we present ourselves, but it is also the conduit for pressures that make these choices most aligned with white supremacy, colonialism, and transphobia.

I'm always thinking of the doorways that beauty opens—how

INTRODUCTION

to make them bigger, more surprising, more worthwhile to travel through or dismantle. Rebecca Solnit describes hope as "an ax you break down doors with in an emergency; because hope should shove you out the door, because it will take everything you have to steer the future away from endless war, from the annihilation of the earth's treasures and the grinding down of the poor and marginal." I'm buoyed by that visual and its urgent optimism, and the lesson that the thing that can save you is often at times dangerous, uncomfortable, and still no less essential to use. These essays aren't meant to serve as feel-good lessons on how to solve the problems of the world. Some of them are lesson plans on specific ways we've failed so far. I wrote out the doors that the world of beauty told me about; I traveled through them, undecided at first if the rooms they led to were worth salvaging or burning down. I made my choices, and my choices made me, in return. These pages are the results.

Italo Calvino writes in *Invisible Cities* that there are two ways to escape suffering. The first is easy: Accept the inferno and become such a part of it that you can no longer see it. This is something I'm good at and used to doing. I still get a thrill when I publish something in a magazine, still get flattered when I'm asked by brands for advice on campaigns or to collaborate with them. I still get free products "for consideration" by brands I know dirt on, and I cannot bring myself to throw them out. I am part of the system I critique, and I have been for more than half my life.

The second way to escape suffering, Calvino writes, is much riskier. It demands constant vigilance and apprehension: You must seek and learn to recognize who and what, in the midst of the inferno, are not inferno, then make them endure, give them space. Give them room to grow. Let the inferno burn itself out and build something new on the ashes. We need new ways of living in this world, new ways of understanding each other. New versions of what beauty, as a precursor of value, even has to mean. Wouldn't it be great if being beautiful didn't make or break your existence in the world? Wouldn't it be nice to not feel like desire was a hunt for self-worth?

I'm not seeking to redeem the idea of beauty as a source of freedom. I'm interested in understanding it as a tool of emergent strategy. How it can be an ax in an emergency or a tool to build a home—a tool of violence or creation in equal measure. This book is the handbook for how I've learned how to wield it, and what I found to be worth saving as the world burns—what is inferno, and what is worth walking through the flames, worth risking everything, anything, to save.

The beauty of the world is the mouth of a labyrinth. The unwary individual who on entering takes a few steps is soon unable to find the opening. Worn out, with nothing to eat or drink, in the dark, separated from his dear ones, and from everything he loves and is accustomed to, he walks on without knowing anything or hoping anything, incapable even of discovering whether he is really going forward or merely turning round on the same spot. But this affliction is as nothing compared with the danger threatening him. For if he does not lose courage, if he goes on walking, it is absolutely certain that he will finally arrive at the center of the labyrinth.

—SIMONE WEIL, *WAITING FOR GOD*

1

Choose Your Own Disaster

Consider this an archive of stories that are typically told separately from each other, stitched together to tell you the story of 70 percent of beauty products in the world. This is the labyrinth that makes them possible.

These narratives are based on actual events, dozens of interviews, nongovernmental organizational (NGO) reports, drone footage, satellite imagery, court documents, video recordings, WhatsApp group messages, correspondences in public archives, previous reporting from multinational media conglomerates and local newspapers, leaked documents from vigilante organizations, independent research groups, and government studies. The annotations will lead you to the reporting each narrative is based on.

Follow the numbers to go through the chapter. You can hop into the other narratives at certain points or stay to the end of the one you began in. You may find circuitous pathways, and each

CHOOSE YOUR OWN DISASTER

reading may offer you a different ending—there are several. The chaos here is intentional, explosive, and planned.

Feel free to explore. You'll probably only die once.

You can begin in three places: a cave in section [1] on page 12, a forest in section [14] on page 30, or YouTube in section [10] on page 26.

See you soon.

ONE

CAVE

You're in search of a mineral called mica. Your day begins in a cave dug with callused hands and a pick. None of this has changed in thousands of years and may not change for a thousand more. Excavation leads to a pearly bouquet of luster, hard-won chunks of purple, rose, silver, gray, moss, and a rainbow iridescent hue, enough to fill up a woven basket a few times over. The farther in the ground you go, the bigger the payday to be driven out of rocks and desperation.

If you're feeling comfortable in the dark today, go to section [2] on page 13.

If the darkness bothers you, go to section [3] on page 14.

TWO

The cave collapses in on you and your skull splits open like a coconut. You wouldn't have felt it coming before it was too late, if that helps you come to terms. You bleed out before your parents arrive. Luck never holds for long.

Another day you would have been fine, been able to collect enough to buy you time at school, eventually move to a town with a Children's Village where this cave would have been a past memory, not your present moment or your endless and infinite future. Not today though, and not tomorrow. That future's past now.

Maybe this was a panic attack, a fever dream. Maybe you're alive. Get back to work at section [3] on page 14.

Maybe you're dead. You want to know *why*—so go to section [4] on page 16.

THREE

Your neighbors are the ache in your back, other children in colorful clothes, and their mothers and fathers, too. Sometimes there is a hammer and scissors, but these are the only modern tools. The tray is cracked plastic and holds a kilogram. If you are in Madagascar, you fill it ten times a day on a good day and it brings you five ariary. If you are in India, you fill it once and it brings you three hundred. Either way it is just enough for a day's survival, never much more.

Given there have been nine deaths in the past month, and that there are *always at least* ten deaths each and every month, you are not so desperate as to offer to be the tenth to never leave what you call the "rat hole." The others around you descend meters to hammer for mica, but not you. Not yet, not now. So you stay close to the sun, able to crawl out a little faster than the others, even if it means you'll bring less home. You almost have enough to buy school supplies now, for the day when you can go back to school.

You sleep next to the tray with your siblings, so no one takes your work. There are other families here, other children you saw at school at one point or another. A two-year-old, a teenager. A mother with an infant strapped to her. Some do go home because they have them.

You wake up and split rice with your family. The manager of the mine gave you the bag as a gift. You later learn he told the reporters that when they came to watch you, but it will be taken out of your wages, because everything—including the scrap of fabric tied to a bare tree as shade—accrues debt. To the translator, you say, "He's never done that before. Don't believe his charity. Do you have some ariary?" The journalist declines. They are here to witness, not to save, which means a different thing entirely. They'll come here in guarded vans with translators and pity, and they'll put you on a stage and say thank you and leave, and everything will stay the same. This, you gather, is reporting.

After two months, the middlemen come to take the mica.

Go to section [4] on page 16.

THE HOUSE OF BEAUTY

FOUR

Mica is a mineral used in 70 percent of beauty products in the world. It lends itself to beauty because of its shimmer. But it has other qualities that make it useful to the other industries it is found in, from electronics to cars. It is flexible, elastic, chemically inert. Any electronic device from your computer to your phone to your microwave to your stove has mica. It is found in a lot of countries around the world, but most of it is mined in India, by children whose hands are small enough to fit in the crevices in the earth where mica is found. There is synthetic mica, but it represents only 10 percent of the market and is not expected to grow by more than 2 percent over the next ten years. Most of the mica mines in India are illegal spots on protected forest land. Satellite footage of the land shows pockmarked caves dotting the tree cover for miles, reminiscent of a porous nose, well excavated.

There are at least 22,000 children working in less than half of the mica belt. The numbers of deaths we know about are an underestimation, as most deaths are not reported to the police, due to them being related to illegal mining operations. Fewer than 10 percent are reported. The ones we know about are from word of mouth or witnessing. Some NGOs spend most of their time on the ground, gathering names of the lost and the dead that will never be publicly mourned, never be written about. Whatever few government surveys there have been, much of the industry's illegal operations go unchecked. Children who are reported dead have their deaths reworked to suit the story. An accident, a fall. One doctor wrote the cause of death for a woman to be falling from a two-story house. Odd, since her village has no two-story homes.

To meet one of the parents of the dead, go to section [5] on page 18.

To get back to work and meet the middlemen, go to section [6] on page 19.

FIVE

Pratap, the father of a deceased child, has chosen not to report his loss. He has chosen to accept payment rather than risk the end of the mining operations. "I was promised 100,000 rupees from the mine operator, but I have not received it yet." He waits, and he mourns. I don't wish it on you or anyone, least of all Pratap.

Eventually, a truck comes. Go to section [6] on page 19.

SIX

The sound of a truck can mean two things: an NGO or a boss. Today the gas-powered roar brings a man in a black jacket from the mica exporting company. He is the man who will pay you. We will call him Bakti.

Bakti pays 5 cents per kilo to you and the other families and then sells each kilo for 9 cents or more, doubling the value instantly. You don't know exactly how much more your work sells for once it leaves your hands, because you are not informed. Still, you know what it gets *you*, and that is what keeps you alive. Two months of your family's daily work gets you no more than $220, and half of that Bakti keeps to cover the loan he provided your mother that fed you while you waited for him to arrive.

There is no negotiation and no cutting him out of the deal. Neither your family nor any other has enough to afford the licenses required to be able to sell the mica as exporters yourself, nor the equipment or education to do so. "Administration" fees are 30 cents a kilo, which is most of a day's wages, not including the loans required to keep you from starving. It is not possible without another loan, and you don't need to know math very well to know that is on purpose.

All you can do is watch him pile bags of silver sheets and scrap of golden rocks onto the back of his truck and leave you in the dust that glitters silver, purple, gold.

To escape the glittered dust, go to section [7] on page 20.

Or go back to work, at section [2] on page 13. After all, a small world you know can be less heartbreaking that one you do not.

SEVEN

Import and export figures are public record, and the numbers speak more honestly than humans do. Once you look at the numbers, you will notice the large gap between what is legally cited as possible and what *is* possible. For mica exports from India, that gap is more than 100,000 tons.

The India Bureau of Mines cites the country produced 18,500 tons in 2013. The amount exported was 127,629 tons.

We are at the docks now in Kolkata along the eastern coast of India, 126 miles from the sea. This place is the oldest operating port still in India, built by the British East India Company, those old conquerors of everything and everybody. This place was initially built to ship Indians as indentured servants all over the world when slavery was formally abolished in 1833; exploitation just wore another name. For a time it was the second busiest port in the British Empire, second only to London, the beating heart of its colonization schemes. It's less important, now, but still very busy, just renamed after more than 150 years of operation. Today you're a crew member on a shipping vessel on a circuit around the world. The mica's been refined and sorted and bought and awaits its new master. You watch the machinery make quick work of the container boxes, the scale and ease of it a bit like a child playing with Legos. Loud but efficient, gigantic but graceful. The contents are neatly packaged, long having rendered a sea of dockworkers moot. It is only a matter of time until you are moot, too, but they still need a crew on these ships for now.

As the supply chain swells and clogs and port capacities across the planet reach their limits and stretch more, they need you more than they'd ever like to admit, actually. There are dozens of ships offshore waiting for people like you, and every minute and every day they wait for their crew they lose hundreds of thousands of dollars of revenue. The cost of shipping just one container has been going up exponentially as the climate crisis escalates—what once cost $2000 to ship may now cost ten times that, and the price gets higher as the temperature does. There are no signs of it going down. Your work is in demand and there are simply not enough people who want to do the job. This gig, this run, will pay you enough to pay your family's rent for six months. There is no "no" possible.

To board, go to section [8] on page 22. The ship will set sail soon.

To get on another ship, go to section [13] on page 29.

I'll meet you in either place, so you won't be alone.

EIGHT

There are more than 100,000 ships at sea carrying the products we use to live, but ask any of their crew what they're transporting for months at a time and most would not be able to tell you. If the containers on a cargo ship were lined up, they would stretch more than halfway around the planet, and yet most of their contents are known unknowns—registries are not the purview of their transporters unless they are flammable and have to be placed away from the sides of the ship so pirates can't explode them. You know as much as you need to know to survive and not much more. Despite the sheer volume of stuff, mysterious *stuff*, two-thirds of ship crews have no internet access at all. Depending on the vessel you're on, you might be able to stream videos thanks to Starlink—or you might be limited to three hours of slow connectivity a day.

Samuel Johnson wrote that "being in a ship is being in jail, with the chance of being drowned." He forgot some things— you might get kidnapped, too, every time you make the journey through the "high-risk" stretch of sea-highway that oil ships and 50 percent of all container ships are advised to take. There is a global task force responsible for monitoring counterpiracy routes, but given that it monitors a popular stretch that is 2,200 nautical miles long, the amount of people per mile is like two police cars traveling 15 miles an hour being responsible for keeping all of western Europe safe and sound.

Piracy is in many ways a theatrical transaction between onshore insurance companies and fishermen driven to gambling

CHOOSE YOUR OWN DISASTER

with fast boats and cheap guns, but the unfortunate part is that the life of your crew is part of the pool. If you are taken, pirates are better off keeping you alive with the boat, because the crew is leverage. Comfort yourself with that while you scan the ocean's horizon, an open and empty jaw.

The universe is gambling on you, your crew. The horizon must be perpetually monitored, and so to reach the end of it you have two choices, which aren't really choices at all.

Pick one:

Take the helm. Go to section [13] on page 29.

Go to the boom section [9] on page 24.

Safe travels.

NINE

YOUTUBE

This is where the story of how beauty is made starts for most of us.

Search for how eye shadow is made on YouTube. A video from Refinery29 will pop up as one of the most popular choices the algorithm provides. It opens with a jar of gold powder, cuts to it being poured neatly into another jar with other richly hued powders of pearl and bronze. It is then blended and added to a liquid base in a laboratory by a faceless gloved person and pressed neatly and efficiently into a jar, less than two minutes from the start. You do not know where any of these powders come from, or how long these workers are in the laboratory where their work is compressed into a staccato montage. Here is a powder. Here is a base. We know what we are doing. Are you not comforted?

Another video, by a cosmetic brand itself. Enter an all-glass building with the bird's-eye view of a drone, drifting into the room with swanlike grace. The building is the same as any other you'd drive by on a highway—an in-between corporate headquarters. You are delivered to a tub of the most resplendent, deep indigo blue. This is the deep and perfect blue that empires fought and men killed over, when it was rare and associated with gods and royalty. Now it is all yours. A tub big enough to swim in if you wanted, if you didn't follow the rules. Then a single drop of a mixing agent—then two. Sleek editing from that to lipstick tubes being machine-poured, to a tray of cheek tints and cream jars. So immediate! So precise! Then out again to a drone shot of the building from before. No voiceover. Just wordless automation and gloss. Labor erased and made magical.

To demystify some of that labor, go to section [11] on page 27.

To see how the magic of branding disguises it, go to section [10] on page 26.

To watch the next video, and then also the next video, and then also the video after that, until you are in an alternate galaxy outside of time, logic, and your body, flip to section [24] on page 48.

TEN

Packaging is a lot like poetry: It relies on sound as much as story, structure that holds a moment or lets it go. It can be extravagant like a libretto or sleekly minimal, a haiku in physical form. A texture dictates. Do you find pleasure in holding something matte or glossy? Do you prefer to twist or pull? Do you want to hear a click or a snap or a silent swivel? To name a product, to brand it into the cultural lexicon, is also a full-time job. It is sometimes the job of a fortunate poet.

The job of branding an item often happens at the same time a formula is perfected, the packaging chosen because of the texture or composition of a product. Airless packaging dispensers ensure that ingredients stay stable longer, tubes are good for travel and for customers to be able to control how much is dispensed. The wrong packaging and composition combination can cause the bottle to melt—it has happened before. Most often, packaging is dictated by customer fancy. People like glass bottles and transparency for aesthetic purposes even if it degrades ingredients much faster. Customers do not usually know that, but they do know what looks pretty enough to justify a splurge. Teams are compiled to brainstorm semiotics to build into copy—Is the theme *power*? Is it *resilience*? Is it glamour? Is glamour *done*? My rent has been paid by determining this stage in the story more than once.

Once the magic words are chosen, the packaging ordered to the factories, the shades polled and ranked in focus groups, then and only then does it go to market and make its way to you.

Go to section [12] on page 28.

ELEVEN

There are typically four pigments used to make a shade: white, red, yellow, black. Sometimes chemists mix too much black into a pigment to make it darker, but it makes the skin look bruised. Too much red or yellow makes you look jaundiced or gaunt. And zinc oxide, a pigment often used to add coverage and provide protection from the sun, can look ashy on darker skin.

In 2014, Black cosmetic chemist Balanda Atis began managing L'Oréal's Women of Color Lab, a team devoted to formulating for different ethnicities. Lupita Nyong'o had signed on to be the latest face for Lancôme, but the brand did not have a shade anywhere near compatible for her when she accepted the position. It was Atis and her team that created it, by adding an aquamarine blue.

Atis took on the shade expansion as a challenge from the head of L'Oréal's makeup division. They did not release her from her duties in the mascara department to focus on the work full-time. Instead, she and two others were welcome to use the lab outside of their work hours to create new shades to prove the merit of her work. After she was able to show them results two years later, they had her work on it full time.

In the PR blitz surrounding the newly expanded shade range, the story of shade expansion was centered on Atis, interviews pitched to frame her to be a success story paving the future for the company, rather than a dark-skinned Black woman who was chronically underresourced.

To see how a thing is packaged, go to section [10] on page 26.

TWELVE

You are some baby girl's first lipstick stolen or trash-picked or bought, either Ruby Woo at a MAC counter ($23, or three hours of a minimum-wage job,) or a Rimmel orange, $3.99, the last one in stock. You are worn through prom night, smeared off girls' brunch, crowning overpriced mimosas and wiped off with a drunk tongue. You are bitten off a nervous mouth on a dark walk home. Smeared onto the collarbone of a lover in the bar bathroom or more fervently in an empty corner. The floor is stickier than you.

You live all these lives in a week, a long night, ten days at the bottom of a tote bag and three months smothered into a diaper bag, a cold few days in an office drawer too. You are lost eventually in a jacket donated to Goodwill. She misses you but forgets you soon. She's got so many new ones to replace you with that are far less used.

This is a kind of happily after ever, if only because it is a normal one. You have some real options now since an end is only ever temporary after all.

Do you want to go into the forest? Go to section [14] on page 30.

Do you want to return to the sea? Go to section [8] on page 22.

Do you want to go back in time? Go to section [24] on page 48.

You could also see what's waiting at the end of the labyrinth. Go to chapter 2 on page 51.

THIRTEEN

After many years and ships slowing down because fuel costs have skyrocketed, the risks get harder to outrun. When the horizon becomes dotted with a fast armed boat and the dot becomes bigger, draws closer, it cannot be outrun by a vessel that takes three miles to turn. And when they board and hang you off the side of the boat with your balls in a vice for a few hours as they ransom you through 12 shell companies and two full-time staffed negotiators arguing over three different time zones, you will wish you had never fallen in love with the ocean.

And the stuff in the containers doesn't even matter then. The mysterious stuff is negligible. It could be people and it could be mica and it could be hospital beds and it doesn't matter as much as the need for it does, the money it represents. Stuff that isn't even yours to give. You are a minor player in the transaction, as a merchant ship crew member on an anonymous ship at sea, and you are—finally, mercifully—passed out, blood having rushed to your head and forcing your consciousness to collapse unto itself.

To survive this, go to section [9] on page 24.

To escape into another story (though be warned: you will come back to a ship and a door), go to section [14] on page 30.

FOURTEEN

FOREST

When you get down to the roots of it, the $50 billion industry of palm oil often hinges on finding an illiterate Indigenous person in a peatland forest to sign a paper that pledges their generational land to the government. It in turn rents that land to a company to burn, flood, log, and farm. The lawyer for Malaysia's Sarawak government describes the process as simple, even elegant, in a meeting with a would-be investor he doesn't know is a reporter.

"Where would you say a majority shareholder should come from?" asks the fake investor, real reporter.

"In the lowest rank we can find in a remote area, where they will not be distracted by clever advisors. We find some guys who are villagers, sign them for all this stuff, and you can't even reach them. Can you imagine, the villager comes to town, and you give them $10,000? He'll go back to the village and he'll be the one-eyed man who's king, in the land of the blind."

Malaysia and Indonesia are the primary exporters of palm oil. The governor of Sarawak seems to have a hand in transactions, and his government directs investors to the personal phones of his family members to further deals along.

A relative of the chief minister is the head of Ample Agro, a top palm oil company. Over tea another cousin, also in on the action, smiles and describes the Indigenous tenants as "squatters" on government property, never mind that it becomes government property only after they find someone for their bargain. You are on the other side of this bargain today.

If you believe in spirits, go to section [15] on page 32.

If you believe in money, go to section [16] on page 33.

FIFTEEN

You sell 100 acres to Dr. Biruté Galdikas, a leading authority on orangutans, for National Park conservation for $100 an acre. It's less than what you would get from a palm oil company, but it spares you nightmares that the *gaip* will come to curse you with disease for tearing down their homes. You've lived with those ancestral spirits walking through the village all your life—they exist here as much as you, their corpses never found, their lives transformed. Even if you haven't seen the *gaip* since you were a child, you feel they exist, and so they do. You felt them at your shoulders while you made the choice. And now, you don't have to watch the land your family has lived on burn in front of you, around you, for months.

That is, until the money runs out, and the palm oil company sends another truck to the slice of acreage you denied them.

To do the deal, go to section [16] on page 33.

To see how they deal with those who deny them land, go to section [22] on page 45.

SIXTEEN

Peat forest is a forest wetland created out of mille-feuille layers of dead things. It took millennia to form these ideal carbon stores, and in Indonesia and Malaysia it's usually thirteen feet deep. When the paper is signed, handing it over, a domino effect of destruction begins.

Bushmeat and forest fruit, vegetables, medicinal plants, firewood, and community plots are razed. When it is cleared the land is set on fire. Hundreds of miles are blanketed in black smoke. The peat is destroyed above and below the surface as the fires are lit, and the fires burn for months, impossible to rein in. It's called the "slash and burn" technique. After it's over, the mechanized plantation process attacks the soil, leading to the pollution of clean water sources.

In 1997, when the fires went out of control, the fumes drifted all the way to Kyoto, Japan, burning the eyes of UN conference goers gathered to discuss climate change. In 2015, the fires again were so bad, so viral, the smoke could be seen from space.

There is typically extraordinarily little compensation for this. Perhaps a few thousand dollars in a one-time deal when the businesses that take over the land could lease the land for thousands a hectare and get charged "administration" costs that are ongoing, courtesy of the government. The Indigenous submission is permanent, irrefutable surrender, and these land grabs affect women especially. In Indonesia, customary laws state that lands may be held by women or by men and women equally, but when they become formalized, the land is transferred to the male head of household. Community rights are erased, then biodiversity is lost as the forest is burned.

To learn what for, go to section [17] on page 35.

SEVENTEEN

Palm kernel oil is used to produce the emulsifiers and surfactants in beauty products. This means that it helps with moisturizing, texture, and the ability to foam. There are several dozen names and by-products of palm oil that are used, and it's not hard to find them in your products: hydrogenated palm oil is found in L'Oréal's Telescopic Mascara, Maybelline's Volum' Express Colossal Mascara, NARS Luminous Moisture Cream, and more. Saponified palm oil, a by-product made from palm oil, is found in most soap bases. The various disguises of palm oil are found across most beauty categories in skincare, suntan, and makeup products, from NARS to Sunday Riley to DHC to the Body Shop to Cetaphil.

Other versions of palm oil are used for soap, cooking fats, and margarine. The beauty industry uses only 2 percent of the global palm oil production, but it is found in 70 percent of beauty products.

The oil palm requires less water, less fertilizers, and less pesticides than other oil plants, and harvesting it takes up much less space and resources than alternative plant options. That much is simply the science of it. That does not mean our reliance on it or the exploitation along the chain of production is not disastrous or magnificent in scope. The exploitation of resources—and of people—is part of the very history of the plant itself. Oil palm is a nonnative plant to Indonesia, imported from West Africa by Dutch colonizers in 1848. Some historians say it was a warfare defense policy to supply food and revenue for importing European countries.

Since then, it has taken over land equivalent to 300 soccer fields every hour, every day.

To go to the farm, go to section [18] on page 37.

To go to the boardroom, go to section [19] on page 39.

To go in between, go to section [20] on page 41.

EIGHTEEN

You work for one of the world's largest palm oil companies, and they have locked your passport in their administrative office. You sleep on the floor of the plantation with no way to get home. They used to keep you in a shipping container, but the metal warmed up like an oven by midafternoon, and you didn't want to burn alive. You would rather sleep outdoors and see the stars. You used to be a fisherman under similarly shit conditions, but when you went to shore to ask for help you were guided by the police to a farm for a new start. You sleep under different stars but suffer the same problems, on land instead of at sea.

You're a long way from home, but home wouldn't have led to better work. Everyone speaks multiple languages since most everyone has been shipped in one way or another. You did try fleeing once, but the fee for smugglers to help you leave the area was more than you had saved up, so they drove you right back over, rendering the hours you walked an exercise in futility. On the drive back you realized you wouldn't have been able to find legal work elsewhere anyway. Your passport was held in storage by your employer. You were charged two months wages as a fee for wanting to leave. That was a few years ago now.

You try not to think too hard about the debts accrued in the process of survival, because you are afraid the despair would render you a ghost in your own body. It is easier to exist in small circuits of moments every day. Waking up early to watch the clouds. Counting the scars on your hands, gloveless most days and weathered with time. Moments spent rhyming in your head all the various words and languages you've learned so far from other workers. You know five different words for home. Three for travel. One day you'll learn three more. And sometimes you watch for visiting planets after dark in the sky and glints of light from binoculars—journalists or overseers?—on the horizon after noon.

To board the ship where the oil drams are placed to return to the sea from where you fled years ago, go to section [8] on page 22.

To become the person who watches, meters away on the edge of the plantation, go to section [20] on page 53.

NINETEEN

Patronage is a better word than bribery, because it is a longstanding relationship; one does not bribe but *patronize* for support. Plantations don't clear and plant the whole land at once. They constantly seek new land licenses and rotate crops every 25 years. Plantings occur continually. As such, they require constant support to make the licenses happen faster.

Plantation firms usually have a board of directors and senior advisers who were formerly in local and national government. In 2012, two former Ministers of Agriculture are respectively the director and commissioner of Bakrie Sumatera Plantations. The chairman of their parent company is also the chairman of one of the biggest political parties in Indonesia. As of 2009, Duta Palma, one of the largest companies, was 30 percent owned by the Indonesian military. Duta Palma is known to have one of the world's worst track records for illegal burning, having had their assets seized in several provinces. All this matters because you need such leverage to get things done.

There are all kinds of boardrooms in beauty. One would be the suppliers' suppliers—these plantation firms, which are powerful quasi-governmental companies. An endless parade of glass tables hanging over metal skylines and soaring profits. Inevitably most of the top 20 most powerful boardrooms in beauty are occupied by elderly white men—no surprise. Because despite beauty being for everybody, as of my writing, only four of the top 20 beauty brands are helmed by women, and two of them are white.

Let's eavesdrop on some conversations with the bigshots.

THE HOUSE OF BEAUTY

You can step into the lives of the Lauders or the Uihlein spouses (who own the packaging supergiant Uline) or a clean-beauty startup's boardroom. These meetings could be about any number of things, so here is a curated menu for you:

To fund the Republican National Convention with cardboard boxes, go to section [21] on page 44.

To expand a foundation shade range to match a celebrity spokesmodel, go to section [11] on page 27.

To hire an auditor team to survey the palm oil smallholders your company proudly buys from, go to section [20] on page 41.

TWENTY

Today you're undercover as part of a trio, and your jobs are that of a car mechanic/crossword puzzle fanatic, a fisherman, and a bird-watcher. You *love* puzzles—that cover isn't hard. After a morning multicountry call with researchers updating a satellite database of the land you're sitting on, you head out along a rutted road in Indonesia. You're surrounded for miles by the trees that the forest has been scalped to foster. The oversize fronds have juicy crowns of fruits. The air is thick with cigarette smoke and distant but looming fires. An hour into the journey the trees begin to form a vector of undoing; you've reached a part of the untamed land still being throttled into submission. The tree cover has gaps like broken teeth in a smile.

There's a smear of muddy orange in a cluster of trees you drive by; as it disappears in your rearview you neglect to hear the crack of a gun, but you see something crumble through the fronds toward the ground. Out of the trees you see humans emerge onto the road, armed with air guns. They are collecting a disoriented orangutan from the native habitat, one less witness to the destruction of its native home. In local Indonesian myth *orang hutan* means "people of the forest," who were deprived of language and banished for blaspheming. This feels sadly appropriate—better to be delivered to a sanctuary, however overcrowded, than burn alive in the deforestation or drown from the floods that follow. An orangutan has an encyclopedic memory of the forest—can recognize hundreds of fruiting and medicinal plants, the same kind humans use. Can use them just as well. Can memorize a forest for the trees, but the forest isn't theirs anymore. It is sad to see a memory outlast its fruit.

Your job is to make these situations happen a little less frequently, but it's also far beyond you, the person in the costume. You have so little individual power here you cannot even safely say who you are. A mechanic with a toolbox filled with another profession's tools: the second compartment stocked with a phone, a DSLR camera, a home-built drone.

You stop in the middle of a plantation and the would-be fisherman takes out a drone from a bait box to use to take updated photography of a plantation a few kilometers over. He is in reality updating all of the satellites responsible for examining deforestation all over Indonesia. When you first began the work, it felt inconsequential. Over time the weekly drives and data uploads have begun to feel like a prayer in a foxhole. Disparate GPS points yield folders compiled into a cascade of small apocalypses. The two of you have helped populate enough coordinates to document dozens of elephants dying, the illegal mills of the five largest palm oil conglomerates in the country, the bulk stations and refineries they use, the millions of hectares lost. In the 30 years since 1985, over half of Sumatra's forests have been lost, much of it caused by companies with all the right certifications, all the right promises. Those promises just happen to be made to people who both are on the company's board and were formerly on the government's payroll.

The fisherman switches the license plate out and you take out a crossword puzzle as the bird-watcher props up the hood. A farmer eventually stops to see if you need help, their truck filled with illegal fruit. You decline the help—you're waiting for a part, you see, before you can fix the truck. It will never arrive, but you don't need to tell him that to get what you came here for. The bird-watcher chats him up and you slowly record the names, locations, and jobs of everyone mentioned in the conversation into the empty spaces of the crossword puzzle. This is your real job. Finding out the small moving parts of the deforestation around you. The human ones.

Eventually the drone footage, the photos, the names, and places are all compiled into reports to send to faceless conglomerates to ask for accountability, for things to change for the people and animals in the forest. Sometimes it works. When it doesn't, you send the information to everyone else. The government first. The press second. Eventually you get people who care deeply. Just like the bird-watcher turned journalist, who is writing a book on all aspects of deforestation. Who knows? Maybe that will help.

To go to the farm, go to section [18] on page 37.

To see who watches *you*, do-gooder, go to section [22] on page 45.

TWENTY-ONE

This is a troll entry for the lawyers playing. Any brand that pays a lawyer knows not to donate money directly to a political party, and what executives and employees donate to in their spare time is on their own dime. As the Lauder company lawyers were so quick to point out regarding an employee letter asking for Ronald Lauder to be ousted, given his millions of dollars of contributions to Republican organizations over the years:

"Employees asked whether a single member of the Lauder family and our board represents the views of our company," the company said in a media statement. "The answer is no."

But the long shadow of their views is given depth and impact by the nature of their association with a company. Can you really say a company is utterly uninvolved? It is a farce to assume so. A million made by an act given to another act owes itself to the original sin itself. Even company presentations say as much. In a presentation for Mary Kay employees, this is pointed out: "If you are in business and are not involved in politics, then politics will run your business."

Anyway, go back to section [19] on page 39 and pick something else.

CHOOSE YOUR OWN DISASTER

TWENTY-TWO

It's a balmy 68 degrees at half past nine at night in late September. It's 2012. There are clouds in the sky but no rain, not yet. You're outside the capital of Honduras, Tegucigalpa, just south, a quick ride back home to anonymity and the chaos of a city and its sounds. You're waiting for a wedding party to clear out of a church. You have not been invited but you are there, an important guest to your circumstances—the host of your purpose for the night. You are looking for a man named Antonio. To pass the time, you consider the etymology of the name, a habit you picked up years ago, in similar circumstances, in other cities looking for other men, for reasons not dissimilar. Antonio is another form of Anthony, the name of a saint of the Franciscan order. Being a Catholic by birth and not by choice, you know these things, and you are grateful for the memories if not the faith you have put down. Saint Anthony was born and raised as a wealthy man in Portugal and died as a priest in Italy. He was devoted to the poor and the sick, known as the patron saint of lost things and the professor of miracles. His tongue and jaw and vocal cords were chosen as relics for veneration. When he was exhumed his body had turned to dust but not, according to accounts, his tongue. It looked as if it were still alive, wet, and pink and glistening.

You consider the church you are sitting across from, which shelters a man with his inherited name, also a guide to lost souls—or at least difficult ones, ones that placed him on the path to you. A guide to lost souls is the most graceful thing you can

THE HOUSE OF BEAUTY

call a lawyer, no? A guardian of another man's problems. Your man for tonight.

He comes out at 9:32 p.m. He's on the phone. You line him up in your sights and your clip empties briskly into his gut. You shoot him five times in staccato. It's messy, and they'll suspect more than one person because that's what you want. He falls clumsily down the steps of the church and you disappear into the night. This is what you were asked to do—end the life of a lawyer representing peasant farmers in a palm oil region in Honduras. One of 92 men killed in the past three years in Honduras alone for being the thing between a business and the land they want. Maybe his namesake will carry him home, you think distantly, neatly palming your gun.

That's not your job, though. Your job's done.

To wash the blood off, turn to section [23] on page 47.

CHOOSE YOUR OWN DISASTER

TWENTY-THREE

In a shampoo you're almost unimportant, the thirteenth player in an orchestra. Marketers pretend you're something else, give you a different name to suit the chorus—they want the hero ingredients to shine on their own. The main ingredients are the usual: silicone for shine and panthenol for elasticity, fiber actives for strength. It gestures to the idea the shampoo will prevent the inevitable breaks, which it won't, but it can offer hope, which is cheaper and more commonly sold. A legion of other fillers—sodium chloride for thickening, an essential sensorial experience for all who buy it to feel a little cleaner afterward. After all of them, eventually there's you. The chemists put you in because you're a cleansing agent and an emollient, you give the right experience, and you're consistent and cheaper than the other options.

You are privy to the best part of an overworked retail employee's day—their bubble bath after an early morning restock. You become a kid's evening bath after playing in the park. You become the soap that washes the oil off a baby duck after yet another oil spill, with donated mascara wands brushing them dry and fluffy. You're in someone's grandmother's tub of Palmer's body lotion she keeps at her bedside table and someone's aunt's vanity in the tiny jar of La Mer cream, unopened and untouched. You're in every product in all the top YouTubers most popular beauty reviews, ten million views and counting. Counting. Counting. Keep counting. That's it. You're everywhere now, riding high on every pixel, all the way to section [24] on page 48.

TWENTY-FOUR

Outside of time and space, there is always more content. Since 500 hours of videos are uploaded to YouTube every minute, the trip below is possible:

You're on your third hour watching videos vaguely related to beauty now. You've passed the influencer wave of beauty gurus loving and hating a new launch, past the reactionary troll videos of influencers throwing away products untouched, past them cutting them in half with a knife. Past the narrator-free ASMR videos of someone destroying a makeup palette and turning it into slime, past someone trying to dye their hair in someone else's kayak, past a vlog of state parks with rock quarries of quartz and mica minerals, into a new space entirely. The algorithm has rendered time into a neat accordion fold, collapsing laws of physics and logic just for you, just this once.

You hear the time change more than you know it—the quiet of no radio, no planes, no satellites, no drones, no cars, nothing with electrical charge outside of your skull for miles. There is a dull cacophony of a whole legion of bugs and birds and other creatures that you have blindly walked into, having sunk into the heat and the stink of life without a human touch. How does it feel to know you're watched not by a robot but by something that might eat you for a few hours' energy and warmth? You're walking around 105,000 years ago, 180 miles outside of Cape Town, South Africa. You're in a cave that smells like death, humid and sticky and warm.

This cave is later called Blombos. There are fresh corpses

buried with shells filled with melted ochre, glittered quartz, crumbled mica. It is one of the oldest burial grounds ever discovered, but it was also a beauty workshop before it became a graveyard. The people here formulated the first glitter cosmetic before *Homo sapiens* even evolved. In typical conversations about beauty, we often think of it as a commercial good. But the act of it is older than civilization. These corpses don't even have the same bones that we do, but they had vanity, and that links us across millennia. I could leave you here to watch this place grow wild until it's a modern landfill, a place where lipsticks die. But 105,000 years is a lot to live alone. So. Where do you want to go now? Be brave, stranger.

Board a ship at section 8 on page 22.

Become a spy at section 20 on page 41.

Become a poet at section 10 on page 26.

Or crash and proceed to the next chapter. No more fucking around.

2

Le Monstre

Every thirty seconds, a bottle of Chanel No. 5 is supposedly sold somewhere in the world. It has notes of bergamot, lemon, jasmine, amber, musk, and patchouli. It smells soapy, clean, and floral all at once. With 2023 revenue standing at more than $19 billion, Chanel has landed on the *Forbes* World's Most Valuable Brands List numerous times due in no small part to the perfume. As many brands floundered during the pandemic, Chanel raised its prices around 15 percent—and increased sales by double digits. The House of Chanel hadn't released their financials for over a century but began doing so in 2018 only to prove how well they're getting on. By photographic and historical association alone, No. 5 will continue to profit indefinitely from free endorsements by the likes of Marilyn Monroe. (In 1952, Monroe was asked by *Life* magazine, "What do you wear to bed?" Her giddy reply: "Chanel No. 5!") No. 5 was one of the first perfumes that ever used synthetic ingredients, and it changed the way women chose to smell. Since its debut, it has so dominated the perfume industry that it earned the nickname *le monstre*—it was, and remains, one of the best-selling beauty products ever sold.

Coco Chanel is a woman I fall asleep thinking about. This has been true for as long as I've known the rough summary of her life story: a designer of very expensive and very fine clothes, the name behind one of the best-selling perfumes of all time, the life of the party—especially if the party is Nazi. She was a Nazi collaborator as well as one of the most famous women in the world for the better part of two world wars. Any decent biography of her life acknowledges this fact about her, but it's rarely closely examined, and the House of Chanel strategically avoids acknowledging her history. The Chanel Beauty Salon in New York—decorated with references to her glamorous life with the names of her lovers, her hobbies, her success stories—has not a single reference to her Nazi beau, though it mentions her other lovers, their names neatly emblazoned on lockers right at the entrance.

It used to confuse me that Coco Chanel's association with Nazis didn't stop her from becoming hugely successful; now I realize she became successful because she so readily accepted fascism into every aspect of her life.

While she sided with the Nazis and slept and dined with one of their high-ranking officers, the Jewish people she found so distrustful kept her business alive, took over production, manufacturing, and advertising, and paid for the rest of her life. At one point they funded the French allied resistance with the money made using her name. I get lost in the possibilities of their mutual storyline. What if the Wertheimers had never funded her at all? What if they'd worked together rather than against each other, on opposite sides of the war?

It is easy to condemn her for her actions, and all those judgments would be fair. But thinking I could condescend to her ghost led me into her life in ways I never accounted for. It made me reconsider all the small, easy ways it's easy to be complicit in harm and the ways redemption can feel like a mirage. But I'm getting ahead of myself.

Coco Chanel was born Gabrielle Chanel in the summer of 1883. Her early days were spent with nuns in France and her family was unremarkable in all aspects but their poverty. Her mother, Jeanne, died in 1895, worn out from childbirth, poverty, and tuberculosis, when Coco was eleven. Her father, Albert, sent her siblings to work and loaded his three daughters onto a wagon to a hillside convent in Aubazine. From then on, she grew up as an orphan.

Being abandoned by her family and being born poor made Coco resentful of her lack in the world; as she grew, the anti-Semitic Catholic nuns became the target for her hatred. The scandal surrounding the Dreyfus affair was a thread of ideology she witnessed growing up. Beginning in 1894, it involved a Jewish captain in the French army being falsely accused, tried, and found guilty twice for passing military secrets to the Germans. Alfred Dreyfus was paraded in front of a crowd that shouted, "Death to the Jew!" The affair divided France into ley lines of anti-Semitic thought and nationalist arguments, with posters and newspapers and rallies everywhere for or against. It would shape Chanel's impressions of humanity in ways that would later influence her career and philanthropic pursuits. Anti-Semitism wasn't exceptional or radical at the time, and throughout her life she lived in a circle of people who shared her prejudice: well-educated men of wealth.

She left Aubazine at eighteen to attend school and become a shop girl in Moulins. She dated officers who took her to bars and thereby introduced her to the world of showgirls. And then she fell upwards in love with Étienne Balsan.

Balsan was the son of a wealthy fabric maker. He taught Coco horseracing, and in turn she became his second live-in mistress on an estate with horses and meticulously maintained gardens. Balsan was a very generous lover and patron, but most importantly he was useful for introductions. He led her to the man who would succeed him in Coco's line of lovers: his own best friend, Arthur Edward "Boy" Capel. Between Balsan and Capel, Chanel gained access to funding for the first steps of what would become her international empire. And so, in 1909, with Capel's blessing and bankroll, she opened a millinery shop out of the ground floor of Balsan's Paris apartment. The next year, she moved the shop to 21 rue Cambon, on a narrow street in the back of the Hôtel Ritz. It's since been replaced by an outpost of Fauré le Page, an old French arms-making firm for European courts that later turned to leather goods. The Chanel store is now down the block.

Coco rose to relevance during World War I for her demure version of charm: wool traveling suits, loose jersey gowns that were photographed in the pages of British and American *Vogue*. By 1915 to own at least one Chanel gown was a matter of course for wealthy women. *Harper's Bazaar* declared, "The woman who hasn't at least one Chanel is hopelessly out of fashion.... This season the name of Chanel is on the lips of every buyer." Customers were paying 7,000 francs (roughly US$3,600 today) for a gown and yet, that same year, the economy in Europe was to come crashing down. In Germany, a loaf of bread that cost thirteen cents in 1914 would have doubled in cost by 1919. By July 1918, instability was so high that German workers demanded to be paid their wages the day of. For most people, their lives were free-falling. Not so for Coco.

By 1920, she had already been a mistress to millionaires for more than a decade. She traveled around France and bought a house in Biarritz. After Capel died in a tragic motorcycle accident, Chanel entered a relationship with Hugh Grosvenor, Duke of Westminster, otherwise known as "Bendor," and one of the wealthiest men in the world. Bendor's anti-Semitism is well documented by history; he was a member of the Link, an anti-Semitic group. It was through Bendor that Chanel befriended Winston Churchill. Churchill wrote to his wife with admiration for Chanel the first year they became close: "She is very agreeable, a strong being fit to rule a man or an Empire." The trio rode horses together on Bendor's estate in the Scottish Highlands and dined together in his Bourdon House, a gem that still stands in Mayfair not far from her London salon. Her romantic and platonic friendships with these men made her much more than a designer of gowns and hats; they made her a nexus of power. When you have friends in high places, you can risk stooping very, very low. It is hard to feel the growing distress of the average European when you only dine with the most powerful men in Europe.

For a successful fashion figure to hobnob with political powerhouses is not unusual and has never been so; there's a running joke in the industry that fashion marries finance—and finance funds politics, after all. Chanel dated dukes and heirs to fortunes in the 1900s; in October 2018, the supermodel Karlie Kloss married Joshua Kushner, the brother of Donald Trump's son-in-law. Kushner is a founding partner at Thrive Capital and, not so coincidentally, one of the Series A funders for the millennial beauty brand Glossier, whose founder Emily Weiss enjoys a public friendship with Kloss. They met when Weiss worked at *Vogue*.

Glossier grew out of the website Into the Gloss, an insider's look at beautiful people's vanities and most beloved beauty products. After a few years of editorial work, Weiss launched the product line arm, promising "your skin but better" through a limited range of face mists, priming moisturizers, and sheer skin tints so people could replicate the glow of the people featured on the site. It grew into a beauty unicorn brand worth over a billion dollars, and Weiss did it in less time than it took Chanel.

In 1920, Chanel decided she would make a perfume. It was around then that she met Ernest Beaux, the man destined to be her coconspirator and alchemist in the world of smell. Beaux was Russian born to a perfumer family that worked for the Russian Imperial Courts. He'd previously created fragrances inspired by royalty and was behind the commercial success Bouquet de Napoleon for the house of Rallet. They may have met through the Grand Duke of Russia, whom Beaux knew from his youth, or through Chanel's friend, the writer Colette. In 1923, Colette and Chanel took her chauffeured Rolls Royce through the Côte d'Azur, where they visited workshops in Grasse, the perfume capital of the world. Beaux and Chanel quickly bonded, and together created what would come to be known as Chanel No. 5 perfume.

Beaux's stroke of genius was to use large amounts of aldehydes, something few perfumers had done before, as it was still a new synthetic discovery. To date, perfumes had been largely floral, natural compositions of great expense and little variety. People who wore perfume chose generally between different floral cologne waters—citrus, lemon, neroli—and were overperfumed at the beginning of the night and underperfumed by the end. Chanel suspected that overscented women were hiding something, and in her world there was no worse sin.

She ordered Beaux to include no hints of roses because she only wanted a "composed" perfume. She was seeking a paradox: "On a woman, a natural flower scent smells artificial. Perhaps a natural perfume must be created artificially." For his part, Beaux wanted a perfume that smelled, according to his notes, like the countryside of the Arctic Circle underneath a midnight moon, when the lakes smelled fresh and clean and quiet. They determined together that there were to be no clichéd floral bouquets to signify the sensuality of womanhood. Instead, women were to smell of a myth built on fantasy, synthetics, and a frightfully cool air, one that edged on the inhospitable.

Chanel's prompt brought Beaux to an unusual formulation of more than eighty ingredients and a huge amount of jasmine absolute. He produced a total of ten formulas for her to sample and lined them up in identical glass flacons distinguished only by numbers. *The fifth one,* she mandated after trying them all, offering no explanation as to her choice.

At first Beaux was dubious, even anxious, about her choice.

LE MONSTRE

He had been exuberant in his use of jasmine for the fifth sample, and he'd sourced it from Grasse, a region with some of the highest-quality jasmine in the world. The expense of making Chanel the perfume she wanted was daunting.

It will be very expensive; it contains a great deal of jasmine, and nothing costs as much as jasmine, he warned her. Chanel was unperturbed. *In that case,* she responded, *add more. I want to create the most expensive perfume in the world.*

In the beginning Chanel was a spy, of sorts. She sat in restaurants with a vial and discreetly sprayed it as her would-be customers walked by, and wondered aloud, *What on earth is that smell?* Her targets were invariably women of wealth. When the collective curiosity about its source reached a climax of rumor and desire among the highest ranks of society, then and only then did she start giving samples away to her customers. She pretended the small flacons of scent were secrets meant only for her favorite clients in her salon and made them beg her for it when they discovered through the rumor mill that she was the source. *Only for you, my love,* she'd whisper conspiratorially to her customers, and only for the next woman, and the next one still. And off it went into her store on the rue Cambon on May 5, 1921, to the vanities of women through France in the shadow of the Ritz, luxury fumes curling out of the windows of the shop doors.

Chanel knew she would need to outsource production if she wanted to expand. The perfume was expensive to produce, and she had other business to tend to. And while she built her perfume to a frenzy of hype and aldehydes, her future business associates were busy building their own empire, too. Their names were Paul and Pierre Wertheimer, and they owned the French cosmetics brand Bourjois. They were also Jewish.

Paul and Pierre were the sons of Ernest Wertheimer, who built Bourjois from the profits of tie-making. Historians can trace the family's wealth back several generations, the definition of old money. Accordingly, the family shied from the public eye and no one in the family was ever particularly open toward the press; there are, at my count, fewer than ten profiles or in-depth interviews with their descendants. They refuse to sit in the front row at the shows of the brands they own. They have always preferred to manage their holdings quietly, and they do have many to manage: the gunmakers Holland & Holland, Eres swimsuits, La Martinière publishing house, etc. But this portfolio sprang out of the family's seminal experiences with the plane manufacturer Félix Amiot and our dear Coco Chanel. The Wertheimers' business relationship with Amiot started a few years before they met Coco. In 1918, Amiot was 23, an aeronautical design prodigy, and was well on his way to securing large orders from the French government. The Wertheimers invested heavily in his company at the recommendation of their cousins, and they were in partnership for several years before Pierre met Chanel. The four of them—Paul and Pierre Wertheimer, Felix Amiot, and Coco—would remain entwined for decades. But for the first few years, they were little more than strangers, familiar to each other, if at all, only because their photographs occasionally appeared in the same newspapers.

LE MONSTRE

Two years after No. 5 launched, Coco Chanel met Pierre Wertheimer at Longchamp while they watched horses sprint around the track.

The meeting was courtesy of the French businessman Théophile Bader. Bader had been a business partner with the Wertheimers' father in the formation of the Galeries de Lafayette, and Chanel purchased materials from him to use in her salon. Impressed with the talent Chanel displayed in her clothes and her fast-growing reputation as an artistic darling of Paris, Bader decided it was logical to introduce his partners to his patron. He arranged for Wertheimer to meet Chanel in his booth at Longchamp in early spring of 1923.

Their conversation was short. Chanel watched the horses race the curve of the Seine from beneath a hat of her own design. Chanel asked if he wanted to produce and distribute her perfume. *Why not?* Pierre responded. *But if you want the perfume to be made under the name of Chanel, we've got to incorporate.*

When the partnership was solidified in 1924, the Wertheimers acquired 70 percent of Chanel Perfumes. The Wertheimers had perfume factories in Pantin, next to La Villette, "the city of blood," known for its supply of animal fats necessary for beauty products. These factories were instrumental to their success running Bourjois. They had been a natural choice for their factory resources, if not for their own Jewish ancestry.

For bringing the Wertheimers and Chanel together, Bader received 20 percent. It is unclear whether Chanel knew of this aspect of the arrangement, but then again, she was content to have someone else stuck with the logistics of manufacturing. For her efforts, Chanel received 10 percent of her own company and 10 percent of the capital of all companies that manufactured her perfumes outside of France. The initial shares that granted her that percentage were valued at 500 francs each.

Keep in mind: It takes 400 kilograms (881.8 pounds) of jasmine flowers to make 1 kilogram (2.2 pounds) of jasmine absolute—this is done by hand, from dawn to midday, from June to October, and each picker can collect only 2 to 3 kilograms per day. Jasmine absolute is a super-concentrated oily mixture extracted from plants through an old process called enfleurage—it is deeply labor-intensive process and, thus, expensive too. Today, each kilo of absolute can fetch over $59,000. Chanel went forward with the transaction and, in fact, they had all initially gotten along so well that they all used the same lawyer for the transaction, one of the Wertheimers' choosing—something Chanel would come to regret later. That critical day at the horse races had cast its seductive glow over the darker machinations of business, turning an easy affair into a binding marriage. The arrangement was one Chanel would regret and fight against for the rest of her life.

People ask me all the time why perfume is so expensive. Perfumery is a complex process. It relies on hundreds of hours of human labor, and the supply of key ingredients is influenced by climate change and political positioning—its farmers are supported and subsidized by government programs or at the mercy of large conglomerates. Perfume ingredients are not consistently uniform, especially those grown in different climates and soils, and specific ingredients are irreplaceable—many perfumers can quickly distinguish between a synthetic version of a material and its original. A well-versed consumer can, too. Once you've been trained in the different breeds of roses, you can distinguish between their scents instantly. You can practice this training yourself, casually, by smelling all the different roses at your local farmers' market. You'll likely learn the difference quickly, though you may not be able to retain it without practice. The major factors in the quality of an ingredient depend on where it is procured. Synthetics vary greatly as well. They are the product of tiresome bureaucracy and often trademarked by large conglomerates for exclusive use. Some natural ingredients are available only out of sheer luck; fisherman and bored scavengers walk stretches of beaches along the South African coast on the off chance they might find ambergris, generally referred to as whale vomit, which has in the past fetched worth more than its weight in gold. Tonkin musk have been hunted to near extinction, making it profitable to use only the synthetic clone of musk, rather than the real thing. Laborers wake up before the sun to pick a thousand buds of jasmine from fields that are kept deliberately secluded and often guarded; pure jasmine absolute can cost thousands of dollars a pound, and the cost fluctuates. The smallest perfume bottles, 30 mL, can contain, on average, up to 1,000 buds—and those blossoms must be handpicked in the morning from June to October and processed the very same day. Tourism to regions in rural France is utterly reliant on a few weeks of precious blooms. And that is just for jasmine—to say nothing of saffron or other ingredients that also happen to be some of the most valuable substances in the world. There have been, and continue to be, crimes surrounding the smuggling of sandalwood and other precious fragrance materials. Nowadays, who gets to even farm rare fragrance materials is often heavily regulated, licensed, and guarded.

Social unrest in harvesting nations can slow production or make it impossible for laborers to get to work. Global warming can and does consistently destroy crops. And exports of vetiver—the oil extracted from bunchgrass that gives a woodsy, citrus scent—were stopped in Haiti after its devastating 2010 earthquake. Climate change researchers are also observing that flowers may be losing the strength of their fragrances due to increasing temperatures associated with climate change—such changes have been observed in at least petunias so far.

Even with the advent of synthetic perfume ingredients, every perfume is a union of labor from around the world, dependent on millions of hands, regions, and livelihoods. That labor is rarely unionized. Perfume laborers operate in a world that is rapidly becoming too warm for sustained production, and farmers are reliant on contracts with the biggest conglomerates in the world to stay afloat. Now imagine the growing instability of the industry in the years leading up to World War II, with land mines and air raids imminent, and our wealthy friend Coco Chanel gaining notoriety for the small fortune she was beginning to build.

Chanel was not satisfied with the success of her perfume. The more money it made her, the more she realized how much more money it was making everyone else involved. As it stood, she owned only 10 percent of Chanel Perfume. Sure, the Wertheimers updated her percentage as they scaled up, but she never fully trusted them: They were Jewish. She didn't believe she was getting all that she felt she had earned, calling the Wertheimers thieves and other names. But even her small percentage was providing her a great deal more wealth than her fashion empire. People could not get enough of Chanel No. 5. While the average fashion consumer could not realistically afford a Chanel dress every season, every tourist in Europe took it upon themselves to splurge on eau de parfum.

By 1928, Coco was publicly insulting the Wertheimers to her inner circle, going on rampages of anti-Semitism. The editor in chief of *Marie-Claire,* Marcel Haedrich, was often a witness to her rants. In Hal Vaughan's biography, Haedrich later admitted, "Chanel's anti-Semitism was not only verbal, but passionate." When Chanel was asked how she felt about her would-be competitors opening boutiques in Paris, she remarked: *I only fear Jews and Chinese; and the Jews more than the Chinese.*

In the early 1930s, she finally hired her own lawyer: the young René de Chambrun. She decided to declare war on the Wertheimers. Her new lawyer would eventually oversee both Chanel's perfume dealings and those of many European companies that worked at the behest of the Third Reich. Chanel's right-hand man was about to become one of the most prominent collaborators of the next world war.

When I flew to Paris to research Chanel's history, one of the first things I noticed walking through her old haunts was that the Ministry of Justice was next door to the Ritz. No one had bothered to mention this in all the documentaries I'd watched and biographies I'd read. It seemed strange to leave out the fact that the heart of the city was a luxury hotel as well as a Ministry of Justice. It seems obvious now that the highest reaches of aesthetic kingdoms have the heaviest gates. Little surprise that the woman wove chain-link into the very clothes she designed to get the exact drape she wanted in fabric. She designed armor for the untouchable woman.

Chambrun once described the relationship between the Wertheimers and Chanel as thirty years of "cold wars, divorce, and reconciliation." It did not matter how many invitations to social events the Wertheimers extended—to Maxim's, to their box at Longchamp—Chanel wanted nothing to do with them. The Wertheimers weren't social creatures to begin with, so I imagine each spurned invitation left a mark. Their social circle was similarly wealthy, though more publicly known: the Rothschilds, the Guggenheims, and the Bichs (of Bic pen wealth). Having a public tiff with a social darling like Chanel weighed on the family. Pierre began calling her "that bloody woman," and she referred to Pierre as "that bandit who screwed me."

Since she refused to enter the boardroom to deal with matters in her own company, she instead sent her current lover. Paul Iribe was a hotheaded, elegant man who worked as an illustrator. Iribe had no business background to speak of, but he was passionately in love with Chanel and determined to stand behind her. He refused to sign documents as an act of protest for the circumstances dealt to her. These operatics were futile; in the end the board voted him out.

Chanel nearly lost all control of her own company in under a decade. She recalled that her agreement had an important clause: her ability to sue if Les Parfums Chanel sold anything other than makeup. She decided a cleansing cream they'd previously released fell into that purview. The lawsuit followed.

That was just the first of many suits that the Wertheimers and Coco brought against each other, not only in French courts but in international ones too. Coco mostly lost, but she did make everyone bleed money, an act of vengeance she seemed to enjoy. It was not as if she couldn't afford the trouble; a 1931 *New Yorker* profile remarked on her wealth and competitive streak: "Each year [Chanel] tries not only to beat her competitors but to beat herself. . . . Her last annual turnover was publicly quoted [not by her] as being one hundred and twenty million francs, or close to four and a half million dollars" ($60 million now).

By 1934 Coco Chanel was no longer the president of Les Parfums Chanel. Determined to control the perfume as sales exploded, she launched a series of lawsuits to try to stop the development of any other products in the Chanel No. 5 line. She would eventually create alternative perfumes and try to sell them to outside authorized distributors simply to undercut the profit margin of the company. These acts of schadenfreude came at great cost.

Chanel lost her throne while Germany gained a dictator. Adolf Hitler became German chancellor in January 1933, appointing Joseph Goebbels to Reich Minister for Public Enlightenment and Propaganda. The position meant he had jurisdictional control over all the communications of Germany. Goebbels decided to name a man called Baron Hans "Spatz" Gunther von Dincklage as special attaché at the Germany Embassy in Paris—a public reward to his longtime master spy. By then Germany was casting a longer and longer shadow on France and the rest of the world. The Nazi party began requiring Jews to wear the Star of David on their clothes. France was beginning to close its borders to refugees from Germany, most of whom were Jewish people stripped of their jobs, citizenship, families, and home.

The Wertheimers watched from Paris with worry while arguing with Chanel over ownership rights through Chambrun. The French Air Force began to buy up bombers from stock in Amiot Aviation. Let me spoil a surprise for you: Spatz, the master spy, was to become Chanel's future lover. So, the roles of this tale have been set: the patron, the designer, the dictator, and the spy. And then there's me, the hapless journalist, chasing a ghost.

To frame Chanel as a powerless spurned woman in this charade would be a disservice to those who worked for her and those who could not afford her work. Though she was a woman without a title at Les Perfumes Chanel, her name and influence were of international repute. The American economy was free-falling, and the loans America had once given to Germany ceased at a time when inflation had rendered necessities exorbitantly expensive. Chanel's company had never been more profitable. She was selling thousand-franc dresses by the dozens each day, tens of thousands a year; she grew her workforce and then grew it again. She paid her friends stipends to fill her apartments with books she would never read; she paid for the housing of her friends and fellow artists; she donated money so the Paris-based Ballets Russes could continue to perform at the request of her friend Serge Diaghilev, and even designed the costumes (this, during the era of Nijinsky). She bankrolled her lover Iribe's weekly newsletter *Le Temoin*, a violent, xenophobic propaganda magazine. She moved into the Ritz in 1934 and kept an apartment nearby just for entertaining. Chanel dined on caviar and ordered fleeing princesses to sew tighter hems on thousand-franc gowns.

The Ritz was never closed during the war; it did what it had always done and accommodated anyone who walked through its doors. Faced with serving the enemy, some employees fled, but not all, and the stalwarts were promoted to emptied posts. The room next to the entrance was turned into a checkroom for guns. One wing of the hotel became the accommodations for non-German guests, and the finer rooms were dedicated to German officers. The hotel bar, not yet named after Hemingway's legendary postwar victory celebrations, became a spy network for bartenders and visiting agents from all sides of the war. The rest of the city became impoverished from restrictions—resulting in an average of less than half the normal caloric intake for most residents, and potato rationing inspired riots. After waiting in hours in line for rations, one would receive half a loaf of bread, crumbs of cheese, and a slice of meat the size of an egg. Even alcohol was rationed and the best, even average, wines were sent to Germany under the Reich's orders. More people died of starvation during World War II than from being killed in combat. But the Ritz never surrendered or admitted defeat in the face of war, and their cellars stayed stocked. They still had access to caviar.

Paul Iribe collapsed on a tennis court in September 1935 while on vacation with Chanel and died in a clinic shortly after. She was still in mourning the following June when her workers went on strike. She was locked out of her own office and squirreled away in her suite at the Ritz while Paris rioted. The French labor movement brought Les Accords de Matignon to fruition in June. This solidified the right to strike, protected unions, ensured paid vacations, and instilled the forty-hour workweek through France and created an example for the rest of the world. Chanel's workers didn't stop there, striking into July and August.

Hitler ordered the murders of Austrian Chancellor Engelbert Dollfuss and all those in power in Germany who had dared to oppose him. He turned his attention to Alexander, the king of Yugoslavia; Dincklage was then supposedly ordered to travel there in 1934. Three months later, King Alexander was shot. In the Paris weekly *Vendémiaire*, an exposé provided by French counterintelligence speculated that Dincklage had been involved in the death of the king, naming him as a Gestapo officer. That was the year Hitler's Nuremberg Rally and Laws came to pass. By 1940, Chanel's lawyer had a boost in social power: His father-in-law had become prime minister of the Vichy government. Legislated slaughter, what was known as the "Final Solution" to the "Jewish Question," had officially begun. And Dincklage, upon returning to Paris, began to court Chanel in 1941.

Pierre Wertheimer left France for America in 1939 to try to secure a plane manufacturing deal with America for Amiot Industries. He was also furtively scoping out how to comfortably relocate outside of Europe before it became too difficult. By then, France's declaration of war and the United States' neutrality meant no deal. When he returned to France later that year, he did have a plan; escape can be bought if you have enough money and time. The cost of escape was about 50 million francs—roughly US$22 million today. It was given to none other than Félix Amiot.

There is no note with the record of the exchange to indicate it was an escape fund. More realistically, it was a fee to ensure that Amiot would act as trustee while they were gone. The French Deuxième Bureau indicates that Amiot received the funds in August 1939, with no record of dispersion. In turn, Amiot used his influence to make friends with Hitler's right-hand man, Reich Marshal Hermann Göring. Göring was the man who would otherwise be responsible for seizing the Wertheimers' companies. Amiot's planes were catching the eyes of German engineers, so he ended up selling to them, too. Amiot provided the distractions and cover, and the Wertheimers began to run.

While the rest of the Wertheimers gathered twenty miles outside of Paris proper in Chevreuse Valley to avoid the bomb raids nearby, Pierre and Amiot met for their final farewell in Pierre's apartment at 55 avenue Foch. It was May 1940, and Pierre was nearly unrecognizable, fatigued from stress and sleeplessness. Pierre asked Amiot to save what was possible and to look after his son, Jacques, who was in the French army and unreachable. They embraced, looked around the apartment, and then they were gone.

The street where the Wertheimers said farewell became the center of Nazi power in Paris. A few doors down from Pierre's apartment, Adolf Eichmann would plan the great roundup that ordered 13,000 Jews to be sent to death camps. The screams from interrogations would travel from window to window down the avenue, and families would be pushed out of their homes and replaced by German officers, their apartments ransacked, and their valuables sold off or hidden away, never to be returned to their owners. Meanwhile, Coco Chanel continued to hold court at the Ritz. Her new neighbor was Hermann Göring. He lived in the wing across from her, two floors up.

The Ritz is a place that seems impossible. It flips me over. I'm not sure I can describe how mythically cavernous it felt to walk through the doors. The wrought-iron staircases, the golden art deco details, the glass canopies of teal steel and thick velvet curtains pooling down to endless halls of Persian rugs, glowing from the lights woven through topiary sculptures. It feels protective because it *is* protective. There are windows, but only to the sky, and they are so far up as to be mere decoration in a place filled with gold and velvet and grand pianos and oil paintings and subdued murmurs of business and laughter from drunken widows. It is a place of decadent refusal, and always has been. The only concession Coco seemed to make while living there was during air raids, when she would enter the hotel's shelter with her maid bearing Coco's gas mask on a silk cushion.

I knew how terrible she was when I walked through those halls, and it didn't matter for a while. For a brief walk through the Ritz, I realized how easy her choices must have seemed to her. It forced an ugly kind of empathy into my skull, one I hadn't been prepared for, and one I didn't want. Her very ordinary weakness capitulated her toward every opportunity. Selfishness is survival, after all. Deep evil can seem unhinged to those on the hard side of it; to others, you are a martyr. Chanel was happy to exploit others to maintain her own wealth, eager to be seen as enterprising, glamorous, worldly, and in charge. She framed her products as worthy of whatever violence and danger it cost to produce such beauty. She was raised in a community of hatred, never sought out different frameworks, and was duly rewarded for her selfishness. The more isolated she felt in the Ritz, the more the suffering of the people around her seemed too absurd to bother acknowledging; it was hard enough, it seemed, to keep hold of what treasures she had for herself, a lifestyle of luxury in a country held hostage. Why would she have ever stood up for people she didn't even like, and flee from one of the only places where life was almost untouched by the sacrifices made in war? It was a conscious choice, never to leave her gilded shell. And it makes sense, really, because *power appears beautiful, and beauty makes time feel conquerable.* Beauty makes cruel choices so easy. Beauty makes empathy a political tool. Why be good, when to be quiet is so comforting and requires so much less work? So much less sacrifice? Who would thank her for giving up everything, when everyone she knew would likely have abandoned her to rot while they continued carrying on? When you have such wealth and power, maintaining it is a constant preoccupation, and every time you say yes to it you get farther away from the other side. Perfume was her way of selling a promise, a promise of success and control she scrambled to maintain for herself.

To feel simpatico with someone you've reviled for years is frightening; you begin to lose your mooring. Context can give you a capacity for evil in the same way and often at the same time that it offers a capacity for good. What I knew of the world was being erased by the memory of her; I felt flattened and forced into her choices and her world. Before then, I couldn't imagine the collusion she was known for, and walking down the hall I couldn't see a point where she would have ever considered another option. It made my worldview narrow down so as to be contained by that single building. I knew then that complicity was a much easier and profitable choice than I'd ever let myself believe.

My righteousness was easy because it was true and felt good. I failed the lesson I thought I'd learned from Simone Weil's writing: *Never react to an evil in such a way as to augment it.* The most disturbing thing about evil isn't how cruel it can be. It is that it makes being good seem impossibly radical. If you were placed in a position of power, after having so little of it, are you absolutely sure you'd make the decisions you'd hoped you would? Would you not think for a second about the choice? If all you knew in your adult life was power and wealth, would you give it up because a stranger was suffering? If it meant that surely you would suffer too? *Really*? Are you absolutely, positively sure?

In the German diktat that stated only high-ranking personalities were to stay at the Ritz, for it was a "supreme and exceptional place among the hotels requisitioned," Chanel was one of the few non-Germans allowed to keep her rooms. This was likely not only due to her own repute, but also her involvement with a high-ranking Nazi official, our man Spatz Dincklage. Her rooms—227 and 228—were on the same floor as the wife of the founder of the Ritz, as well as Nazi collaborators Charles Bedaux and André Dubonnet. It's safe to assume that during the war, Chanel dined nearly daily with Nazi personnel.

While Chanel was becoming acquainted with her new Nazi neighbors, Amiot's factories were destroyed in bomb raids and nineteen people were killed. Chanel closed her fashion salon and tended to her new relationship with Dincklage, while Amiot raced against the clock to evacuate the factories he owned with the Wertheimers. He had to evacuate 3,000 people to the South of France, alongside equipment and materials. He was given orders to reroute the staff to the south. He transferred the research unit to the Free Zone, a short drive away, where the space between occupied territory and "freedom" was demarcated geographically.

Jews were being removed from positions of power and being killed or shuttled to camps by the thousands. As the Axis soldiers bombed the borders and crawled their way into France, Amiot doctored the transcripts that proved the Wertheimers were ever involved in his aeronautical company. This meant that if the Vichy government were to come calling and demand the Aryanization of his business, he could still retain control. The Wertheimers asked him to do the same with their cosmetics empire. So, in October 1940, Amiot fictitiously bought Bourjois. The letter to the Wertheimers' representative assigned to the exchange was short but essential: "I have sent to you by registered air mail the power of attorney signed by Paul and I. A pleasant task! This power, you understand, must be used to sell to Félix only. You can fill in the date and place of creation and, if necessary, notarize our signature at the police station. We are all in fine physical health. Morale is less high. Mother and Paul send all their best wishes. I embrace you. Pierre."

With that, control of Bourjois and Chanel Perfumes was transferred to the hands of Félix Amiot: forty-year-old aviation manufacturer, Wertheimer dummy, and ruse.

It was a good plan, but not a perfect one. The first doctoring was passable, but the Bourjois transaction caught the attention of the Vichy watchers. The sale was questioned by the Germans, and Amiot's friendship with the Wertheimers was brought to speculation on and satirized in a flurry of publications. On April 3, 1941, Amiot was summoned to the Hotel Majestic, which housed German Military Command. It was a room with a view of Pierre's old apartment. *The Wertheimers are your friends and also your associates. You are their cover. All of this is naive and dangerous for you.* An engineer by the name of Sturm interrogated Amiot and stared him down, obscuring the nostalgic view. The government had appointed an administrator, Georges Madoux, to look into the company. His conclusion: Les Parfums Chanel *is still a Jewish company.*

Then Chanel arrived. She met with the lead investigator to campaign for her cause and then, in a letter addressed to Madoux on May 5, 1941, she wrote: "I intend to acquire the totality of the shares of Les Parfums Chanel, which are still the property of Jews and which, as per your mission, must be given up or given to Aryans." The plan seemed to look like it was bound to fail right up to the moment the lead investigator discovered that Madoux had been commercial director of Chanel Perfumes years before and was fired for "unjustified withdrawals from their fund."

The French administrator eventually sided with Amiot. *I can conclude, in good faith, that the Bourjois perfumery has*

LE MONSTRE

passed into Aryan hands in a legal and correct manner. It is unclear how Mr. Amiot seeks to safeguard the interests of the Wertheimer brothers, since he is associated with the Junkers Flugzeug Motorenwerke for the construction of 370 aircraft. The Wertheimers and Amiot placed their bets on both sides of the war, though bombers ended up saving them all in the end. The months of interrogations and suspicion slowed but would start up again via the press in 1942, and Amiot would be called in for interrogations again on several occasions.

Coco Chanel didn't kill anyone. She merely slept with a spy who probably did—we don't know. She only tried to get people she distrusted removed from positions she wanted herself. She only had meetings with people who could make that happen. Coco Chanel didn't kill anyone, but she wrote letters to the people who could have made it happen. Coco Chanel didn't kill anyone, but she lived in a hotel with the men who did and wrote letters to the men who did and paid for the publishing of a magazine that encouraged them to do it.

Hannah Arendt was writing her treatises on organized guilt and totalitarianism in France not that far from Chanel's neighborhood. They were living in Paris at the same time, though they did not run in the same circles. (After all, Arendt was Jewish.) Arendt wrote that "guilt implies the consciousness of guilt, and punishment evidence that the criminal is a responsible person." She recorded a conversation between an American correspondent and a German paymaster at a camp in 1944 that I think about often:

Q. Did you kill people in the camp?

A. Yes.

Q. Did you poison them with gas?

A. Yes.

Q. Did you bury them alive?

A. Yes. It sometimes happened.

Q. Were the victims picked from all over Europe?

A. I suppose so.

Q. Did you personally help kill people?

A. Absolutely not. I was only paymaster in the camp.

Q. What did you think of what was going on?

A. It was bad at first but we got used to it.

Q. Do you know the Russians will hang you?

A. (Bursting into tears) Why should they? *What have I done?*

As the Wertheimers settled into their new homes in Central Park, a six-foot eight-inch behemoth of a man named Don Armando Guevaray Sotto Mayor passed through border control in Paris under the eyes of German guards. His real name was Herbert Gregory Thomas, and though he informed the press and customs officers that he was traveling for the New York Toilet Goods Association, he was the vice president of the Bourjois Company in New York. The Wertheimers had sent him on a mission to get a hold of the safeguarded formula for Chanel No. 5 and bring the necessary ingredients back to New York without anyone finding out. With a history of practicing law in Paris, Geneva, and

The Hague, and time spent as president of Chanel's competitor, Guerlain, Thomas had been tasked with the future of the production of the best-selling perfume in the world.

No one was to know he was there—especially not Coco Chanel. In *The New Yorker*, John Updike estimated that it took more than 700 pounds of jasmine to keep production up. After converting it to absolute, the weight is much more discreet: only 50 kilograms of the liquid were required to keep production going through World War II. Thomas needed to hide bottles of fragrance roughly the weight of a teen girl in the lining of his clothes.

While Thomas never explained how he pulled it off, his colleague Peter Sichel, another early agent in the OSS, speculated he smuggled the coins to pay for the ingredients in the lining of his suit, inside his suitcase, and in false-bottom shoes from train to train, international ship to bus, along with Louis d'Or coins as currency to finance the espionage. Depending on the date of the coin, each one could be worth thousands of euros: the 20 Louis coin is still the largest and most expensive French gold coin ever minted, much more valuable than francs, dollars, or euros.

By any account, it was a fortune to smuggle, through coin or purchased absolute: The New York Toilet Goods Association told the State Department in 1941 that "a pound of precious natural aromatic product [like jasmine] may sell for four or five thousand dollars in 1941." Amazingly, Thomas managed not only to smuggle ingredients, but also retrieved the No. 5 formula from a Chanel company safe; we still have no idea how. He also managed to find Pierre's son Jacques, who had been hiding in Bordeaux. Jacques had escaped from a prisoner camp, and Thomas brought him back to America, where he reunited with his father on the steps of their Park Avenue home.

Wertheimer's lawyer Claude Lewy described the adventures of Thomas with the sort of admiration usually reserved for war heroes. "The feats accomplished by Gregory Thomas are out of a James Bond movie."

With the formula and ingredients finally in the Wertheimers' possession, No. 5 was enjoyed as the best—and most popular—perfume of World War II and beyond. Since the ingredients were stockpiled well out of reach of Aryan administrators, the perfume maintained formulaic integrity throughout wartime restrictions. This was remarkable, especially because so many competitors suffered the restrictions and toppled because of them. Having production based in America helped distribute the perfume to foreign customers, too.

The Wertheimers took their move to America to heart. Not only did they manufacture Bourjois products entirely in America during the war, they came out with a propaganda perfume to capitalize upon it. While Coco Chanel continued to try to seize control of the European holdings of Chanel Perfumes through Aryanization laws, the Wertheimers settled in to manufacturing in New Jersey. From the same factories that produced the perfume of a now well-known Nazi collaborator, a perfume called Courage was released by Bourjois. Another layer to the story: The Wertheimers got help setting up their Hoboken factory from

Estée Lauder's boyfriend. During World War II, the beauty empires of America were entirely Jewish run. "It is monstrous," Chanel screamed when she learned about this in 1945. "They produced it in *Hoboken*."

The Wertheimers made the executive decision to sell No. 5 at military post exchanges shortly after they moved, and as a result, No. 5 was one of the only perfumes to make a profit during the war. Chanel was infuriated and considered it déclassé for her perfume to have been sold next to dry goods and supplies for sergeants at war. The Wertheimers used the profits to help fund their involvement in the anti-Nazi Free French movement led by General Charles de Gaulle. They held fundraisers and were often the most prominent supporters of the general's cause. And in May 1941, the Wertheimers met with anthropologist Claude Lévi-Strauss and Bertrand Goldschmidt, one of the scientists behind the French atomic bomb. A few months before, the Wertheimers provided the financial means and network to biochemist Louis Rapkine to orchestrate the rescue of dozens of scientific researchers from France—Lévi-Strauss and Goldschmidt included. Rapkine said, *It is only thanks to the donations of the Wertheimer family and the Rothschild families that I was able to pay for the steamship tickets.*

While the Wertheimers dined with and plotted with the founding members of Free France and the Allied resistance, Coco Chanel was enrolled in the Abwehr Berlin Registry in 1941 as agent f-7124, code name WESTMINSTER.

Each bottle of perfume sold with her name sent profit to both sides of a world war.

THE HOUSE OF BEAUTY

All was not well on the Parisian front, and Spatz Dincklage decided Madrid would solve that problem. Dincklage proposed to use Chanel as cover on a diplomatic mission to Madrid, where she had friends and connections that he did not. He was under pressure from his advisors to leave Paris, and Chanel was eager to join him after Free France intelligence obtained a recording of her declaring *France got what she deserved* at a lunch party on the Côte d'Azur. She wasn't exactly popular. Over the last year, Coco and Spatz had both been seen dining among the Nazis many times over at the Ritz Hotel, and the year before her lawyer, Chambrun, had been among the prominent names listed in *Life* magazine as known collaborators. Besides dealing with Chanel, Chambrun also edited confidential documents for his father-in-law, politician Pierre Laval, and he also represented US companies operating in Nazi Germany. Until the North African Allied landings, he cohosted business lunches at the Ritz, where Nazi officials and collaborators met to plan business ventures as part of Hitler's European New Order. The blacklist that *Life* had issued warned that "some [were] to be assassinated . . . others to be tried when France is free." With her lawyer mired in public scandal, and herself not far behind, Chanel and Dinklage were living on borrowed time. Documents from Chanel's police files reveal that the escape plan meant Spain, through "the intermediary of German authorities." They arrived in Madrid for a mission ordered by Heinrich Himmler and were given the task of establishing a point of contact with the British, since Coco was a known friend of British Prime Minister Winston

Churchill. Her codename was shorthand for her value, a relationship not easily bought.

Coincidentally, Herbert Gregory Thomas was in Madrid at the same time as Coco, but temporarily working for the OSS. While Coco was stirring the pot, Madrid was a nest of spies from all sides of the war in those years. In fact, we know little of her Madrid trip at all—the documents directly communicating the events that transpired have been mysteriously lost in libraries around the world. I have spent the last six years trying to find their ashes to no avail, and have been told through the grapevine of editors close to the House of Chanel that any surviving documentation will likely be released only when all living descendants die.

There was a period of the war when German officers were the main ones buying Chanel No. 5 out of the boutique on rue Cambon. They needed no language to order it, they just raised one hand: five fingers for an ounce of No. 5. It was a sign of their success and travels under the New European Order guided by Hitler. All that ended on August 25, 1944, when Paris was liberated.

An expert at guerilla strategy, Chanel wasted no time running out to hand out free vials of her perfume to British soldiers and American GIs. Two French soldiers armed with revolvers went to arrest her regardless.

As she was guided out of her room at the Ritz, thousands of other collaborators were being dragged through the streets or guided into jail. Some were forcibly shaved or branded, retribution for sleeping with the enemy. Chanel was more fortunate. She was imprisoned for only a few hours.

She was shown a photo of Dincklage and asked if she knew him. *Yes.* So it was true that she consorted with him, a known German? As she would tell photographer Cecil Beaton later in her defense: *"Really, sir, a woman of my age cannot be expected to look at his passport if she has a chance of a lover."* Coco was 61. They let her go.

More than her wit, it was her friendship with Churchill that protected her from immediate punishment. She took the opportunity to run away to Switzerland while other collaborators went to trial. In Switzerland she came out with a predecessor perfume called Super Chanel No. 5. She sent it to her stores, and the Wertheimers had it confiscated at the ports. Chanel sued them shortly after. She couldn't sell it, so she did something worse: She gave it away for free.

It was the last straw for the Wertheimers. When Coco returned personally to Paris, she sued the Wertheimers for abuse of majority shareholders, and they sued her for counterfeiting. When the dust settled, the Wertheimers ended up settling out of court: They bought up Coco's final shares, her latest perfume, and never let it sell. They met for the final negotiation in an office on the Champs-Élysées.

Chanel and the Wertheimers argued behind closed doors, while Chanel paced her apartment and tapped her cigarettes out of the window. In their suits, the lawyers threw shadows on the reflective brass and gold wallpaper. Their final negotiation took eight hours.

Coco ended up with 2 percent of the gross amount of perfume sales throughout the world on top of a sum calculated to cover past royalties. She was richer than she had ever imagined she would be. The rest of the tale may be familiar to you: She continued running her fashion house, though by then she was well into her seventies. The Wertheimers continued to pay to produce Chanel No. 5 and the advertisements for it, and bought up Chanel's fashion line. They supported her through the decades she was out of sight or out of fashion and paid for all her life expenses until the end. When Chanel eventually died, the world mourned. The price of Chanel products under Lagerfeld (and now post-Lagerfeld, too) has only climbed.

Chanel No. 5 is still a best-selling perfume. To this day the Wertheimers have never entertained interviews on their participation in the Free French movement; indeed, they have rarely taken any interviews at all. Gregory Thomas died before he explained how he smuggled the world's best jasmine resources through a world war. He left no children, and much of the evidence of his past in the OSS has quietly been scrubbed from the digital skeletons of the internet. The archives get harder and harder to find and descendants get older and rarer, still. The one hundredth anniversary of Les Parfums Chanel passed recently; they have launched a new perfume called Gabrielle Chanel in her honor. The timeline of her life on Chanel's website makes no mention of her complicity in the war. In a later launch, they sent comically large compacts of product to editors, celebrities, and influencers, and built out a replica of Chanel's apartment in Los Angeles for selfies. To mark the hundred-year anniversary of No. 5, they hosted a gigantic party in New York. I was invited. I declined. Shortly after, they held another celebration in Los Angeles, a few miles from where I live. They had a flock of drones fly across the sky in the shape of her logo, a paramilitary bouquet I couldn't help but laugh at, knowing what I know. It was a cruel joke well told.

On a recent trip to Paris, I stayed in George Whitman's apartment above Shakespeare and Company bookstore as their visiting writer. On one of my last nights, I invited the volunteers at the store up for wine after the workday, and we stared out the window to Notre Dame and the flock of crowds. It had been foggy and raining for weeks and we had spent most of the day in paranoia over the Seine flooding. The Seine had settled a foot short of the barrier that kept it from flooding the beloved bookstore. We talked about Chanel, the feeling of Paris then and the feeling of Paris now. We couldn't agree on what makes a person irredeemable. As my friends left, one of them turned and shrugged. *I do not think there was ever a chance of saving her, you know. Everyone did what they had to do. Wouldn't you?*

3

An Empire of Hair

[Where are you from? No, really?] [Can I touch your hair?] [Oh, sorry, it's hard to tell you guys apart. You look like someone else.] [I didn't recognize you with your new hair!] [Go back to where you came from.] [Is that your real hair?] [Are you mixed?] [Where are you from? No, really?] [Is that your real hair?][Can you make your hair more ... professional?] [Where are you from?] [Can I touch your hair?] [Where are you from? Where are you from? Where are you from?]

When I was in sixth grade, I was meticulous about brushing my hair. I carried a travel-size bottle of Pantene detangling spray in my backpack constantly and I always smelled like soap. Pride goes before the fall: Lice found me, and they greeted me with horny aplomb when I woke up one day. I screamed. I cried. I crushed them.

Once I saw those bugs on my bangs I immediately went without sleep, terrified they'd burrow into my bed, into my clothes, into the walls.

My neighbors were a Hispanic family that I grew up alongside while my father took care of our other, elderly neighbors for grocery money. When the lice came, my neighbors took care of me. Tia stripped me down, hosed my naked body in the bath, and promptly cut my beautiful, bug-filled mane while I cried and watched the strands fan out along the tile like so many caterpillar legs. I felt betrayed by the thing I loved best: my own empire of hair.

I wrote my first short story after that, and it immediately got me into trouble with the school principal. It was a short story about my hair being forcibly cut. The climax of the piece was me throwing my hairbrush into the vanity mirror that I spent most of my days staring into. The mirrored glass cracked into chunks, and story me wrenched out the shards to use as a weapon against those who would make decisions about my body without my regard. Adults asked if I was being abused at home. Was my assignment a cry for help? I was just processing my summer of lice. I missed wearing my hair like a cape, braided like a crown, long enough for its own centrifugal force. I wanted it weaponized, but not against *me*.

I understand why they were concerned. But my rage wasn't wrong; hair's power is too much, too important to feeling good about yourself when you don't yet know who you are. I articulated that power in a way that frightened someone who saw it differently. I had been told all my life that I had beautiful, TV-commercial hair, even if people often asked where did I *really* come from—no, *really*. I was told it was the best part of me, because it could be sold or donated to others less fortunate if

I treated it well enough. People debated all the time if I looked more like my white father or my Asian mother, but on one thing they usually agreed: My hair was the best of both. My vanity felt like my worth. To lose that was startling.

I knew then as I know now that hair is a portal, a means of escape or assimilation. Hair is indicative of audacity, jubilation, rebellion, elegance. It can say, "I need to speak to the manager"; it can say, "I am a swindler, the future of blood technology and Silicon Valley"; it can say, "Black Power"; it can say, "I am a Hitler Youth"; it can say, "Every ribbon and bead woven into my hair is a legacy that colonizers did not manage to kill." Hair is a measure of beauty, of respect, of wealth, of professionalism—it is a measure of identity that people register before they may even know your name. I knew that even as a little girl: that lice-filled hair was shorthand for filth, and that it must have reflected poorly on my home life, my parents, and my upbringing.

People have read their own prejudices into the textures of hair for centuries, used it to shortcut their interrogations into one's humanity. Forced haircuts and race-based policymaking have long been part of how assimilation and humiliation have been forced onto human beings. Corporate and military codes of conduct list hairstyles as professional or not; children are sent home with their braids cut, their Afros cut, accused of myriad things. Unprofessional, unkempt, unclean.

The story of hair is the story of people. For people of color, it is braided into how we navigate a hostile world.

Even cursory research shows that most cultures have complex messages delivered through hair and its upkeep. During the Han

Dynasty era in China—206 BCE to 220 CE—women wore their hair in loose buns. You can trace time through the style of hair throughout decades; coils and combs are shortcuts to marriage status, virility, social class, military success, divinity. Bun angle and complexity could define an era, nine buns were a shortcut for nobility, a high bun and loose strands signaled your rank as a courtesan—every style had a meaning. As a child in Taipei, I remember my aunts and grandmother teaching me how to recognize royalty in paintings and sculptures by their hairstyles when we walked through museums.

In Indigenous cultures in North America, hair is a tribal identity. For Native Americans, when hair is cut, it's not to be thrown away. It's meant to be burned ceremoniously with sage. When it is cut, people know you're mourning something, experiencing a watershed change of your very existence. In the Navajo Nation, hair is cut to mourn death in the immediate family. For the Mexican American artist Danié Gómez Ortigoza, braiding is a way to ritualize her connection to her Indigenous matrilineal roots. "I remember my abu speaking the Mayan words 'In lak' ech, Hala ken,' which means 'I am another you, as you are another me,' [which means] I don't exist without you, and you don't exist without me.... [These words became the] principle behind the ritual of my daily braiding practice," wrote Gómez Ortigoza in 2022. As an organizer for women's rights, she has ritualized braiding the hair of the women she brings together for political change, too. Hair was a medium and a material that linked her both to her ancestors and to the women she was building political coalition with.

Hair is linked to family legacy and a door to divine relationship across cultures and geography. Mohamed Mbodj, professor of African Studies at Manhattanville University, explains that in Senegalese cultures, devotees of certain gods and goddesses have hairstyle requirements to honor the power of their faith. "The hair is the most elevated point of your body, which means it is the closest to the divine," explains Professor Mbodj in *Hair Story*. Across borders, cultures, and centuries, people have made medicines and spells with single strands of hair. It is not merely a thing, but a capsule of legions and lineage intertwined. It's a soul-keeper, a signature not just of your DNA but of your spirit, your place in the scheme of things.

Little wonder that there are persistent myths of conquerors like Alexander the Great ordering soldiers to cut off their beards after losing battles: They lost to the Persians when their enemies pulled them off their steeds by their beards and slit their throats before they hit the ground. Much later in modern Empire, boarding schools for Indigenous children would forcibly cut children's hair once they stole them away from their families. Hair holds you in place.

In Empire's eyes, it holds you back.

In the history of hair, an anecdotal story lives: escape routes braided into the hair of the enslaved. Plaits as secret message systems, braids as cartography. Colombian stylist Ziomara Asprilla García relayed it in its most well-known form: to signal the desire to escape, women braided their hair in a style called departes: "thick, tight braids, braided closely to the scalp, tied into buns on the top."

It is hard to verify these stories because of how archives are decided. Whose histories are safe to keep alive with paper evidence; whose lives are threatened by their retellings? I choose to believe there's a version of this that was true, because someone recognized a need to escape and heeded the signal. That they survived and kept their crown and that there is at least one happy ending kept secret from suffering. That hair didn't merely keep a secret, but it helped you find freedom. And its story could only be repeated intimately, not best by words but by gestures from someone's hands to your scalp, something they'd hold and cradle tenderly. A story held close to your body, a ritual focused at the highest part.

There's a Confucian idea that parents live on through their children's hair; the idea of filial piety is linked to your body, your skin, your hair—you receive all of this from your parents, and so you must not desecrate them by cutting it. This made forcible cutting a traumatic experience for East Asians who have also had to endure it repeatedly throughout history. The image of an American soldier forcibly removing a Chinese man's hair became commercially available on greeting cards shortly after the Chinese Revolution in 1911. Newspaper cartoons across the United States at the time replicated the humor with varying degrees of racist mirth. You can still buy these cards on eBay. Last time I checked, one ran you $3.55 plus shipping.

I did not know any of this when mine was cut as a tween. I had very little historical context for the racism my vanity was trying to circumvent. I had long sorority-girl brunette hair, sun-streaked, squeaky clean, and neatly brushed, because I hoped it would racialize me into safety. It did not. All I knew was that

AN EMPIRE OF HAIR

a bowl cut was embarrassing, and I was regularly greeted with racist slurs as I entered class for weeks. It's a common story often told, and it is offensive for many reasons, the lack of originality being one of them. What bothers me isn't the names others used but the disgust and the distrust in my own body. There were hostile forces filled with my own blood, living on my scalp, procreating literally *in my face*, even after days of every holistic and pharmaceutical remedy. I refused to shave my head bald, even as I felt the lice breeding in my sleep. I wanted to run away from my body, trained myself to float outside of it for reprieve. Tia tried to console me with talks of wigs. I didn't want wigs. I wanted the truth of my hair to be beautiful and clean and for no one to call me racist Asian stereotypes when we were on the playground at lunchtime. I wanted beauty to mean safety. I wanted to belong in America and have the people around me see that in me, as plain as day.

Before a hair piece is ever clipped or braided onto your scalp, it travels through the market. Before the market, there was a port. Before the port, there was a sea, and so many lives on every coast of it. We all came from somewhere originally. Even Americans. *Especially* Americans. And our natural-born braids.

I am telling these stories simultaneously to honor my debts to a history that crosses borders and erases names. I know the names of none of my ancestors, no one beyond my grandparents, no lineage to claim. But I know what roles people who looked like my family have had to play in this country. People of color have every claim to every role in the history of hair. All of them. Merchants and customer and merchandise. I am following the braid.

Along the Atlantic's arteries, you can trace how flesh merchants advertised the quality of a person by the descriptions of body, of personality, of hair. A strand from *Hair Story: Untangling the Roots of Black Hair in America*: "Straight hair translated to economic opportunity and social advantage . . . the hair was considered the most telling feature of Negro status, more than the color of the skin. . . . The rule of thumb was that if the hair showed just a little bit of kinkiness, a person would be unable to pass as white." Hair heralds.

The description of a runaway slave in the *New York Weekly Journal*: "A mulatto man, age 23, pretty fair with his head commonly shaved in order to make himself pass for a white man."

Yet shaving hair was also one of the first things slave traders did to captives, a way of stripping the enslaved of their identity. Denied palm oil and combs to care for their hair, they would turn to whatever was available. Goose grease over a butter knife for a curl, coils wrapped in strings, lye mixed with potatoes to straighten a strand. But lye eats the skin off your head. It's a slow-burn chemical scalping.

Elsewhere in New York City, another man's fortune is much improved: One Pierre Toussaint, a Haitian man, arrived from Santo Domingo in 1787. The third-generation slave of a well-off French family, he used his skills navigating the hair and society of New York's elite to support the family of those who enslaved him and his own family. He was released from servitude on his enslaver's deathbed, and went on to open a home for orphans, both Black and white. His name changed in the transfer paperwork, shearing off his slaver's: Bérard to Toussaint. The leader of the Haitian Slave Revolt was named Toussaint L'Ouverture.

Toussaint the barber died on the path to sainthood, buried at St. Patrick's Cathedral. But plenty of people consider his success to be a reward for servility: 139 years after his death, a reflection of his life in the *New York Times* was titled "Canonizing a Slave: Saint or Uncle Tom?" Black Catholics were skeptical of his inclusion in liturgy by the church. "The man was a perfect creature of his times," said Reverend Lawrence E. Lucas from Resurrection Catholic Church in Harlem, quoted in the piece. "He was a good boy, a namby-pamby, who kept the place assigned to him." He could have bought his freedom sooner. He could have slit his keeper's throat with his straight razor like Sweeney Todd.

Elsewhere, in the histories of barbers in America, he's considered a hero—a philanthropist—a muse.

A year prior to Toussaint's New York debut, a new law passed in New Orleans: "Excessive attention to dress" was seen as evidence of misconduct. Free Black women were forbidden to wear plumes and jewelry in their hair and were to wear the tignon, a handkerchief that bound the hair, and no longer permitted to assemble at night.

That misconduct was a fear of Black women seducing white men and confusing the racial economy of slaves—too much freedom meant, for white overseers, too much temptation. To mitigate this, the salacious surveillance of whiteness, Black women wore the tignon but wrapped their hair in jewels, chose sumptuous fabrics, swaddled their curls. The defiance, in illustrated portraits of the women of the time, makes them look like royalty. A few decades removed from their ancestral homes, where they might have been royalty—once.

The earliest ship manifests considered Asians, like the enslaved Black people who arrived before them, a form of product, not people. Asians were loaded onto the flesh merchant ships that earlier brought Africans, their ships having been rerouted from Africa to Asia. In a "Secret Memorandum from the British Colonial Office" to the East India Company in 1803, just after the Haitian Revolution, colonial administrator John Sullivan explains the substitution baldly, writing that bringing over Chinese laborers would "effectually tend to this danger [of a spirit of insurrection], a free race of cultivators into our islands, who, from habits and feelings could be distinct from the Negroes." We were framed as a solution to suppress Black slave rebellion and still grow production. We weren't slaves, we were *indentured*. Lesser than white, better than Black, with a debt that could be surmountable. Supplementary, surmountable, servile. Alien and suspect, just the same.

Trying to find the names of indentured Asians on the earliest ship manifests is as hard as you'd expect, even if the fact of them existing is well repeated in academia and history books. The archives are the ghosts of the slavers. Their names are mistranslated or not recorded at all in some cases. In others, the only records of them are of the white overseers who managed the debts they struck a bargain for, the gatekeepers of their journey to the United States.

I find my people in the trail of hair. I find them in reports of

Asians in Chinatowns, being chased through the streets, lynched, or forcibly shaved. In cartoons printed cross-country—in the *Herald*, in the *Times*, in the *Tribune*. I can find them written about in the National Archives, through documents of people regulating their freedoms out of existence. I find their descendants in the comments, asking plaintively for more information on their great-great-great-grandparents, by name, generally to no avail.

When I move from those newspaper archives to the news home page, I now see their descendants, beaten in the streets. Pushed onto train tracks down the street from my old apartment. Stabbed on the corner across the street from my favorite dumplings. Chinese elders who are grandmothers now, but still their daughters' daughters' daughters' daughters—attacked on their way to get groceries.

Eventually, I leave. I leave for California, a place of sun and where many Asians first stepped foot in America. I try not to think of it as an escape. What is hardest to digest isn't a specific trauma that decided the departure, but the terror of its anticipation.

One hundred fifty years before I touched down onto the tarmac, Southern plantation owners shipped indebted Chinese to California to "punish the Negro for having abandoned the control of his old master." They were also brought to factories in the Northeast to keep the wages down.

The railroad magnate Charles Crocker testified, "After we got Chinamen to work, we took the more intelligent of the white laborers and made foremen of them." Upward mobility for white laborers relied on the subjugation of everyone they worked alongside. Central Pacific railroad workers were at the time 90 percent Chinese, white laborers having shunned the dangers of that labor for years. But the Chinese also cost one-half to two-thirds of what white workers cost for the same job. Many more of them died, being tasked with most of the explosives and high-risk scenarios along the railway. And their deaths were never recorded formally, their names never acknowledged in any way.

The Chinese railroad workers who survived their jobs were forced to walk the many miles back to their homes from the celebration of the railroad's eventual opening. It was a celebration that they were discourteously not invited to, despite a speculated thousand-plus bodies buried in its creation. One 1870 newspaper reported that 20,000 pounds of bones were dug up from shallow graves and taken by train to repatriate the workers, approximating anywhere from 50 to 1,200 fragmented bodies. There is no real way to bridge the estimation into reality. Historians who study the sites have folders of unmarked graves and remnants of the laborers' camp sites. Combs, porcelain and tin cups, and stoneware, mostly. Some forgotten picks, some hair.

A few years after they finished their duties as railroad workers and other kinds of labor, a mob of 500 people ran through the streets of Los Angeles's Chinatown and lynched 18 Chinese men and boys, wiping out 10 percent of the entire city's Chinese population in an alley known then as "Negro Alley." In the reporting on the massacre, the *Los Angeles Star* called Chinese residents "barbarians," the cartoons showing white men pulling Asian men by their braids.

AN EMPIRE OF HAIR

My mixed lineage makes my family likely to be implicated on both sides of this act of violence. I see my family in both caricatures. I remember every evening I've ever braided my father's hair, had my hair brushed by my mother before bed—the feeling of her pulling my head straight, yanking the tangles, calling me tender-headed in Chinese. I am protected, perhaps occasionally, from the experience of the victim by the whiteness of the historical perpetrator.

This, too, is part of the braid.

The queue, a braid that men in China wore at the emperor's behest as proof of loyalty, was a symbol of their difference. Soon, anti-Asian sentiment came together in the Pigtail Ordinance of 1878. Officials believed the threat of losing queues would keep Chinese immigrants from overcrowding jails, and so San Francisco jailors began cutting queues off imprisoned Asians. One might assume they were imprisoned for theft, for violence, but it was often simply poverty. Ho Ah Kow, the plaintiff for the case that led to the ordinance to be overturned, had been imprisoned in the county jail for failure to pay a fine concerning the square footage of his lodging in San Francisco. Two years earlier, California had made it a misdemeanor to occupy a room or apartment containing less than 500 cubic feet of space for each person occupying it, otherwise they would be fined up to $50 or imprisoned.

Given the racial segregation and job limitations that Chinese immigrants experienced in San Francisco, they often slept in apartments in larger groupings than those requirements demanded. The people considered misdemeanor criminals were poor immigrants who could not afford and were chased away from better options. Or they were poor immigrants who refused to pay the fine on principle: They wanted to protest the injustice of being presented with only bad options.

When they went to county jail, their hair was forcibly shaved to assimilate them in a country that didn't want them to stay but made it harder for them to go. They came to this country with long hair and left jail shaved of both their hair and their dignity.

Early America loved hairpieces and hated Asians. An article in the *New York Times* in 1921 warned that 9 out of 10 American women were addicted to hairnets and wore them on a daily basis; American girls used over 180 million human-hair nets from China that year. Hairnets are like snoods, woven of silk thread and hair, and can be both wraps for your hair—like a tignon, but a net—or an extension in and of itself. The hair ideal for all hairpieces for its texture and durability was Chinese.

This was in an era when the Federal Chinese Exclusion Act, made permanent in 1902, denied citizenship or immigration to Chinese, and where Asians already living here were given "separate but equal" schooling, were prohibited from buying land, and the act of marrying outside of their race would render both parties ineligible for citizenship. America was built on imported labor from Black slaves, indentured Asians, and forcibly assimilated Indigenous Americans. It appreciated the bodies of people of color in pieces if not full personhood. While the full human lives of people of color repulsed America, it considered us productive, as in products to use.

It was cheaper for American firms to export the raw hair

from China to the United States for bleaching and dyeing, import it back to China for hand-knotting, and re-export the finished product. During the entirety of the hairpiece wave in America, the Chinese were banned from immigrating, but their hair was on nearly every woman's head in America, and the sparse Asians moored on this continent were being chased through the streets and forcibly shaved.

Queue cutting and the tignon laws and forced haircuts came about as petty and violent responses to seeing us living and surviving in our own enclaves. But I don't want to talk about the various means of degradation people of color have experienced. In spite of everything, we lived.

People still kept oral histories and secret braids. Loss feels so much like drowning in a tide that won't break. I can swim, but not against memories I can't articulate, and memory is tidal. But now I am trying to accept the unknowing. Maybe it's provisional. Maybe belonging isn't something given but something you create in the absence of things.

My neighbors didn't have to take care of me, but they did. And many people, across many decades, have walked the path of the railways for remains to return to families.

I know plenty of elders who refuse to engage in English, and I imagine our ancestors did the same, uninterested in being constantly surveilled by white debtors. I can consider the idea that their missing names was an act of violence done to them, but there was always a chance they were uninterested in being seen by people who clearly disdained them anyway. Despite contempt and constant policing, they built pathways. Tunnels and underground railroads against death, captivity, explosives, kerosene, lynching. They made maps of their bodies to places most of them were never guaranteed to see.

They were segregated into their own neighborhoods, yes. They were turned away from places, yes. But that also meant there were places they could be amongst their own people. Places where they did not need to translate. Places they didn't need to code switch or be servile or look down respectfully, fearfully. Places where their bodies and hair weren't quite as policed. Beauty salons and barber shops in their own communities.

These spaces became places they could plan.

One of the greatest planners of these spaces was beauty entrepreneur Madam C. J. Walker. Her legacy is the blueprint for many beauty businesses today. It's also a key example of the fact that while racism was constantly used against her, her Blackness was the source of her strength.

Born Sarah Breedlove on December 23, 1867, in Louisiana, Walker built a million-dollar empire on hair products for Black women, inspired by the problem she solved when her own hair had begun to fall out. She started with door-to-door sales, eventually establishing a hair institute and the largest factory in the nation. Her company turned out hundreds of stylists who would join her or start their own salons. Walker organized a national business union in America for her agents and rewarded attendees for highest sales *and* largest charitable contributions.

She and her students built an empire at the same time as Jim Crow segregation laws were built up to entrap them. Louisiana enacted some of the first Black codes in December 1865, right after slavery was abolished by the 13th Amendment. The codes were modeled on former slave laws and in some states required Blacks to have written evidence of employment for the coming January. Walker was born two years later, the first freeborn person in her family. At the same time, former Confederate soldiers became Southern judges and police, which reinforced criminalization of the Black people who had the misfortune of ending up in their courtrooms. The North was no safe haven either. The NYPD developed through its enforcement of the Fugitive Slave Clause, which meant that through the early 19th century, they kidnapped free Black people and sent them back into slavery.

Jim Crow also checked access to credit, so most Black American beauty companies could not utilize banks or other institutional means of financial support—which has led to an economic fact that they have less intergenerational wealth than their white counterparts. Consistently, Black brands began from household enterprises, and successful businesses were built on the fortunes made from your own profits, not through institutional favors or family nepotism. It required on-the-ground networking, which was a great risk to take. As soon as she could afford one, Madam C. J. Walker hired a chauffeur in order to avoid segregation on the train as she traveled from city to city, state to state. Louis, her driver, would remain in her employ for the rest of her life, and be named in her estate.

Once, one of Walker's most loyal and influential employees, Marjorie Stewart Joyner, went on a business trip where she was refused boarding privileges for a train in Texas. An agent informed her that the train carried no Jim Crow car, so her ticket would not be honored. A porter who knew Joyner convinced the agent to let her make the trip in a baggage car. Joyner later sued the Burlington Rock Island Railroad for racial discrimination, asserting that not only had she been denied equal accommodation, but she'd had to share accommodation with a corpse on its way to an out-of-state burial.

Traveling Walker agents had to deal with roadblocks like this all the time. Madam C. J. Walker became a millionaire during *this*. In the face of this. In spite of it.

For Black women, the beauty industry was one of the few avenues of work that they could enter and flourish in. Salons were some of the first prevalent Black-owned places nationwide, and they were integral to organizing for local communities and political outreach. Barbershops were also one of the first avenues of business for Black men to enter in successfully—white folks didn't consider it a huge leap in class and viewed it as a servile profession, something that wouldn't threaten class structures but reinforce servility. This contempt didn't dissuade beauticians from harnessing possibility and making presentation a powerful tool. "Presentability was a factor in the fight for desegregation," according to Professor Julia Kirk Blackwelder. People used to life under surveillance understand that optics are a matter of life and death. Salons were a place one would become "acceptable," and plug in to the community.

Besides offering stable jobs to people who had no previous experience in the industry, hairstyling offered mobility. It built a network for you to lean on and connect with. Walker kept extensive records and regularly offered training to women who couldn't pay up front, across the country. Once the course had been paid for, the agent could set up a salon in her home or begin offering door-to-door services. Walker never forgot where she came from and utilized cross-class divides to strengthen her organizing.

Walker and her competitors invited friends into their homes to demonstrate their creams and lotions and troubleshoot problems in their community. These home demonstrations evolved into household salons and freestanding parlors as their clientele grew larger and more resourceful. Black American churches were also an essential venue for Walker and her competitors, because their basements and halls were offered at minimal cost and already had built-in organizational structures to piggyback on. Walker recruiters relied on clergy to introduce them to clients and to locate safe accommodations for women stylists on the road during segregation. Once they had the pastor's wife on their side, they had the congregation. Walker also encouraged sales agents to have local chapters of the organization that pooled membership dues for fundraising for local needs, much like church groups. Each formal meeting opened with the "Hairdressers' Ode to Madam C. J. Walker," which was to the melody of the Christian hymn "Onward, Christian Soldiers."

Time and time again, Walker utilized the power of her network to focus on causes like equal-opportunity education and anti-lynching advocacy. She offered to fund Black colleges across the country if they would institute classes featuring a syllabus she curated for business-minded Black women. Walker clubs ensured medical leave and burial funds, and did annual grocery giveaways to the local club communities. Walker created a community that was at one point several thousand strong. She is a unique example of a Black woman who created her fortune from a problem she dealt with directly: Her hair had been falling out due to stress and poor living conditions, and it was from the pursuit of a remedy for her own experience that her brand was even born. The only surviving manual of Walker's business enterprise opens with a photo of the plantation on which she was born, placed directly across from the Walker estate she purchased, designed, and built, one sale at a time. One head of hair to a millionaire's estate.

Walker died in 1919 at the age of 51. She'd been advised to work less to combat her hypertension but passed away returning home from a business trip through the Midwest. She'd been lobbying for the rights of Black Americans in World War I just before. Her daughter A'Lelia took over the company after her death, but the Great Depression hit every business in America hard and Black businesses doubly so. She sold off heirlooms and antiques to try to keep the business afloat and her own quality of life up to the standards she'd become used to. In the end, it didn't make much difference, though. She died younger than her mother, at the age of 46 in 1931 from hypertension. The business went on as a modest echo of its former greatness until 1985, when the family finally sold the company.

The Walker Estate in Irvington-on-Hudson is in the hands of the New Voices Foundation now, preserved as a monument and standing legacy to the family and Walker's success. The last press-magnet bonanza there was in July 2021, when Black American couturier Kerby Jean-Raymond hosted his couture debut in the rain. Every look was a reference to Black invention. Eventually, a showstopper look walked down the steps to waiting onlookers: a model wrapped in a tower of hair curlers draped around an orange and blue robe.

In a piece on Madam C. J. Walker, Doreen St. Felix wrote, "On Black hair, the drama of freedom questions itself, closed off from whiteness and invisible to men. The freedom lies . . . in the possibility to do something with it, to change it as if on a whim, that kind of hapless freedom."

＝

The years of A'Lelia's stewardship of the company and after her death were difficult and transformative in America. The 1920s to the '80s held a lot of history and consequently a lot of changes in beauty: There was the Great Depression, Roosevelt's New Deal, World War II, the Korean and Vietnam Wars, the car industry booming and Woodstock and hippies and lipstick shortages and fabric shortages and war drafts and nuclear bombings. Chaos and history, economic disasters, and the reshaping of national identities. Hair got short, then long, Marcel waved and tucked in perfect wigs, often depending on the year and the money you had to spend on beauty. Christina Jenkins, another Black woman from Louisiana, patented Hair-Weeve in 1952 while working for a wig manufacturer. While hair extensions have been around for centuries, protective hairpieces and synthetic, affordable extensions are far more recent, and their development has been culture-shifting. The quest for respectability and economic freedom are deeply tied together, something both Asians and Black Americans have navigated through beauty spaces. By the 1960s, they did so from the opposite sides of a business exchange.

In November 1965, the global wig industry was restructured by the US Department of the Treasury in response to China's participation in the Vietnam War. The Treasury placed an embargo on "Asiatic hair," targeting China's hair industry. In a year when Chinese troops had been dispatched to North Vietnam, they wanted that currency flow to stop. The treasury ruled that hair from US allied countries could be used in wigs regardless of whether it was "Asiatic" or not, as long as it was not from a Communist country. The embargo was described by an economic official in South Korea as "manna from heaven," because it allowed Korean wigmakers to get ahead of their competition, and by 1971, they firmly overtook their competition for the following decades.

When South Korea became a center of wig manufacture in the 1960s, it didn't have a strong factory trade yet, but it did have plenty of people with capital that regenerated itself millimeter by millimeter, every day—and that was a start of something. "You can say the myth of South Korean exports grew out of wigs made from the hair of our grandmothers, mothers, and sisters," journalist Sangju Bak wrote. Hair traders went from village to village buying hair from women and young girls. You could tell when the hair traders came to town, because long hair tied in buns transformed into short bobs.

South Korean officials worked with the US government to link US wig buyers to South Korean factories and sent Korean executives to the States; USAID facilitated US investment in Korean firms, and the embargo created preferential access to the US market for Korean firms. The US market received more than 95 percent of South Korea's wigs. Korean banks established branches in the US near military bases and offered loans to migrant businessmen hoping to sell wigs through family connections back in Korea. Many Korean businessmen in these situations came here trained as skilled doctors or teachers or in the hopes of becoming them through US universities, but the racism of these institutions shut them out.

Hair became their most realistic option; a window opened when a door was shut in their face. The overwhelming majority of the new customer base for these mass-market wigs were Black American women, and so it was in Black neighborhoods where the first wig stores were established. Plenty of now well-established wig suppliers sold their products out of the back of their cars, from Harlem to Chicago to Detroit to LA. Mutual marginalization became the birthplace of a very specific, imperially funded modern economy.

Dr. Afiya Mbilishaka, hair historian and professor at the University of the District of Columbia, explained to *InStyle* that "wigs were used to address employment. There were actually certain hair requirements when a Black woman had to comply with a style that her natural hair maybe couldn't do. It justified the respectability of that person, or people gave them feedback that their hairstyle or texture was not acceptable otherwise."

Wigs were the third most popular export for the beginning of South Korea's industrialization. The first was military contracted supplies to America for the Vietnam War. The trade agreements around war in Asian countries shaped, however unexpectedly, the beauty industry and race relations for decades in the United States.

Now, it is estimated that 70 percent of beauty supply stores—the primary purveyor of wigs in America—are Korean owned, and the main consumers of synthetic wigs are Black American women. And all this because of an embargo stemming from America's anti-Chinese sentiment. These politics coalesce into the average experience in any beauty supply store in America.

A century after Madam C. J. Walker's entrance into the hair industry, there are new entrepreneurs in the beauty space creating new legacies.

There's Paris McKenzie, who in 2020 became a 16-year-old Black teen beauty supply store owner in Brooklyn. "My vision was to have a place that was very accessible, affordable, and comfortable for anyone who walks in. If you're Black, you're white, you're Asian, whoever walks in, I wanted them to feel comfortable no matter what. And especially because I'm Black, I wanted to push more on the Black products and making Black people feel comfortable in an area that we very much frequent. . . . I just want us to feel comfortable in a space where we spend the most money, and not like we're being followed, watched, or accused of stealing. . . . I have experienced people telling me that my dreams were invalid or I couldn't do it or laughed at me while I was working just because of my age. I don't want others to feel the same way."

There's Rebundle, a plastic-free hair company for Black women, founded by Black women, which recently raised $1.4 million in funding in 2022 for their alternatives to synthetic braids. The origin story is an echo of Madam Walker's. Founder Ciara Imani May had been dealing with scalp irritation from her braids and wanted a nontoxic alternative to synthetic hair. Rebundle uses banana-based fibers that are compostable, and they have a recycling program for used synthetic extensions, too. The past few decades of hair have been made of plastic fibers and as a result, none of it is biodegradable. One in two Black women experience hair loss in their lifetime, in part due to the chemicals and scalp allergies to synthetic hair and relaxers.

AN EMPIRE OF HAIR

Rebundle claims that plant-based fibers mean no scalp irritation from chemically treated hair fibers, which can lead to balding for particularly sensitive scalps. It can mean, for some, far less pain. These options prioritize the comfort and variety of Black womanhood over the sacrifices they often make in the name of "respectable" hairstyles. There are more ways to comfortably express hair visions now: Braids can come with less pain, and less plastic waste to boot.

The CROWN Act also recently went into law in California in 2019. The legislation, now law in 20 states, demands protection against race-based hair discrimination in the workplace and in school systems from K-12. It eventually passed in Louisiana, in 2022: Madam C. J. Walker's home state.

Over the years of metabolizing hair history, I've slowly begun learning new braids and new hair techniques. There's so much to learn, and every technique has a lineage so much older than you'd imagine it to be. There are endless kinds of braids—crochet braids, Dutch braids, French braids, box braids, fishtails, feed-ins, goddess braids. I can't do most of them, but I could spend hours watching them appear in a flurry of expert hands and combs and extensions and careful sectioning. I learned how exhausting it is to properly blow-dry my own hair—sectioning, heating then cooling, heat protectants, hair smoothing serums, hair wax and braid balms and four-strand weaves. And when I do watch or practice on myself, I think of all the history that goes into the gesture, all the secrets, the countries, the persistence, and artistry. But on myself, I also endlessly and habitually check for lice and fleas. A force of habit.

By now I've lived many lifetimes of hair since I saw the lice swinging. I shaved my head in the bathroom to Portishead, dyed it blue in a friend's bath while they hosed me down, laughing. I used to dye my hair gray and now it's going gray prematurely. I look more like my elders every day.

Even when you die, it looks like your body keeps growing hair for a while—did you know that? As your body breaks down, your hair refuses mortality. When your skin dehydrates and your bones decay, when death comes for you, hair stays. It heralds: tells people who come after you so much about how you existed, who you belong to, all about your family. You carry it everywhere, and it will stay when you leave. All the bugs that eat your body take that story wherever they travel, too. Little adventurers, secret keepers, storytellers of nature and beauty even if they are repulsive (to me).

When I think about all that, I never feel lonely. Because when I die and the bugs finally do eat me and my body feeds the trees, I'll have been scattered everywhere I've ever been, across time and space. The evidence of my existence will be far beyond me, and I will belong everywhere I travel. There will be no name-calling, no anxieties of passing in a white space, no pressure to negotiate other people's discomfort or racist expectations. I will be just another fact of a legacy much older than myself, another step on a ladder of generational resilience beyond oceans and countries and empire. These things—they will be rendered meaningless in the face of death and where it might take me. I will just be joining a million ancient names—another branch among the faceless many and the treasured remembered few. I'll be home, and everyone who ever made me possible will have called me by my name.

4

Nailing the Landing

For my early twenties I subsisted on an anemic $25 weekly grocery budget eked from freelance gigs, plus free empanadas from the nail salon down the block from my apartment. I would be fed them during my monthly nail appointments, one of the only indulgences I could afford, and my salon was a no-frills Dominican place with no website, no Instagram, and no credit card processors. It had soap operas playing at max volume and a pack of children always playing on the floor in the back near the sink; neighbors would come in just to talk and there was usually someone's grandmother napping in the corner. This was not glamour, but the nail art they offered was flossy. Where more publicized salons in Manhattan would charge $225 and up for a full set with nail art, my nails would top off at $50 plus tip, as well as the bonus of being fed empanadas during birthday celebrations for neighbors, regular customers, workers, and the workers' children. They welcomed me, and it always felt like homecoming.

Over the years, I would bring them nail polish and UV lamps sent to me by brands to review, and I would wave when I walked by with groceries. I tried to come in monthly, but sometimes it would be less often, and I'd often come back with mismatched nails done in a city I'd traveled to for work. We'd joke that my nails were a passport, that the replacements and repairs I'd get on my return were the real stamps to certify I was back home. It's an echo of how nail salons came to be so popular in America to begin with: Being a manicurist is one of the most available jobs to get "fresh off the boat." It requires minimal English, and you can find work even if you are undocumented. You don't need to know a place to know the rituals for a manicure.

It's this placelessness that built the nail industry after the Vietnam War. This world was built by refugees, by loss and what it bought.

America went into Vietnam in the 1960s hoping to use it as an example of how it could crush a communist government, having failed spectacularly in Korea in the '50s, a war often called the "Forgotten War" by the generations old enough to remember it. More than 10 percent of the population of North and South Korea died in that war, having had napalm and more bombs dropped on the island than what was dropped in the entire Pacific theater in World War II. The bombings were so constant and all-encompassing that entire towns were moved underground, and peasants came out to farm at night to avoid famine. This largely failed. By 1952 every significant town, city, and industrial area in North Korea had already been bombed. There were no more targets left to hit, more bombs dropped than there were people, but still no one won. An armistice was instituted instead, and fighting was replaced by sanctions still in place to this day.

The United States helped rehabilitate South Korea by offering military contracts for industrial projects, and it was on those contracts that a newborn South Korean industry cut its teeth. In 1960, South Korea was ranked as one of the poorest countries in the world. Three years later, South Korea was the United States' biggest military ally in Vietnam, and many of the cars and guns shipped in for the troops were Korean made. The first two years of war created 40 percent of the country's foreign exchange earnings, and the South Korean troops sent to Vietnam were paid for by the American government. Outside of military contracts, the biggest industry was wigs, with the hair collected from poor villagers across Korea and hand-sewn into caps for American consumers, primarily Black Americans.

The American liberal attitude going into the Vietnam War can be neatly summarized by then Senator John F. Kennedy's speech at the 1956 Friends of Vietnam conference: "If we are not the parents of little Vietnam, surely we are the godparents. We presided at its birth, we gave assistance to its life, we have helped to shape its future.... This is our offspring. We cannot abandon it."

And then with heartbreaking concentration and insolent devotion and an absolute metric fuckton of money and bombs, America lost that war. America lost badly and quickly and painfully and stayed there, insisted on it, obliterating and reshaping the forests and trees and land—for years.

America took from every family, it took a family from every hamlet, a hamlet from every province, whole slices of land burned into dust, paddies and brush fertilized with mines and Agent Orange and body parts. It got high on grass and high on war. And millions of people fled their country as it burned under their feet, then drowned at sea trying to find refuge.

When the capital of South Vietnam fell in 1975, it was the end of a war and a country. April 30, 1975, marks the fall of Saigon in western narratives. It is called Ngày Quốc Hận, "National Day of Resentment," by the refugees who survived but had to flee. Flee, as the situation would have it, right into the arms of the American military carriers that were just offshore as the country imploded into flames. The 1975 Refugee Act was passed one month after the fall of Saigon, and 130,000 Vietnamese began entering the United States.

After the fall of Saigon, the actress Tippi Hedren worked as an international relief coordinator for Food for the Hungry. She visited a refugee camp called Hope Village established near Sacramento, set up in a former tuberculosis treatment center. At first, she visited with her seamstress and typist in an effort to help teach the women marketable skills, with the hope of getting them work in America. But they had little interest in pattern-making and tailoring clothes. They were fascinated with her perfectly manicured nails. So Hedren flew in her personal manicurist and support from a local beauty school to teach twenty women for free, and later helped them find work in salons across Southern California. In a documentary on her impact on the salon industry by Vietnamese filmmaker Adele Pham, second-generation salon owner and president of Advance Beauty College Minh Nguyen called her the "Godmother of the Nail Industry." His wife, a manicurist herself, is best friends with a woman who studied under Hedren's patronage. The founding owners of Advance Beauty College, Minh and Kien, had fled Vietnam in 1975. Minh had been a Navy lieutenant, then became a social worker, assisting refugees with the transition into nail work and later acquiring a license himself.

More than fifty years after the Vietnam War, over 50 percent of nail technicians in the United States are of Vietnamese descent. The influx also changed the price point and accessibility of the beauty practice. Once up to $200 in the 1980s—the equivalent of more than $440 today, the typical manicure now costs $20. Manicures in New York are on average cheaper than even that, at $13.71 according to a 2021 industry survey. Once a luxury experience only the moneyed could afford, manicures became something middle- and working-class women could indulge in and find in their own neighborhoods.

This could be partially attributed to developments in technology that shortened the time necessary to provide a manicure, like acrylics and electric files, but the stories of Asian manicurists waiting for a customer, surrounded by white colleagues fully occupied in a busy salon are too numerous for me to believe that's all there is to it. The story of Yan Rist, one of the manicurists who studied under Hedren and from whom Hedren secured a job, is also skeptical. "I worked on Rodeo Drive, but I am a refugee, and I didn't dress well at the time. All the rich women coming in—they didn't want to try a newcomer." Rist was once a military intelligence translator and then a secretary for the State Department, but her job as a nail technician in wealthy white enclaves proved to be too costly for her both emotionally and literally. While rich women snubbed her services, she paid $8 a day ($45 today) to park her car, and so she left to find another opportunity.

People would initially go to Asian manicurists only if the deal was too good to pass up. So while manicuring offered economic opportunity to escape a war-torn country, it didn't prevent the devaluation of that labor in comparison to their white peers. It was one field that required minimum English skills, no college education, and crucially: The licensing exam was offered in Vietnamese, after community organizers championed language options to offer in locations not far from refugee camps and the newly established ethnic enclaves. And for the first twenty students, the classes were free.

Most of the time this story is shared, it's told with starry eyes at the savior that Tippi Hedren became. A woman gathered a class of women who became the next wave of industry veterans in a booming industry that broke barriers in class and race, coming soon to your TV as a prestige Television Event. But these stories are also stories of respectability, imperialism, and the cost of capitalism itself. Vietnamese women were "empowered" to leave their war-torn country for a new opportunity, but it was a situation created by the US's involvement in the first place. The women Hedren worked with were also not "typical" Vietnamese women but wives of high-ranking South Vietnamese military personnel, some working in military intelligence themselves. Knowing this complicates a hero's narrative—when we consider *who* is "worth" saving first, it's usually those who are most recognizable to those in power, anyway. It perpetuates the myth of the compliant and exceptional model minority. It frames all participants in stark lighting as either hero or victim, when neither is altogether true. They got chances at a new life because of military and intimate family connections, after having been traumatized into having nothing left to lose.

In his novel about beauty, love, and his mother—a Vietnamese beauty worker by trade—Ocean Vuong wrote it best: "To be or not to be. That is the question. A question, yes, but not always a choice."

Until the 1980s, the United States did not have a separate policy regarding "refugees" and instead called them "parolees," with some countries having a stronger claim to the term than others. A scale of suffering. The lowest would be alienated, literally classified as "illegal aliens" as if descending to the planet from some void in space.

The 1948 Displaced Persons Act prioritized accepting "some" Europeans who had been "victims of persecution by the Nazi government." The 1953 Refugee Relief Act focused on Europeans "escapees" who had "rejected communist-occupied areas of Europe." This political purity was hard to achieve since Communist Party membership was often a requirement for educational and job opportunities behind the Iron Curtain. The 1965 Immigration Act eradicated the former quota system, whereby refugees were up against slots to take, and weighed against their professional skills and if they were uniting with family.

All acts were directly linked to responses to US military engagements and had ties to US-backed governments or military aid. American Empire fostered the environments that created the crises of refugees in the first place. Out of chaos comes power, debt, and transformation. Is that not the summary of the American Dream? Bootstrap your way out of burned fields we set on fire, bootstrap your way into becoming an exception to the rules we arbitrarily made to define who you are. But don't dream too close to our homes. Not in our backyard.

The 1970s and '80s became a time when Asian American businesses popped up by the dozens in poor and working-class neighborhoods in major cities across America—Los Angeles, Atlanta, New York. They took over the leases or bought businesses from Jewish landowners in the communities who'd worked the hair trades before them, who wanted to move to more white spaces. These were the locations newcomers could afford to rent after collectivizing their funds and taking out loans from places that would give them to Asians. Before, nail services were part of a salon experience, but not the singular offering someone went in for. That rapidly changed as the Vietnamese began offering nail-*only* salons at more competitive price points in nonwhite neighborhoods.

The first chain salon popped up in a South Central Los Angeles neighborhood and catered specifically to the Black and Asian community surrounding it. The unassuming salon in a strip mall, with a neon rose in the window and a corner spot on South Central and East 103rd Street, was owned by a Black woman named Olivett Robinson and a Vietnamese refugee named Charlie Vo. They named it Mantrap Salon.

Robinson taught Vo English during appointments elsewhere, and that was how they built their friendship. They went into building Mantrap with relatives of Vo who had also studied nails. The business exploded, with people lining up around the block for Vo's designs, and at its height they had nine locations across California. A competing, unassociated salon named Nail Trap opened just across the parking lot of their main location—they were so popular, they had imitators.

Their business and friendship are legendary in the nail community, the origin story of racial solidarity, beauty, and successful partnership. Many manicurists across America first got their start at Mantrap before opening their own salons. There are salons owned by the children of these first women still open in Florida, Maine, New York, California, New Jersey—decades old, by now, well worn into their own communities, having transformed the nails of thousands of people across the United States. By now, those salon owners are teaching their children how to take over their businesses, having successfully learned how to franchise their own salons from Mantrap's example.

When Mantrap opened, the price was $150 for a set. But as the industry exploded, competition became fierce, and prices went down and hours got longer in order to make the same money as before. But their interracial business is also a singular exception to how nail salons ended up—largely Asian owned, with Black women defining the trends that create the demand itself. In interviews with manicurists generations down the line, Mantrap is spoken of like a fairy tale they wish they'd been able to see up close. It isn't famous outside of nail culture, and yet the imprint the unassuming salon made onto beauty culture is still felt, and the loss as an example of cross-racial solidarity is still an open wound. It had been wildly successful for years, but it didn't last as a commercial chain and the brand did not release its own products. The digital evidence of its existence hardly remains at all. We're losing the recipes of community partnerships when we should be using them *more*.

When nail acrylics were first popularized in the late '60s, it was Black women who were the first to bear them on magazine covers, with Donyale Luna wearing them on the cover of *Vogue*

UK in 1966. When Olympian Florence Griffith Joyner, known as FloJo, earned her several gold medals in 1988 and graced the cover of *Sports Illustrated*, she was wearing acrylics she did herself. While training for the Olympics she worked part-time as a nail technician in a salon. It was probably a salon not unlike Robinson's and Vo's.

The programs meant for refugee Vietnamese, alongside immigrant enclaves created out of necessity due to racism, made group economics even more vital. They also privileged the middle class and those more easily assimilated into America, those with English proficiency and those with military connections. After the first group of trainees, mostly middle-class, English-speaking, and with military connections, more and more refugees coming from more rural areas or with lower proficiency levels also entered the industry. The success of these new immigrants in a racist institution fostered resentment among longer-standing American minorities. Asians were shaped into a myth of the model minority that many of us took to the bank: our own banks, our own familial networks, or government-sponsored programs. We were also expected to fight against other minorities for space and economic opportunities that white people had no interest in, redlined into the same housing markets and expected to betray each other, told that there was scarcity. It often worked, because racist communities across the United States created scarcity through refusing to lease or lend to nonwhite community members. People implemented racist clauses in housing deeds and rejected or offered outrageously predatory lending terms to nonwhites, permitting exceptions occasionally to Asians only by assuming their proximity to whiteness or to American militarism. Redlining, the shorthand for race-based exclusionary tactics in real estate, has been actively evolving since the term and practice was coined in the 1930s. It has been seen in all the major United States cities: Los Angeles, New York, Atlanta, Chicago, Detroit. All of which are beauty hubs, too.

Mantrap's legacy disappears in the shadow of other nail stories now. The biggest nail salon chain, Regal Nails, is in more than 800 locations like Walmart across America, and it was founded by Vietnamese immigrant "Charlie" Quoy Ton. His wife was a nail salon owner in the mid-1990s, and he turned to nail salon product distribution when he couldn't get a job as a chemical engineer in the United States, despite it being his vocational training. He began an import business for mail-order nail supplies, and when he approached Walmart to begin a nail salon in their stores (having observed the success of a hair salon chain already in existence), he was refused at first. A year later, they relented, and he was given less than a week to open his first one. From there, he opened 1,000, and it's since scaled up and down in size over the past decade. It is by far the biggest nail salon operation in the United States.

As Regal Nails is a franchise business, the salons don't have as much corporate oversight but still operate within certain constraints of rent cost and service pricing. Regal operates on a license to franchisees and an ongoing royalty system in exchange for the usage of branding and knowledge. Franchises have been a doorway to economic growth for minority-owned businesses in America for decades, with fast food and nail salons as key examples reflecting Black and Asian business success. But such success has had shortfalls. While a manicure at Mantrap may have been $150 in the 1980s, at Regal Nails salons across America 40 years later, the same labor is priced around $17. You can expect 60 percent of that to go into the pocket of the nail technician directly. No benefits, no job security—just mobility, and tips at the mercy of the consumer's whim. "This form of commercial development allows corporations to pass on their liabilities to third-party suppliers, franchisees, and to some degree, local governments," explains Marcia Chatelain in her work on franchise models and Black America.

If the history of capitalism can tell us anything, it is at least this: Economic growth is not indicative of things going well for workers providing a service. It is merely a sign of expansion. Refugee training programs nowadays, like CalWORKs, have stopped offering refugees nail technician trainings, stating that the field is now so competitive and overcrowded it isn't worth the time.

In 2022, Black nail technicians made up less than 10 percent of the industry, even though Black women spend 80 percent more than the general market on beauty products. Since the majority of the nail salons across America are Asian-owned and hire within their race, it is not a surprise so much as a consequence of racial capitalism and white supremacy fostering competition and ethnic isolation that repeats itself in communities big and small.

It begs the question of what problems are worthy of restitution and repair, how those reparations are afforded and considered doable, and which are ignored in hopes that they will disappear. And when they aren't ignored, who exactly is to be held accountable? The easiest villain is the one who doesn't hire you over someone they knew from back home. The easiest villain for *them* is the person they dread serving for fear of the trope of an angry Black woman, because white women don't even enter the salon. Both are easier to castigate than the idea that racism can harm all kinds of people differently—and make you harm others who don't deserve it.

The enmity collapses oppressions in a way that benefits white supremacy. Both experience racism and replicate it in response to lack of access and opportunity. Asian Americans have individual ethnic histories, but when the nail industry is discussed, we're considered interchangeable. The different countries and languages that make up salon worker backgrounds collapse instantly under the flag of Orientalism—we're all just Asians to outsiders, anyway. In interviews with cosmetology school teachers on the commonality of Asian beauty workers, several trainers have the opinion that the talents of Asian manicurists are "innate," as if half-moon manicures are part of our body memory—something to do with our patience and small physicality. We're mistaken for each other and our grievances compound. "Chop shops" and "manicure mills" reported in news articles and review websites are always Asian. What *kind* of Asian? Negligible.

When you walk into a nail salon, you walk into a living history that fills the air alongside all the acrylic particulates. There is a racial hierarchy you walk into, a play that you participate in over and over again in salons across America, one that compresses race, immigration, exploitation, and solidarity into something that looks innocuous. But ask a Black manicurist how hard it is to find a salon that treats them well versus a Vietnamese manicurist in New York, ask if they are paid equally, if they've had to pay a fee to get a job. Ask if there's resentment there. They'll say yes if they trust you enough to hold their truth. These are the whisper network conversations of radical honesty about race and solidarity that many beauty professionals are afraid to acknowledge. Editorial nail artists are more likely to discuss this openly, as they don't rely on the employment of a salon owner to pay their bills—and it has always been Black editorial nail artists who have been outspoken about it to me first and foremost. They've walked away from salon booths, from steady hours at a shop, finding it less frustrating to work entirely on their own. When pressed, most of the nail techs I spoke to at length brought this problem back to the Vietnam War, the flooding of the market and shifting price points, the economic opportunities given to one community but never offered to their own.

For the Vietnamese refugees who first encountered Hedren, the initial deal had conditions. They had senior military connections to army generals. Under these conditions, the debt was transformed from an American apology to an immigrant's debt to a country that took them in and expected them to start over. This is a debt, even if it is a gift. It is not grace. "There is no gift without debt, which is to say, no gift without claim on the other's existence. . . . To be freed, as [Saidiya] Hartman remarks, is to be a debtor forever," writes Vietnamese American beauty theorist Mimi Thi Nguyen.

The reality of a miracle is that it is also a story of devastation. It demands scars and sacrifice in return for prosperity and democracy. It is a violent transaction, and it is often a trap.

The beauty industry is a parable of transaction, one where a past generation's sacrifice is traded for a present generation's success. It's easy to swallow the myth of miraculous empowerment often offered by brands when it comes to their founder's tales of overcoming, but they usually present either the most tragic or the most simplistic story possible, flattening out the dynamics that produced their circumstances, rendering them unimportant. This is also how the myth of the model minority perpetuates itself: Bootstrapping, funded by American imperialism, becomes disguised purely as an impulse to work hard and prove yourself better than everyone else, regardless of what barriers may prevent them from proceeding along the same path you took. You escaped, you succeeded—so why can't they?

Tippi Hedren's manicurist Dusty Coots has said in interviews that she once felt regret for her participation in the initial trainings. She had no idea that her assistance would end up contributing to the drastic competition and price devaluation of her work for the rest of her life. She felt resentful for many years: displaced by people she once helped. And then she remembered that *her* mother came to America as a war widow, and that the opportunities she was given were not so different from the women she'd helped teach those years before.

In order to feel belonging here, immigrants and their children are supposed to feel grateful to be here at all, and not get too good at what they learn to survive when everything they know is gone. A refugee, an immigrant owes this country something even though this country may have been the reason they had to flee to begin with. An immigrant is a refugee that the state accepts for conditional care, indefinitely. And the children of both are doubly indebted—we owe our parents a better future than the ones they escaped.

But this country taught us something terrible. It taught us, too, how to forget things in order to forge our own futurity. It taught us to compete and constantly prove our loyalties to a country that has never really loved us, only tolerated our existence conditionally. It taught us to abandon each other to try to create our own mythologies. It taught so many of us—and our parents—that upward mobility is the only worthy endgame. That's the reality of Manifest Destiny. That is the American Dream. It's simply white supremacy.

In *Minor Feelings*, Cathy Park Hong writes about the failures of solidarity even among Asian Americans, and she does this by describing her experience of getting a bad pedicure from a Vietnamese teenage boy, who clearly hated the process, too. She writes: "Capitalism as retribution for racism—but isn't that how whiteness recruits us? Whether it's through retribution or indebtedness, who are we when we become better than them in a system that destroyed us?"

I once deviated from my neighborhood Dominican salon to a Chinese-owned one in Crown Heights. I went for acrylic removal and gel application, and there was only one other customer in the salon: a Black woman scheduled for a full acrylic set. They gave me a bad removal—instead of soaking my acrylics off, taking time, they used a nail file to flip them off my nailbed, ripping them off hardened glue and the natural nail, which feels not dissimilar to your real nail being ripped off. In fact, your real nail *can* be ripped off this way, if done carelessly. It is an unpleasant, brisk, and ruinous shortcut that damages your nail health. I squirmed but said nothing, not wanting to seem difficult, just relieved my nails were still attached to my fingers. The other woman watched and winced in sympathy and refused the same treatment herself. The manicurists complained about the inconvenience in Mandarin, which, unknown to them, I understood. I said nothing, still. It was one of the more isolating moments of beauty I've experienced in a salon. I minimized my desires and didn't want to be inconvenient and ended up dissatisfied and embarrassed because of it. The other woman and I both left that salon resentful. We probably would have had a better experience if we had advocated for each other.

As the academic Elaine Kim wrote in 1998 regarding Asian Americans and US race relations: "Coalition work is not easy for anyone. Moreover, a coalition is not right for everything we do. Perhaps it might help for us to view coalition not as a site of comfort and refuge, but a site of struggle.... We must reach far beyond simple-minded celebrations of identity and resist the seductive claims of victimhood. We must scrutinize our warts. We need to be critical and self-critical.... It is 'both/and' rather than 'either/or.'" We have to work together in struggle not to take up the same place but as companions toward a reality we both want to live in: where power doesn't mean a hierarchy over the other, where scarcity isn't real anymore. "We have to move away from always speaking to the dominant"—whiteness, who may not even be in the room—"and rarely speaking to each other." After all, so much of the idealized salon experience is the patter of talk between clients and customers. When there's trust, we learn things about the people around us that we would shrink to tell our mothers.

"Talking service" has a financial cost in salon spaces, as much as an emotional one. But in communities of color, it builds solidarity and helps us keep each other safe and understood. Safety itself is relational; it requires connection to be maintained. And that is also why it is so expensive, and so valuable. We are afraid of being misconstrued, and silence sometimes feels safer than not being really heard at all. Being quiet means you're less likely to feel vulnerable. But to be in community with somebody is to be vulnerable with them. Silence strangles.

───

The cost of a manicure is much lower than it has ever been before. The empire of nails has led to plenty of wealthy Asians—Asians are now the wealthiest racial group in America, but the ethnic makeup is a gap like never before. That income inequality gap began stretching in the 1970s, right around the time Asians began opening nail salons. It has also led to the exploitation of newer migrants in the salon space. As a 2015 *New York Times* two-part exposé addressed, most nail salon workers often experience wage theft, to the point where only a quarter of workers interviewed were paid close to minimum wage—the rest had wages withheld. When the New York Labor Department performed sweeps to investigate labor violations (something they'd never done in a salon before the exposé), they discovered wage theft 80 percent of the time. In a lawsuit filed against their salon owners in New York, workers said that they were paid $1.50 an hour for a 66-hour workweek, that one salon charged them for drinking water, that they were kicked while they sat, working on pedicure stools. One worker was fired after she had to pay hundreds of her own wages to an angry customer for marking her Prada sandals. "I am worth less than a shoe," she said, remembering the moment with perfect and heartbreaking clarity. While the piece did expose the exploitation of the workers, it also led to an increase in government surveillance in communities under the guise of protecting workers, undocumented immigrants being afraid to show up for work, and nail salon owners banding together for lawsuits on the basis of race discrimination. The cost of a manicure still didn't go up, so most workers didn't get raises—they were simply more afraid and more in the spotlight than before. A year after the piece went live, New York ordered 143 nail salons to pay $2 million in damages to 652 employees. That is just a fraction of the workers harmed; that number is merely the number brave enough to speak up, risking all their future jobs.

But the exposé did initiate more community-based organizing across the country. It led to the New York Nail Salon Workers Association and more visibility and support for the already existing California Healthy Nail Salon Collaborative, both founded by community organizers, philanthropists, and nail salon workers. And both are deeply invested in organizing nail salon workers and owners to teach the industry about workplace rights and how tied the industry is to social justice within the communities they serve. They have managed to sponsor legislation for product ingredient transparency, healthy salon core requirements, labor law information to be listed within beauty service licensing applications, and translation services for their members. This work isn't glamorous, though it centers on beauty labor. It is, however, transformative, and deeply necessary. The typical day requires foot-on-the-ground outreach from salon to salon, bilingual or trilingual WhatsApp group messaging and phone trees, grant research, and learning the labyrinthian maze of nonprofit fundraising and governmental lobbying. It's a far cry from sitting across from a client and offering a nail treatment, but the work done by these collaboratives is helping mitigate detrimental health conditions of nail salon workers and offering them needed resources as underresourced and overexploited care providers across the country. Both collectives conduct local, statewide, and national studies alongside researchers to document the statistics within communities in a way that doesn't risk their citizenship status or make them more vulnerable to policing. They aren't alone in this work, either. There's VietLEAD in Philadelphia, the Michigan Healthy Nail Salon Cooperative, Women's Voices for the Earth in Montana, the Healthy Nail Salon Network in Toronto, and the Manitoba Federation of Labour Occupational Health Centre in Winnipeg. Some of these organizations have already been on the ground for several decades.

They've collaborated on educational programs for owners and manicurists for language programs, business services, and, most recently, how to protect yourself in a pandemic. They center around community boards made up of the salon industry veterans their work serves. And some of them provide direct mutual aid in times of crisis, too. No questions asked. Mutual aid funds as part of a salon environment aren't unusual, but those involved shy away from any press or publications for fear of government penalties. At the end of the day, most of the time it's the under-resourced and undocumented, cobbling together support to lend a hand to a friend so they can survive another month of rent so they have more time to buy their way to a better opportunity—perhaps a seat at a better salon. Perhaps a salon of their own one day, one they can open together with trusted friends.

The easy story of nails in America is that the economic opportunity gave the disenfranchised a new start. It's the story of a heroic, pretty, white actress. But an industry can't be a hero. The nail industry—and the hair industry—operate on exploitative labor conditions buffeted by state connections and nepotism.

NAILING THE LANDING

They offer individuals the opportunity to be their own boss, but this also means they have little labor rights in a salon setting and can't unionize, and the very conditions that make staying in an ethnic enclave for work easy make it harder to leave an unjust situation. The vulnerable are still vulnerable here; the vulnerabilities are simply different. They come from inside the salon and inside America as opposed to elsewhere, that's all. It's only been the work of direct community organizers building trust within the community that has made change possible for the workers and the people they touch.

Beauty is a state of entrance, opportunity, and exploitation, just like the geographical locations it plugs into. Beauty doesn't save anybody. People do. People can be relentless. They can be resilient. Sometimes, the dreamers—who are all of those things—they even win. The wins might be small in comparison to what they lost to get there. Say, advocating for Vietnamese-language forms instead of English-only for educational training across disciplines. Making sure classes are free, eliminating barriers for entry. Offering Zoom workshop groups on labor rights in multiple languages with captions and recorded videos for those who can't leave work or family to attend. Offering accommodation that simply prioritizes your need of the knowledge, of what it might bring, so that you can do with it what you have to, when you can. Small things. Small wins.

But a win is a win is a win. Small wins after devastation.

The first time I met Kesang and told her I was a journalist as she dipped my nails in acetone, she took her hands away. She was suspicious of me at first. Previous reporters had treated the relationship between them as transactional and offered her exposure as a form of payment for collaborative work. They had her do videos of her work—impeccable, joyful, meticulous work—but didn't credit her for her labor. They forgot about her after their articles were filed. She was asked about bad work conditions but not offered protections for speaking out against them. She felt disposable. She had created most of the designs in the well-heeled salon's design booklet herself, and yet she was uncredited in the press surrounding the salon or salon workers. An artist, forgotten. It's an old story familiar to a lot of women artists.

Every month for three years, I would visit her for her work and just asked her to do whatever she wanted to my nails. She replicated couture gown folds onto my nailbeds, she drew magnetic auras out of bottles and placed them on my nails. She's mimicked coral reefs onto fingertips, conjured clouds from thin air. She made every nail a different intricate design in under an hour and she did it so perfectly that strangers were convinced they were stickers, not hand drawn. We still prepare mood boards for each other, we share memes. I can't apologize for the lack of care given to her by others, but I can always thank her for taking care of me. When she did a manicure fundraiser for refugees from Cambodia, where she's from, she raised enough to help 10 women flee. Her appointment books are filled up for weeks. She's opened her own studio now, a room of her own she built from taking care of other people. I am one of them, and happy to be. When this book is finished, she is one of the first to whom I'll gift a copy. When I know what this book will look like, she is the first opinion I plan to seek, because I want to see her version of it on my nails one day. I live across the country from her now, but every time I return to New York City, sitting with her is part of my homecoming.

I've started learning how to do my own nails lately, messaging Kesang and making friends with nail techs around the country through pure admiration and fascination of their skills, learning their favorite products as I learn their life stories, buying whatever they recommend like I'm being timed against the clock. It's given me so much more appreciation of the time and skill that goes into even the most basic salon manicure, the lessons I must learn and the journey I have to experience to even compare to anyone else's work—to be good enough to even have someone else's hand in my own. I was compelled to learn from constantly trying different salons but never finding the same camaraderie I had with Kesang in New York, and now I can't stop my obsession with learning. I spent years metabolizing the political history of the craft, but now I'm learning the art of it, and it keeps stretching my world with joy, filling in the pathways of loss that learning the history of the industry gave me. To marbleize a nail so that it looks like stone, or moving water, or a rose petal—that is *so hard*. To magnetize a nail so it looks like a cat eye, or an amethyst, or the sharp edge of a knife before it cuts—it takes practice, technique, the right tools. Cuticle work is meticulous, patient work, and it forces me to be patient with myself, too. I'm learning how to take care of myself on an infinitesimal level, millimeters at a time.

It makes me notice myself in a way that I can find playful, that I can learn from. I'm noticing the world and other people differently, too. Their hands and nails are not something I notice in terms of want, of consumption—manicures are not something I'd have to buy to replicate for myself—but the art becomes something I can learn to do myself. And when I see sets that I so clearly *cannot* achieve, I celebrate them with the fanaticism of an ESPN sports commentator. My god, she recreated a David Hockney painting on a pinky nail, call the Met. My god, she made a perfectly anatomically accurate tiny heart out of 3D gel for a press-on nail? She's a genius, and I would die for her. I feel like a child again, bad at something that I love, surprised by it, and thrilled I can keep going anyway, because I've learned how much more I can learn to do.

When I do go to get my nails done at a salon, I can talk craft as much as gossip, truly appreciate how much time my wildest dreams take to translate. I am more capable of understanding the barriers of existence, safety, respect, and artistry they've had to navigate to sit across from me. And when I'm home and invite friends to my place, I ask if I can do their nails. Let me hold your hand. Tell me what you're dreaming of. Let me take care of you. Tell me everything, anything, and let me give you beauty. When I do this, I hold in my hands all the contradictions that led me to the knowledge, too, but it's a gift, you see—to hold all this loss and redirected dreams and still make something beautiful from the remains. To know bone-deep that resilience can create art and comfort and connection, despite what makes resilience necessary. Cursed gifts like this are bigger than the world, and yet they fit so neatly and invisibly into the nails on your hands. Isn't that marvelous? Isn't it devastating?

I want you to act as if our house is on fire.

GRETA THUNBERG, speaking at the World Economic Forum, January 2019

5

In Case of Emergency

I could tell you about how many species have gone extinct this week. How many baby ducks were bathed by volunteer researchers in dish soap, brushed gently with clean mascara wands after another toxic oil spill. But you can find these stories too. You may already know about these victims of climate catastrophe, and you may already be one of them. Power grids are already failing, gas prices are soaring, and droughts are common. The impact of pollution on our bodies is already being documented as smog worsens. Long-term living in polluted air throws your skin's microbiome out of balance, disrupts your skin barrier, and makes you more prone to breakouts and long-term illnesses. The surface damage is just the beginning, though it's plenty enough. Yes, you can get brown spots, dull skin, wrinkles, redness, and dry, itchy skin from poor air quality. You can also get respiratory illnesses and other long-term full-body horrors that will make worrying about a zit or two feel quaint or even comical. Beauty's approach to the climate crisis is to use it as a marketing opportunity—but the consequences it claims to address are canaries in the coal mine of the climate crisis. It simply hopes we'll buy more coping mechanisms as cold comforts before we figure out how to repair our impact on the planet.

Seven out of ten Americans already know climate change exists, and the beauty industry has already spent a lot of money trying to adapt products and marketing to navigate a world with more pollution, more drought, and fewer resources. The term *clean beauty* emerged in the 1970s from a CoverGirl ad in reference to "fresh-faced" makeup and has since ballooned to stand in for all kinds of promises around toxicity and harmful ingredients. The thing is, what people deem harmful varies wildly and is often based in inaccurate interpretations of outdated scientific studies—one study from 1990 with 20 people and no control group does not a substantial claim make, but it is so often the evidence presented on "watchdog" websites claiming to monitor product toxicity. These watchdog organizations also happen to get affiliate commission on their choices, so it's not as if they are unbiased observers. What is meant by "clean" or "sustainable" is not legally and consistently defined. The FDA and its sister organizations internationally do not define cosmetic ingredients as "clean," "hypoallergenic," "sustainable," or "natural." These are marketing promises built on a mirage of fear-based assumptions, not universally defined scientific terminology of safe-for-skin science. When we indulge them, we're buying into the idea that purity might protect us. But lard can be organic, and you wouldn't put that on your face, would you? Something natural is no indication as to whether it's something suitable for any given purpose.

There's a lot to know and to unlearn—marketing jargon, power dynamics, conspiracy theories, real-life systems analysis. I'm not going to exhaust you with all of it at once—info dumping won't help you retain knowledge or motivate you to do anything with it. What I will do is break down the immediate practicalities of how the beauty industry is linked to the climate crisis, what current hot-ticket PR terms are just hot air and greenwashing, and what measures you can take to help effect change at every level, from your house to the rest of the world. Because even if it is not our own individual responsibility to fix the planet, we live in relationship to other people, and we can still effect change at a local, community, and immediate level—so shouldn't we try? "Greenwashing is meant to make people doubt themselves," explains Nicole Loher, an educator at NYU on climate communications. "And the doubt creates a bigger psychological problem around how we view climate change and talk about the solutions involved." The industry has offered so many possible Band-Aids and promises to be doubtful over: water-free skincare, clean beauty certifications, organics, vegans, anti-pollution themed products, the list goes on. Here, we will examine what aspects of the beauty industry are worth second guessing, and what answers from corporations we have to collectively push for, sooner, together, right now.

I believe that you have the wisdom and agency to make your own choices once you have these pillars of guidance. Hero ingredients might change, and trends certainly do—but the ways people have come together to disrupt structural inequity are always available to us. They are available to us right now.

Because as Mexican Chilean climate activist Xiye Bastida reminds us in her writing: "You don't have to know the details of the science to be part of the solution. And if you wait until you know everything, it will be too late for you to do anything. That's why this is an emergency."

How is beauty linked to climate crisis?

Most conversations around the beauty industry and the planet have to do with packaging waste, because there is certainly a lot of it: More than 120 billion units of packaging are produced every year by the cosmetics industry, contributing to the loss of 9 million acres of primary forest annually. The most common materials used in cosmetics are plastics, and all those plastics have varying degrees of recyclability. The end packaging varies in terms of sustainability, but scan your beauty products and it is probably looking grim. Lipstick bullets? Right to the landfill. Plastic-tubed deodorant? That too. Only 9 percent of all plastic has ever been recycled. But the cost of beauty is not just in terms of what containers are used to package them but in the carbon usage of all these processes and the production of the ingredients themselves. These are not typical costs companies admit to, but still, they're there: the resources needed for farming and shipping, waste from water, crude oil to make plastic, oils distilled for use as an ingredient, the deforestation required for ingredients and factories, not to mention the pollution accumulated for a 2-day rush order. These are all part of the story of every product in your makeup bag and on your face.

Marketing focuses on our individual consumption as the arbiter of environmental change, but none of that necessarily means a natural product is better for the planet than a "chemically laden" product such as, say, Cetaphil. An all-organic product may be less sustainable than a product with synthetic alternatives. Synthetics are commonly used in perfumes, for example, because many organic alternatives are hideously expensive due to being over-hunted, incredibly rare, or labor- and resource-intensive to procure. For example, it can take 4,500 pounds of flowers to produce 1 pound of essential oil. In these scenarios, a synthetic option is more feasible. When it comes to skincare, if brands opted to use only the plant-derived form of high-demand ingredients like L-ascorbic acid (also known as vitamin C), it would require a mind-boggling amount of land, water, and resources to get the number of plants required. "Organic" and "sustainable" are in these cases ideologically opposed. The value here isn't what is seen as "pure" but what is most important—being organic or being good for organisms besides you.

Don't trust anything that purports to be "chemical-free," because that is a fundamental misunderstanding of how beauty products work. Every single product you use, even if it is water and olive oil, has chemicals. And olive oil doesn't have only one chemical. It's made up of chemical structures! Everything on the planet is. *We* are made of chemicals and gore and electricity, and Earth is, too. Unlearning the fearmongering of "organic only" beauty marketing is one of the first lessons you're taught in cosmetology school—because organic materials can harm your skin as much as synthetics can. Preservatives keep products stable longer, which can help *minimize* waste, maximize usage time, and prevent bacteria from causing skin infection. In the years that I have been interviewing dermatologists and aestheticians, many have noticed an uptick in skin infections from clients who use "natural" skincare products. Dermatologist Anjali Mahto has observed a pattern in patients called "chemophobia," when patients get confused and turned off by long chemical names and a fear of what they don't know. Cosmetic chemists have jobs creating formulas in stable environments for a reason—a DIY sunscreen has nowhere near the same stability or efficacy as one purchased. Some things *are* better off bought.

That being said, buying a "green" beauty brand from Amazon shipped from, say, Australia to a third-party distribution center in America and then to you requires a lot more fossil fuels than buying a locally sourced product. The convenience of buying online is built on artificial costs: costs the consumer would be happy to pay, not the actual cost to the planet or to people at large.

Another complicated, sticky conversation around "eco-friendly" beauty products revolves around the fact that many of the base materials and systems the beauty industry relies on for ingredients are by-products of fossil fuels—the grand extractive addiction we haven't been able to loosen our grip on. Two of the most common personal care ingredients are petrolatum and mineral oils. Petrolatum is a by-product of petroleum that has been refined to become safe for skin. It's an occlusive, which seals the skin off from water and air when applied topically, allowing the skin barrier to heal itself faster than it would otherwise. In other words, it seals in your serums and moisturizers and protects your skin. A journal article published by the American Academy of Dermatology recommends its use for injured skin as a means to reduce scarring. You'll recognize it in some household staple products, like Vaseline and Aquaphor, products that every dermatologist I've ever seen or spoken to advocates for as part of your beauty roster. Fossil fuel companies love that what was once considered a by-product of fuel extraction is now a very valuable commodity in and of itself. "Why do you think the petrochemical industry sells ingredients into the beauty industry? ... The most profitable ounces or kilos that you get are the ones that go to the beauty industry," explains John Melo, CEO of Amyris, a synthetic biology company with a stable of beauty brands in its portfolio. He also happens to be the former president of US fuel operations for the oil giant BP. He's seen it all, sold it to us, and walked away from it, in search of alternative solutions.

The most valuable ounces of every cracked barrel of oil go to the beauty industry, and yet the beauty industry uses only 0.3 percent of the petrolatum produced. It seems like such a tiny number in the scheme of things, which makes it seem permissible. That permissiveness is supported by the fact that even with that marginal number, the beauty industry is still one of the biggest polluters on the planet, but there's no international standard on how much information regarding recycling or product ingredients to share with consumers. While there is a Fashion Industry Charter for Climate Action supported and researched through the UN's Climate Change program, as of my writing, there is yet to be one for the beauty industry. Our ignorance might be our downfall—we're running against the clock, having to rely on individual brand promises with few ways to hold them accountable on a global scale. "We are living at a time in our world where the transition to sustainable living is going to be critical," says Melo. It *is* critical, right now. We have lived the hottest days on record for many years in a row.

We should be ending our dependence on fossil fuels, not complicating our relationship to it further—but the onus isn't on us as consumers but on the companies to prioritize large-scale changes that put the planet before profits, and to educate their consumers on the reality of what that choice entails. Fifty-five percent of consumers are willing to pay more for products that work to improve the environment already—companies need to heed that majority rule if any material change is going to occur. Professor Loher is adamant about us collectively choosing a path where we stop trying to justify ourselves and focus on climate solutions: "Using by-products is not a solution in any way. The solve is to work towards not using fossil fuels *for anything*. All the energy that anyone, anywhere, spends on *not* solving this problem, is just trying to make a profit. To me, that is ethically wrong. Yes, we all have to make money, but at what expense? Killing humanity? Killing the world?" There *is* a human cost that we cannot ignore. As the planet heats up, more and more people are displaced from drought, from wildfires, from deforestation. People go farther to get to work for vanishing wages and exploitative work practices. This is true (and well documented in the garment industry), and these same geographical regions are involved in beauty ingredients procurement and exploited just as much.

One long-standing example are the people forcibly removed from their homes and factories built on their homeland every day in Palestine. Some of these factories package Dead Sea salt scrubs and Moroccan oil shampoo. Moroccan oil is a mixture of argan oil and other extracts, but the company Moroccanoil is Israeli. Same for Ahava, a skincare brand that uses Dead Sea products and operates in an Israeli settlement in the West Bank. The brand—and others—are on a boycott that emerged around 2005 when the Boycott, Divestment and Sanction (BDS) movement for the liberation of Palestine launched. A coalition of 170 Palestinian civil rights groups, the BDS movement asks for people to boycott brands that have factories on occupied land and from brands that profit from the occupation. This has a relation to the climate crisis because the land "reclaimed" by Zionists is ecologically safer from climate change, while the places Palestinians are forced to flee to are more prone to flood, drought, and frost. It's been proven in studies again and again that marginalized communities and poorer countries are more prone to feeling the violence of climate crisis. It follows logically that those same communities are more likely to feel the consequences of capitalism's demand on factory farming and product manufacturing. Costs don't disappear; they're mitigated.

They're often mitigated into Indigenous communities. The great irony of this is that Indigenous communities are also the caretakers of the world's most valuable land. I don't mean value in the sense of how much a developer would pay for it, but in the very literal sense that these lands are essential to the survival of living creatures on Earth. Indigenous people manage much of the land that acts as a carbon sink, absorbing carbon and thus playing a crucial role in fighting global warming. Eighty percent of the planet's biodiversity survives in their keeping. They have been protecting and preserving the most important tracts of land on the planet for generations, and Western science and scientific research has only recently begun catching up and affirming their approach to ecological preservation. Indigenous-led protests have also stopped or delayed nearly 1.6 billion tons of greenhouse gas emissions per year—which is around a quarter of the combined emissions of North America.

Outside of fossil fuel industry pressures, wage theft and bad labor practices are found in beauty spaces as often as they are in others. Factory and sweatshop workers everywhere from Bangladesh to Ohio are passing out from dehydration and lack of air conditioning in spaces that are over 100 degrees Fahrenheit in the shade. While the fashion industry's labor practices are by far more publicized, these same regions also have substantial beauty industry arms, and the supply chain transparency is somehow far more opaque and harder to hold accountable. Yet the harm is still done. There is no beauty product or sweater worth dying to make, no product worth displacing another human being for. Our vanity isn't worth the world.

What ingredients are "bad" to use?

There are different banned ingredients across different regions—the US and the EU specifically—and they're typically banned because they pose unsafe health conditions for humans. But ingredients aren't usually considered through a lens of harm reduction to the *planet,* just to the consumer. Environmental organizers and lobbyists have made a difference in this by advocating for the ban of microbeads in beauty products, because now our oceans are full of them. By avoiding microbeads, you are avoiding eventually flushing down these ingredients into the lungs of baby turtles. When you look at the banned ingredients list from the EU, you'll find rocket fuel, the cancer drug methotrexate, antibiotics, fuel gases, and carbon monoxide. There is also arsenic and cyanide. And while the Personal Care Council, an American trade organization, assures these substances would never be used in American cosmetics—and I would hope they are right—it is not out of historical impossibility. Cyanide and arsenic have been famously and quite commonly used. Queen Elizabeth I used to smear lead mixed with vinegar as a kind of powder on her face, and arsenic complexion wafers were used for pale skin. Radioactive chin straps, blush wafers, and timepieces were a thing in 1915 before scientists realized radioactive materials were lethal. While the idea of these ingredients being banned seems obvious and even a touch absurd now, they're banned out of historical knowledge of their past impact in the industry. Banning dangerous ingredients is not a waste of time, even if the ingredients are now obviously dangerous. Given the long history of medical experiments just *happening* to be done on poor people (and in particular, poor people of color), it is better to have the regulations than expect people to not cause harm. But the self-congratulatory nature of brands that tell you what they *don't* use more easily than what they *do* is a red flag to watch out for. It is easy to greenwash by distraction and fearmongering. Pointing out a problem and positioning yourself as the only way to solve it is the story of branding, politics, and hero complexes across history. Look for companies that are transparent about the science backing their products, update it regularly, and are not afraid of answering questions with unbiased citations when you have concerns. They ought to treat progress and success as moving targets because they are. They should be able to trace their supply chain, they should acknowledge the resource drain of their packaging, and they should be able to explain why an included ingredient is important to the formula. The fact that it works for you should also, somewhere in that list, be mentioned.

Research on long-term effects of ingredients we already use changes all the time, constantly revealing new depths of impact on the planet, as well as the impact of specific chemicals on us. Given that we're always learning, it's not helpful to conceptualize a "pure" ingredient as any better for us than any other kind. It's more about what causes the least harm and provides the best, most controllable effect you're looking for. Parabens won't kill you, but microbeads will kill something later on. Benzene, found in many sunscreens, *can* harm you, but not in the percentage typically found in beauty products that you apply *topically*. A lot of the panic around what we find in products stems from misunderstanding how substances interact with your skin barrier. A lot of brands get away with overpromising what their products can do by way of allegory and influencer-led advertising—but neither method means their products can permanently fix any problem your skin may be having. If they truly could, they'd be pharmaceuticals, and they'd have to face medical testing and the FDA for health-related claims. When a brand touts clinical trials as proof of the efficacy of their products, the value added isn't the trial itself, but how rigorous the trial was—Was it conducted by a licensed third-party group? How big was the sample size? How long were they studied? What were the recorded results compared to? The answers to these questions determine the rigor of their claims. A clinical trial has different substantiation requirements and disclosures than a survey emailed to consumers, labeled as a "study." You as the consumer shouldn't be expected to be an expert patent lawyer or cosmetic chemist, but being able to spot a red flag when someone is bullshitting you will save your skin, quite literally.

What kind of products should I look for?

Plenty of retailers already offer "waste-free" packaging, plastic-free shipping, and solid shampoo/conditioner bars. These are all viable options. Rather than opting for individually wrapped sheet masks, makeup wipes, or cotton pads and swabs, consider reusable cotton pads, jars or tubs of face masks instead, and so on. The easiest thing you can do is use less and *use what you already have* before buying other products. There are already many marketplaces that focus entirely on offering "sustainable" and "eco-friendly" versions of products you use, and there have been for a while. You can also find retailers that offer refill stations for products, which are more common outside the US but are growing in popularity stateside. These are places where you can buy products in refillable containers and come back to refill them at a lower price. Some of these retailers also offer recycling stations for you to dispose of empty and cleaned beauty product containers for store credit. Credo is one such retailer that offers these options, and LUSH has been a champion of no-waste packaging for many years.

Ultimately, reusable and refillable products are less wasteful than travel-size and sample packaging. Buying in bulk does create less of an impact than buying piecemeal. In 2020, Credo announced it would stop its sampling program to reduce plastic waste, and other retailers will likely follow. *Allure* magazine ceased to refer to any type of plastic as "recyclable" that same month, stating that they're not going to use the term "as a crutch to let us tell ourselves—and for packaged-good companies to tell themselves—that it will be used again! Nope. It will most likely live in a landfill or our oceans for a very long time. . . . It's on manufacturers to use less plastic, period." This has always been the case, but it is our awareness of their responsibility that has changed.

Polluters have long known the solutions we have are imperfect ones: Recycling was never meant to be the only option. In a PBS investigative documentary on the plastics industry, Lewis Freeman, the former VP of government affairs for the Society of the Plastics Industry, stated: "There was never an enthusiastic belief that recycling was ultimately going to work in a significant way." Tom Rattray, a retired recycling expert, explained it more plainly in 1996: "Petrochemical companies and resin producers viewed recycling as 'internal competition.' They don't want to see it succeed." They knew the true scale of the issue *decades* ago, and they've just been distracting consumers for years to save their bottom line. That means we're behind, and we have a lot of bureaucracy to cancel out.

Supporting policy changes at a local and federal level that put the cost of recycling programs onto those that produce the waste is totally feasible and still necessary: In New York, Senator Todd Kaminsky, the former chair of the Environmental Conservation Committee, recently tried to pass a bill to shift end-of-life responsibility for packaging and paper products from local governments to in-state corporate producers. It's not the first bill of its kind—a Maine law was signed into effect in 2021 after failing in different forms a few times. Oregon's version was also signed into effect in 2021, making companies pay to expand existing recycling services. Public pressure makes a difference; we need to know where to push and then keep showing up. There are versions of laws that make producers pay for packaging recycling being introduced in states across the country, and many of them aren't new but are restructured versions of attempts that failed before. They need more public support to make it through. Some have already done this elsewhere; the EU passed a law in 2019 to ban the most common single-use plastic items. It is relentless consistency in the dull rhythm of bureaucracy that sometimes sways the arc of history.

It's not all doom and gloom. Perfume houses are opting for

partnerships with synthetic biology companies for sustainable, alternative versions of materials required for beauty products. There are more brands that are utilizing waste materials for packaging and product, too—they need shelf space and funders to scale up. Packaging that focuses on using recycled and easily recyclable and reusable packaging must become more available and more affordable for more brands to offer. Outer packaging for products could be eliminated or reconceptualized to be 100 percent compostable at the very least—there are more and more mycelium-based packaging options available for beauty brands to switch to. Yes, mycelium, as in mushrooms! It's a packaging option as well, currently utilized primarily by smaller mid-range luxury brands, and it degrades within a month in a home compost pile. Beyond packaging innovations and putting pressure on brands to prioritize circularity, investing in auditing systems and labor networks that center human rights and racial and gender equity is an obvious pathway to a better future. The fact is, we can't trust any conglomerate or corporation in fossil fuel *or* beauty to have our personal best interest at heart, and certainly not that of the planet—so why should we trust their self-reporting on the math behind their sustainability efforts? The data we have at state levels has serious gaps, too: The New York State database has more missing reports than available information right now. The bar for improvement is so low it is truly possible to make immediate collective good occur sooner rather than later: Brands could, at the very least, provide better communication and education on how to recycle their products properly.

Prioritizing brands and pushing government organizations to be transparent about their production, sourcing, and reports, and to partner with organizations within the communities they serve, are always going to be your best bets. But try not to be too impressed by brands offering limited-time tax-deductible donations to nonprofit initiatives—while it's a write-off for them, it's not enacting a comprehensive investment toward a global solution.

Do water-free products help? What about anti-pollution skincare?

The long-term effects of bad air quality from pollution impact us in ways a skincare product has no chance of resolving. Diseases stemming from high concentrations of air pollutants are numerous: chronic obstructive pulmonary diseases (COPD), asthma, lung cancer, central nervous system dysfunctions, stroke, diabetes. It's estimated that air pollution is responsible for nearly 7 million deaths globally. Anti-pollution skincare products focus on "improving" the impact of pollution on your skin, but they don't do anything to improve the environment they resource materials from, and so consequentially are Band-Aids on a seeping wound. Ultimately, they're just targeting fear of climate crises and inventing a new category because of it. As for water-free products framed around using up less resources—these products still require water to get to you. They also require water to *use*; they're simply not liquid at the point of sale. They rely on the idea that you have clean, potable water to combine with the product itself. Many don't around the world, and that lack of access is getting worse. Poorer countries, countries with smaller carbon footprints than America, are the ones that are harmed the most and the fastest by climate change and water scarcity. These problems won't be solved by more products. Pollution won't be solved when we conceptualize it as an individual problem through skin products, and it won't be solved through a donation of 1 percent of your order. Long-term health concerns from fracking and factory pollution and lack of potable water and toxic air quality cause intergenerational health problems in families, towns, zip codes, countries. No moisturizer fixes the scale of neglect that can cause, and has caused, organs to shut down. Systemic racism will not be exfoliated out of us.

More products aren't a scalable solution. They're a neoliberal coping mechanism. Which is still a comfort some of the time, but not a way out.

What do I do with the beauty products I already have and am going to use up?

The bitter pill to swallow at the moment is that recycling beauty products is a logistical nightmare that varies from county to county in the US, and the impact is vastly different from country to country. There is no universal standard on to how to recycle products. Here is what you may not know:

- The symbols on your products mean something, but the meanings can be misleading. An open jar with a number and an M indicates the expiration period *after* opening. A flame indicates it's a flammable product; this is most likely found on aerosol canisters and products containing alcohol.
- Multilined packaging, such as paper lined with bubble wrap, often can't be recycled unless you split the layers. That white and blue Amazon packaging with

the recycling logo covering it? You cannot recycle that unless you bring it to an Amazon drop-off location. Otherwise, it is going to go right into the trash unless you reuse it for something else. And realistically, there is *no* mainstream solution for recycling mutilayer plastic packaging in the next 5 to 10 years.

- Unless you're removing all remaining product from a beauty product before you put it in recycling, all you are doing is contaminating that batch of recycling, which ultimately means it will be thrown in the trash anyway. You *must* wash out the containers so there is little to no residue. China stopped taking US recyclables in 2018 because they began implementing much stricter contamination protocols, and ever since, even more would-be recyclables from the States have been going to landfills. Even before the ban, 79 percent of plastic waste was accumulated in landfills or the natural environment.

- If you do plan to recycle products, you have to check your local recycling ordinances: You may need to break them down into the individual pieces they were built in—a cap might not be permitted to stay attached to the tube, for example. This varies for different regions.

- "Compostable" products are not legally obligated to specify if they can be composted at home or elsewhere, so unless they say it on the packaging or their website, do not assume it will break down in your at-home compost bin or garden. This varies from state to state.

- Glass packaging takes more resources and carbon than plastic to produce—and as such, it is not necessary the more sustainable choice. The color of the glass and if it has stickers on it or not also factors into if it can be recycled. Lighter-colored glass is more likely to be recycled. There are specific manufacturers of glass that prioritize using recycled glass for new products, and brands like Guerlain use it and claim that they've been able to reduce the carbon and water footprints of their products as a result. There's been no outside verification of the success for this—recyclability measurements in the beauty industry aren't vetted and monitored by the EPA. The FTC provides guidelines to help companies avoid misleading claims, but so far, there have been no penalties for beauty companies that don't use them.
- The smaller the beauty item, the less likely it is to be recyclable because the automatic sorting machines at recycling centers simply cannot identify them properly. The culture of beauty samples and travel-size products is incredibly damaging to the environment for this reason.
- If you have unused and unopened products that you do not want, there are plenty of organizations around the world that accept donations for people in need of them. Do not throw them away! Redistribute them in your community after sanitizing them thoroughly on the outside. Reach out to your local women's shelters and adjacent organizations to see what they need or would be happy to take.

- You can advocate for your housing community or local municipality to install recycling bins for specific products, too. Local mutual aid organizations also often have composting and clean-up chapters you can plug into. You can also ask beauty retailers near you to host a recycling bin of empty products at their stores. Some, like Credo, have recycling boxes at their cash registers and offer store points in exchange for recycled products. I've personally made it a ritual to save up my empty containers until they fill up a large tote and then recycle them for points all at once. Counting them as they disappear into the chute is deeply satisfying, and I recommend it to you. Do we have statistics on how effective this is in the large scheme of things? Is it moving the needle? The jury is still out.

Will carbon neutrality save us?

You may be noticing that more and more brands and buildings are promising to be "carbon neutral" or "carbon negative," phrases often written in enthusiastic green across product packaging and building lobbies. Even the oil companies are greenwashing with influencer partnerships: Shell Oil paid a series of influencers in 2021 to advertise their gas stations on Instagram and encouraged them to mention you can pay a few extra pennies at each fill-up to pay for carbon offsets. Carbon neutrality just means that a brand paid someone else to "cancel out" their impact on the world; it does not mean that the CO_2 in the atmosphere has been reduced by the production of what you're looking at. The success rate of such programs isn't monitored by an oversight committee, and they've been investigated by third-party groups to have a terrible success rate preventing deforestation and carbon loading the atmosphere. It's essentially carbon as currency that the rich can afford, but it still disproportionately affects the most vulnerable. Climate activists call it climate colonialism. It is not a solution. It is an IOU to the future that will never be paid off. Once the carbon credit is bought, the company is allowed to immediately claim they have "canceled" their emissions—but nothing has been done to mitigate its harm. Every former carbon capture company employee I have spoken to is adamant about this: "There's no company out there that has been able to prove, at scale, that carbon capture works." It is worthless to the point of fraud.

Indigenous academic Elizabeth J. Jackson explains, "Indigenous climate activists have been involved in resisting carbon offset programs since they started to be discussed. . . . Indigenous rainforest peoples state they will be displaced and denied access to their lands through this program. They also state that the deforestation will only be moved to a different location or, due to corruption and lack of regulation, the lands will be logged anyway." This has proven, time and time again, to be true.

One infamous example is from 2013, when the Paiter Suruí Indigenous people in Brazil sold 120,000 tons of carbon offsets to the Brazilian cosmetics giant Natura through the REDD Program, the first deal of its kind. But then gold was discovered, and diamonds shortly after, and the money generated from the latter fueled the conversion of the forest to pasture. After these resources were discovered, the territory deforestation rate increased 256 percent above the project's allowed limit, and the program stopped.

Who are some leaders in minimizing the impact of the beauty industry on the planet?

There are so many people and organizations that address climate change in different ways at different scales, and to assume a hierarchy of knowledge about who has all the answers is part of how we got into trouble in the first place. It takes work at every level and in different industries that include the beauty industry but aren't exclusive to it. There's 5 Gyres, a nonprofit focused on reducing plastics pollution in general. There are human rights organizations like World Vision and Terre des Hommes that focus on eliminating child labor in places where the labor is utilized by companies that contract the results for cosmetics. WE ACT for Environmental Justice seeks to ensure that people of color and low-income residents can meaningfully participate in the development of environmental protection politics and practices, and Women's Voices for the Earth is a national organization that organizes around eliminating toxic chemicals in beauty products that cause harm to communities. There are human interest groups and union organizers like California Healthy Nail Salon Collaborative and the New York Healthy Nail Salons Coalition that lobby Congress for protections for salon workers across America and for more sustainable products to become the standard at retailers and spas. There are auditing companies and supply chain organizations that go into companies and claim to offer more eco-friendly options to materials the companies require for their products—but, again, their processes *also* aren't transparent, and some have been accused of greenwashing themselves. To remedy the beauty industry's impact on climate means understanding how intertwined the industry is with so many others. It requires a comprehensive solution that touches on labor issues, management accountability, ingredients auditing, logistics management, and more. There's no international policy or formal guidance provided by the UN regarding how the beauty industry should mitigate this crisis—a crisis they are so clearly involved in. There's a lot for us to fight for. A planet to fight for—our own.

Every company approaches the task in their own way, the biggest ones establishing their own foundations where their profits pass through for tax write-offs, and because they are private foundations, it is impossible to monitor the financials and how effective they really are. A 501(c)3 organization is transparent with financials in specific ways that a 501(c)4 organization doesn't have to be. And the reality of matching employee donations plays out a story of corporate hierarchy and political leanings: Employees across political positions all have equal opportunity to donate a portion of their paychecks, but it's senior management, often conservative white men in executive roles, that donate the most money per quarter to candidates and political parties. Estée Lauder's sons Ronald and Leonard Lauder alone have donated many millions to various organizations and Republican political campaigns. A 2022 *New York Times* profile on Ronald Lauder's contributions describes him as a "gale-force disruptor, throwing millions of dollars behind conservative causes and candidates. . . . There is little doubt that Mr. Lauder has single-handedly tilted the playing field for his party." Every employee may have equal opportunity to donate, but they do not have equal *equity* when they do so, and political parties and lobbyists are funded by the *amount* of money in their coffers, not by the number of donors they can tally. America's culture of independence plays out imperfectly in practice, rendering political contributions from a few billionaire donors more effective than many small donations from everyone else in the country. But there are other models of community we can turn to.

There are beauty brands founded by Indigenous people that are great examples of how Indigenous cultures' ethos of interdependence and community care plays out wonderfully in the beauty space. Cheekbone Beauty, for example, is an Indigenous-owned Canadian cosmetics company that cites Anishinaabe roots in its ethos and brand playbook. Its products fund donations to the Navajo Water Project and One Tree Planted, and they utilize a sustainability standard for their packaging, ensuring it is either plantable, refillable, or reusable. It set out to be zero-waste by 2023 but realized that it would be near impossible, then provided transparency updates and explanations of the setbacks it is experiencing in minimizing waste. It donates funding to Indigenous youth collectives and has long-term relationships with both local and national organizations for Indigenous youth. Prados Beauty is another company that donates time, money, and mentorship back into the Indigenous community across Turtle Island (an Indigenous term for North America), and they raised money for supplies like PPE and shoes to distribute throughout remote Indigenous communities straining under COVID. Youth to the People is a skincare brand that focuses on specific pillars of give-back: climate, human rights, and gender and racial equity. It partners with organizations empowering people from marginalized backgrounds they're hoping to support, and it has the partners take the lead on how best to support their missions.

Companies of all sizes are banding together to make statements on climate change, though it remains to be seen how effective their campaigns will be. CodeRed4Climate, a coalition of more than 200 brands, has written an open letter to Congress asking them to support the Clean Electricity Payment Program, direct 40 percent of funding to frontline communities, and end subsidies for fossil fuel corporations. But directing their consumers to call their senators is less effective than tactics that are proven to work: Oil and gas companies talk to Senator Joe Manchin every week, and he made more than $491,000 in 2020 alone from his coal company holdings. He was the deciding vote in Congress over climate change policy. Americans live in a country that listens to money more than phone calls. That's how we got where we are.

Our conversations around climate crisis must be decolonized—as well as our minds, wallets, and beauty closets. The way we approach our relationship to beauty products, brands, and the very world we live in—all this must change. It's not a funnel system directed toward our own nervous systems, though we all thrive with daily little treats. We're in a network of connectivity with each other and the planet we live on. The brands we use and the ways they conduct business ought to reflect the fact that *we all make each other possible*. And the fact that we make each other possible means that we can help change each other, too. Beauty standards across regions have long been intertwined with colonial powers, and it's those very colonial powers that protect the profits and interests of corporate institutions rather than the land we live on. Decentering the ideals they've projected is to disinvest in the power they wield. To buy differently is to weaken the impact of their own coffers. To use less is to starve their voracious appetite for growth by any measure. And it is the negative feedback that makes the biggest difference—corporations invest in what makes and loses them money; they are not directed by the impact they make on the world. The truth of the matter is it's more profitable to innovate temporary solutions than invest in true fixes. It's why those fixes haven't happened yet. To make them happen means that collectively we must make any other pathway less desirable to choose.

Do small brands have as much onus to think hard about these problems as bigger brands, when they have less resources to address them?

Yes. Every big brand started off as someone's baby. Pointing fingers at someone else to take over the problem is how problems just fester over time. If anything, small brands can make change happen exponentially *faster* than big conglomerates, because there's far less bureaucracy to slow them down. By choosing better options from the beginning—and within your own community and network—you're directly impacting change that could otherwise be *worse*. And consumer demands reflect wanting to support both smaller, up-and-coming brands *and* brands that are more interested in sustainability. If you aren't listening to your consumers, who have time and time again said that these are their exact demands, you are wasting your time and everyone's resources. Setting an example early on also makes your company more valuable at scale as a disruptor if we're talking money moves. Beauty founder Melany Dobson (who uses mycelium packaging from Ecovative for her products) explains it simply enough to *Vogue*: "Multinational companies [look to] small brands once they get attention. It helps set trends. If [we use] Ecovative, L'Oréal starts thinking about it, too."

Huge beauty conglomerates are still, proportionately, buying a significant portion of Earth's supply of palm oil. These purchases then justify the allocation of more resources to create the supply for the demand they have shown. It is a self-sustaining problem. Yes, they participate in the hopeful promises of green solutions we've already mentioned—the carbon credits, the recycling programs. But they're still creating a huge supply of product and investing their money in new ways to drive demand—and growth of their businesses and, therefore, unavoidably, waste—in the world. Unless they're all invested in closing the loop of waste and environmental damage and consider it as important as, if not more important than, the products themselves, they are still bad actors. More sustainable solutions are usually not the most profitable options. Values are important, but it's their bank accounts that keep the lights on.

The ultimate goal for many beauty entrepreneurs, regardless of their identity, is to become incredibly wealthy beyond imagination and to sell their company to a conglomerate. But more billionaires is ultimately not a success story if their wealth is still just an accumulation of exploited workers and an exhausted planet. You don't become a billionaire from doing a public good. The world's five richest men have more than doubled their fortunes to $869 billion since 2020, while the world's poorest 60 percent—almost 5 billion people—have lost money. Joining their ranks implicitly means you are relying on the labor of billions of others—what is to be congratulated here? A diversion of capital changes things for the group of people who now have wealth accumulated, but it doesn't make change for their extended community if their new economic power isn't distributed, and systems of equity aren't shared. While there is plenty of good that wealthy people can contribute to the world, the long arc of history has proven that just because a wealthy person *can* do something good, that doesn't mean they ever do. Any billionaire could end world hunger at any time at all. They do not. This is a choice. And any human with a lot of power wants to preserve it and wants more of it. This is how power works. We have to prioritize new ideas of what success can be that doesn't center profit over the people who raise you up.

What can we do when we feel helpless at the scope of it all?

In an open letter to a fossil fuel executive, the model/organizer Cameron Russell wrote: "The more I learned about the industry, the worse I felt. I stopped working for a while. Have you ever done that? It's a privileged response to despair. I think we often allow ourselves to be ignorant. Not ignorant of the issues, you know where all this leads . . . but ignorant of another way forward." Having an empire of knowledge means little if you are so despairing of the facts you can't react to them to protect yourself and change the circumstances you were dealt. Your reactions of grief and trauma mean you're paying attention and you're hurt, but if you stay stuck in them, you are actually no better off for knowing how fucked up things are. You *do* have to move through them.

The best way to do this isn't always to learn more about how tragic the possible futures are, but to focus on the small, immediate, and actionable ways you can feel more empowered to change your circumstances and the circumstances of your direct community. This kind of intervention can happen at any level of your life or your interests. Russell, after witnessing the direct connection the industry had to systemic injustice, organized the model community alongside Áine Rose Campbell in 2017. The Model Mafia is now 200+ strong and operates internationally and has helped raise tens of thousands of dollars to support Indigenous activists, create community picnics, and collaborate for fair pay, climate justice, immigrant rights, animal rights, childbirth education, and more.

So we're supposed to stop buying things? It's not very practical. I'm going to still need soap.

It *is* not very practical, and you *do* need soap. But do we need to spend, on average in America, $3,342 a year on cosmetics and beauty services? No. We need to use less, and the process can't end at the garbage can. We need more closed-loop solutions that are invested in restoration and expansion of what we lose in the process of our enjoyment. There are already many people and coalitions working on this. But these problems must be addressed in every community, not just in hubs.

The world can't sustain our desires. And at this point, even the most dramatic individual sacrifices by an as-yet unseen number of regular consumers isn't going to save the polar bears or the coral reefs. These will, unless a true miracle of international political bravery happens virtually simultaneously to you reading this very sentence, be lost to generations after us. It is about mitigating *more* loss and trying to turn the ship around before we destroy the entire ocean it's been traveling on, rendering the ocean uninhabitable for every single creature in the water. The COVID-19 pandemic did not change our consumer habits for the better of the planet—in fact, carbon output and packaging waste skyrocketed, despite fewer makeup purchases. Four years into a worldwide pandemic, and makeup purchases increased despite a recession. We are already behind scientists' most conservative goalposts. It truly sucks to suck, which is to say we have some work to do. To solve this crisis, we are faced with a moral reckoning, on a personal and global scale, on the reasons we use beauty products or contribute to their usage and sale. Are you willing to use, buy, create, or promote beauty products at any cost? What if the cost is the planet? Is it more important to feel beautiful? If the answers to these questions conflict with one another, what do you plan to do about it? My answers to these questions change all the time. Answering these questions honestly and dealing with the consequences continue to transform my life—for the better, even if the better is more difficult than before. I sleep better at night. Your answers might lead to the better for you, too.

At the end of the day, I'm not trying to become the Earth Police and make you feel bad about resources you may not have access to, but it's also deeply paralyzing to shrug off the mere *possibility* we can all do more work to find local alternative sources, accept slower shipping times on things we must get online, and advocate in our local communities to make big changes easier at a local level. No one is asking you alone to convince politicians to save the planet. But shrugging off little changes is fatalistic behavior, and it does not make organizing easier for anyone else to do. The sentiment "There is no ethical consumerism under capitalism" is true, but it's not a license to shrug off any obligation to the planet's future. It is not a pass to condone or become complicit in further exploitation of the planet's resources or other people. It is not license to abandon each other.

To consider this conversation a moment of joy-killing or to be entirely defeatist about it is self-involved. It could be seen as a moment you can connect to histories and mythologies and systems much older and bigger than you are. You could choose to feel more connected to the planet around you and more inclined to explore the knowledge waiting around you. It doesn't need to feel like despair. It could also feel like waking up. It could feel more like reaching out to someone else who is just as scared as you are for the future. It could feel like helping them feel less alone. Beauty was never just about you or how it makes you feel. We are simply its current keepers. It was never only yours, just like this planet is borrowed from the future. We are not the center of the universe or even the axis on which the present revolves. We are part of something much bigger than us—we are the future's ghost, the past's wildest dreams, and just one version of the present's possibilities. We can always work on better options. All it takes is us trying to do so, and somewhere, somehow, it might work. That is how the present becomes the future. That is how the impossible gets done.

6

How Beauty Survives a Plague

When I was sixteen, it took me three weeks to find someone willing to dye my hair green like Enid's from *Ghost World*. This is a very stupid problem I miss. As I write this, every nail salon, hair salon, spa, tattoo parlor, and beauty supply store in New York is closed. There are no more beds in the ICU or the morgue. We are weeks into New York being the epicenter of COVID-19 in the United States, and there will be months, and then years, of this death and isolation. For many people, salons have been spaces of shelter, community, transformation, and rehabilitation, the places we go to be comforted by others as we're polished and trimmed into different versions of ourselves. But as of my writing, these places have all been closed. Some open again for a few weeks in between shutdown orders, their hours changing in an accordion of desperation. Some of them will open again, but their staff will shift in staccato as workers get sick, die, or quit for fear of being exposed. Many salons won't reopen at all.

Their technicians are without work, and if they *are* at work, they are exposed to a virus that can damage their respiratory system for life, if not kill them outright. Nail technicians are already exposed to vapors and particulates on a daily basis and supposed to wear face masks but sometimes don't, for salon compliance is rarely enforced by the government. This is a disease that targets them when they are already more vulnerable than most. Before COVID-19, most salons didn't consistently adhere to CDC regulations, and many do not provide gloves to their technicians—because many aren't salon employees but *freelancers*, and so the burden and responsibility is on them, an individual, lucky for a day rate and a warm room. Being forced to pay for these materials out of their own pocket cuts into already diminished daily wages, to say nothing of hands so raw from sanitizing that some sleep in moisturizer-filled gloves.

Right now, as research develops on the coronavirus, we're turning to the bare necessities of beauty as means of harm reduction: soap, hygiene products. Salons that do ordinarily provide masks and gloves to their technicians have donated them to hospitals; art museums have donated their restoration department supply closets of gloves and smocks and masks to frontline workers. Tattoo parlors and hair salons have done the same. Cosmetic conglomerates like Coty and Unilever and L'Oréal have converted their factories to produce hand sanitizers and have donated the products to frontline workers. Beauty, as a tool of daily life, still matters as a place of possibility—only now it is about community health. On an individual level it is essential: Wash your hands, lotion them, repeat the process until you feel a little less close to the void of death around the corner. It is a tool of emergent strategy and a preventative measure against burnout.

HOW BEAUTY SURVIVES A PLAGUE

═══

The beauty industry profits when it adapts feel-good "self-care" measures into a system often used to constantly "improve" ourselves; it simply profits less than when things are "running normally." But—and this is an important *but*—it also helps us endure our conditions, which permits us to fight the larger problems at hand. In an interview with Democracy Now, Naomi Klein said, "The future will be determined by whoever is willing to fight harder for the ideas they have lying around." In moments of crisis, people focus on daily emergencies and put their trust in people in power. Beauty is typically used in daily emergencies, but when utilized wisely, it can help us fight harder, for longer, for the shit that really counts. Beauty matters when we remember that we can use it together for something bigger than our own vanity.

Crisis brings opportunity. Beauty doesn't leave; it adjusts to new conditions.

═══

May 2020. A specific photo of newly reopened Georgia salons went viral. Picture a Black nail artist at the feet of a faceless elderly white patron, in a wisp-thin plastic cape and surgical mask. She is gloveless and has no visor on, but photos from technicians at other salons have visors and other protective gear on—they look similarly clothed to surgeons in an OR, though rather than sewing up a heart, they're shaping and buffing a nail. Nurses died a few weeks earlier from exposure to COVID, having been so severely underresourced that they were forced to turn to trash bags as surgical gowns.

Meanwhile, white protesters are on the streets demanding

salons reopen so that they can get haircuts. A white woman protesting in Sacramento, California, is seen wearing a surgical mask over her eyes in a protest organized by local conservatives to reopen salons. Another white woman in a protest elsewhere is seen holding a poster with an illustration of a Black woman in a cage mask with the text: "Muzzles are for dogs and slaves. I am a free human being." A protest in Michigan called "Operation Haircut," organized by Michigan's Conservative Coalition, features primarily white Americans cutting hair. They file their taxes under the name of Michigan Trump Republicans.

It's mostly white protesters in middle-income neighborhoods protesting that salons open, where employees are mostly Black and live elsewhere, with higher rates of COVID. A month or two into shelter-in-place and there is now a citywide curfew in LA, New York City, Chicago, and Atlanta, and protests in every state in the United States of America. According to the Associated Press, over 9,300 people have been arrested so far in protests against police brutality after the killing of George Floyd. Since his murder on May 20, four other people were shot by the police in the protests, one woman miscarried in police custody, at least eight people were partially blinded, and another man's skull was fractured by being pushed down by the police (a video of which went viral on June 4, 2020). At the time of my writing this, there are now 387,898 dead from COVID worldwide, and the numbers are already known to be underreported. Another 6,018 will be reported dead by the morning. Counting, counting.

June 6, 2020. I'm on my daily morning walk, the 20 minutes a day I go outside to breathe fresh air. There's little movement on the streets; construction projects have stopped, and half-built condominiums stand skeletal next to boarded-up storefronts and empty bus stops. The signs of life are mostly in parks and grocery stores, lines snaking out the door in staccato clumps. Church parking lots fill with volunteers and people searching for sanctuary. There's more life in the less gentrified neighborhoods that my walk eventually expands into. I take an hourlong walk past my old neighborhood in Crown Heights, past the Black-owned barbershops, and there—there's music, still. They proudly have signs on their windows and doors, even as more and more are shuttered and boarded up as I walk by, weeks turned to months of this crisis. The signs remain— "Immigrants are welcome here," "Emergency Community Organizing Space," "No Justice No Peace"—all up and down Fulton Avenue. They have street art as their store decor, Haitian and queer flags outside their doors. Before and during protests against police brutality, many of them were supplying water, food, sanitizer, and music to marches as they passed by, flashing whips of light.

Beauty only matters when you don't think of it as just aesthetics but as a matter of capacity and connection. It is a nexus of social power and accessibility. Its spaces offer sanctuary, and its tools offer more than that, sometimes. For example: Soap saves lives.

"We're Left for Dead": Fears of Virus Catastrophe at Rikers Jail

In a March 30, 2020, *New York Times* piece covering the pandemic as it invades Rikers Jail, the kicker is all about beauty.

"One inmate used an alcohol pad that a barber had given him after a haircut to sanitize a frequently used Rikers Island jailhouse phone. Another used a sock to hold a phone during a 15-minute call. A third said he and others have used diluted shampoo to disinfect cell bars and tabletops."

Jail officials state that inmates have access to soap and cleaning supplies, but that clearly isn't entirely true. Rikers at the time of my writing is the most infectious place in the entire world. Its infection rate is seven times higher than the rest of New York City, which is already the center of the pandemic in America, which is already the center of the pandemic in the world. They are running out of soap. You cannot *send* soap. Inmates are required to purchase it through the jail system with their commissary funds. This is the case in jails across America. A study by the Prison Policy Initiative compared prices of beauty goods to that on the outside and discovered prices were sometimes higher than the outside for items like soap, shampoo, and conditioner. A 12-ounce bottle of VO5 shampoo costs $0.99 at retail, but costs $1.69 in the Illinois commissary. Per-person commissary sales in a 34-state study averaged $947 per year. This may not seem like a lot, given it also includes food and beverages, but the typical hourly wage for an incarcerated person is less than $1 an hour. To put that into perspective, according to the Bureau of Labor Statistics, the average amount spent on personal care annually in 2017 was $762 alone.

Mutual Aid Fundraisers floated around the internet a week or two before the *Times* article came out. The National Bail Fund Network put out a call to organizations around the country to demand incarceration rates be lowered, and to make sure people in prisons and jails across the country had access to the supplies they need, and organizations raised money for commissary programs, like Black and Pink Boston's $33K fundraiser to send money for soap to commissary programs across the country. These funds often rely on immediate community members of the incarcerated, though, and are not a long-term solution to a problem that is based on neglect and profitability.

In New York, there is a 20 percent transaction fee for all money put into commissary accounts. Costs for using the prison message system (similar to email) just to assess needs on the inside vary, from free to $0.50 per message sent. The prison system has created a profit margin in the ways it refuses to care for the people they imprison, down to soap and the means people have to communicate with the outside world. Soap is supposed to be part of the necessities they have inside, but it is still being withheld, so they can die faster and be less of a burden on the prison's bottom line. Ultimately, figuring out better means of justice goes beyond soap drives, but it's still an immediate action to prevent a lot of life lost. When we do manage to bail people out, they need care supplies and community.

According to reporting from *Business Insider*, the Texas prison system has spent more than $1.1 million in legal fees countering a lawsuit presented by prisoners who had been denied hand sanitizer and masks during the pandemic—geriatric prisoners who, no surprise, eventually did get COVID. The legal fees accrued from March 2020 to April 2021 amount to $1,146,278. The prisoners won, but the case was later overturned. So far, more than half a million people incarcerated in prison have gotten COVID, and that number is likely an undercount. That $1,146,278 could have bought 5,731,390 bars of soap.

While the Texas attorney general spent over a million in

taxpayer dollars denying soap to sick people, mutual aid organizations have continued to show up. A typical post-release request package compiled by organizers in New York City includes the following: a MetroCard to get home, a personal guide to shepherd them back and greet them at the door. Body wipes, a snack, toothpaste. And soap.

As the lawsuit moves through appeals court, Texas has the largest number of infections and deaths among prisoners in any state in the United States, and by the end of it I have used five bars of soap in their entirety while watching the numbers rise and waiting for letters from incarcerated pen pals to reach me. Three letters I wrote were returned, refused by guards, because I drew flowers with colored pencils on the cards. They are only permitted letters in black or blue pen. It took three months for them to be refused and returned. Counting, counting.

There are days where I feel sure that the best thing beauty can be is an anesthetic, that fleeting relief is the only possibility it offers, that it dulls rage just enough to make our lives livable. That the numbness and comfort it provides misdirects our energy from bigger fixes and better solutions. A great deal of the beauty industry is a waste of energy, resources, emotions, and time. But then I get a letter from a pen pal in prison, and every letter asks for the same kind of help: descriptions of beautiful things and places I've been to lately, Polaroids of girls, of flowers, of food, to feel seen by someone outside the walls they're confined in, and commissary money for soap and stamps, so they can keep writing to me, stay clean, and stay alive.

HOW BEAUTY SURVIVES A PLAGUE

When I think about beauty in times like this, in the time of a plague and the denial of it, it's a hand to reach out to when you're already over the cliff—and I'm not sure how long we can keep grip for. I'm not posturing that beauty is the solution to our problems; soap is not the cure, but it is part of the solution to saving the lives of thousands of incarcerated people. It is a lever in a system, a system that is broken and must be dismantled entirely. It is not a method of "reform" but a method of direct action to minimize harm. We don't know the magnitude of our impact in small ways—we only know what happens when none of us bother at all. So why not bother? It doesn't numb the pain felt, but it does help you live through it. It makes it endurable, a kind of hapless freedom.

March 31, 2020. Sephora laid off thousands of employees across the US via a conference call. Most employees were told about half an hour before. "You could hear everyone absolutely sobbing," said former employee Brittney Coorpender. "Sephora was pushing all of us to go to school to get a cosmetologist/esthetician license and said in return they would compensate us for it once we get the license. So free school. . . . Now what? You fired us. How are you going to repay everyone now?" Another employee wrote on Twitter: "Sephora promised to take care of their employees when this virus shut down stores, only to turn around and fire them off today via conference call and that was that. So, before you say, 'Who gives a fuck about makeup during a pandemic?'—it's not about makeup, it's people's jobs."

Sephora's tagline is "Let's Beauty Together." Apparently not.

Sephora is owned by LVMH, the world's largest maker of luxury goods, worth over $500 billion. The CEO, Bernard Arnault, is the third-richest person in the world, with a net worth of more than $190 billion. Half of LVMH is owned directly by the Arnault family. The ownership group LVMH has $5.67 billion in cash on its balance sheets for 2019. The third-wealthiest company in the luxury market, Hermès, has $4.55 billion in cash and cash equivalents, which let it keep paying all its 16,600 employees without government subsidies. LVMH is worth more but did not do the same. While they have converted factories for sanitizer, their media impact value—MIV, also known as the impact of publicity and advertising in monetary form—is now up more than 43 percent from this time last year, before COVID, according to analytics firm Launchmetrics. They have made $11.7 million in good publicity from responding to the crisis, with $6 million directly from their COVID response, in spite of firing a portion of their Sephora workforce while senior executives took no pay cuts. In her coverage of the luxury market during COVID, *Business of Fashion* writer Lauren Sherman wrote: "Helping the nation in a time of crisis is a power play. Such gestures not only wield influences with the government, but they are also a powerful brand building opportunity."

Black-owned businesses are far less likely to be able to reopen, relying on community support rather than institutional networks of power. Uoma Beauty founder Sharon Chuter began the #PullUpOrShutUp challenge on Instagram, demanding transparency from other beauty brands to highlight the staffing diversity in their companies and reflect on how they could do better. A transparent diversity report isn't a new concept, and media companies like the *New York Times* and my former employer, BuzzFeed, offer their numbers on a yearly basis to little effect. But this was the first time in recent memory that beauty brands of all sizes, from Estée Lauder to independent cosmetics brands, offered to do the same. Chuter also began a grant fund for Black-owned brands, underscoring the fact the grants offered do not require you to provide equity in your company for access to institutional and community support.

The organizing impulse reached editors and publishers, too. Early in the pandemic, beauty editor and former nurse Cheryl Wischhover began sending beauty packages to hospitals around the country, alongside other beauty editors. Her average day looks a lot different than it did before, with PR events and endless press releases. She sets up work in her living room, where she answers a backlog of emails, plugs addresses into a terrifyingly long spreadsheet, and packs up boxes for hospital staff in need of products to combat N95 mask bruises. She has a Zoom meeting scheduled with three other beauty editors for a state of the union on their donations project. They've passed 300,000 products now and 60,000 more healthcare workers to help. The number of products could fill up her entire three-bedroom house in the suburbs. Counting, counting.

―

April 6, 2020. Shirley Raines is driving to LA's Skid Row early Saturday morning, as she has done nearly every Saturday morning for three years. She's got a full face of makeup on, eyes resplendent like a Lisa Frank rainbow, neon green eyeshadow bouncing off her brown skin like a strobe light that matches her dyed buzz cut exactly. She has a nonsurgical bedazzled face mask on. Her car smells like burgers (600 of them) and roses, too. There are 1,000 small bottles of hand sanitizer packed under the burgers, jugs of water it took her days to buy enough of, and a line of cars following her on her journey down. There is a motorcade of bikers roaring alongside her, her friends and bodyguards, in various kinds of masks and scarves as they whip through a nearly empty highway to their destination, a uniform of leather vests and studs. They are the Fighters for the World biker club, providing her security and crowd control for the work they do together every weekend. Together, they are all driving toward a mass of people they recognize as their friends, tents hitched the length of littered avenues. People light up when they arrive, waving at the cars.

On an average weekend, Raines sets up hair coloring stations at the sinks installed by nonprofit mobile hygiene provider Lava Mae. There are "solar shower" bags filled with hot water from home she pours over the sink and red Solo cups to hold store-bought boxed hair color. Alongside her McGyver'd beauty stations she has a trunk stocked with hygiene kits that include toothbrush, lip color, tampons, and soap. Some brands have donated boxes and sometimes even crates of products to her cause; ORLY donated 500 bottles of hand sanitizer, as did Greenerways Organic, Laura Geller, and Manic Panic. But the costs of products and difficulty to acquire them has more than tripled since she began this work three years ago, and her usual suppliers are denying her access as they prioritize other orders first, fearing hoarding and resellers capitalizing on the pandemic supply chain. It used to take around $500 to feed the line of regulars each week, somewhere between 300 and 400 people. At the beginning of the pandemic, that crawled up to $800 and by 2022 reached $22,000 a month. Homelessness in LA has increased 80 percent over the last eight years, and more are estimated to lose their housing in LA due to pandemic-related circumstances. There are approximately 5,000 people on Skid Row alone, and the rate of infection there is skyrocketing.

"This is a Band-Aid—I am trying my best while people in power deal with policy. This is what *I* can do," explains Raines. In an interview with *Vogue* on her work during the pandemic, she confessed that doing the work with the pandemic crowding the city is skyrocketing her anxiety. "It's very unsettling for me and my team. Of course, we're paranoid and washing our hands 24/7. Of course, my family is concerned. My kids and my sister beg me, 'Please, don't go out there,' and I'm just like, 'I gotta. We can't give up on them right now. [I have asked the people here to] lay back, close their eyes, and trust that my Fighters for the World will make sure nobody will run up on them. We gained their trust with consistency by coming every Saturday. And that can't end now. It is essential that we don't lose that love and trust we've worked so hard to get from this community." Raines lost her job recently due to pandemic budget cuts, but she's still coming out every weekend with donations from her online network of supporters. She is still handing out roses from her car window and apologizing for not being able to hug the now-familiar faces on the street who call her mom, who call her godmother, who ask her about her health and her family.

Raines has received industry accolades and celebrity recognition, but not long-term institutional support for her work on the streets. Individual brands commit products but not long-term support in monetary funds, which would make a real difference as community resources for donations dry up while unemployment skyrockets.

Beauty as a community exists when we create relationships where we feel more capable than we were before. Beauty as a commodity exists when we only feel more capable through our purchasing power and product acquisition. We're usually there, in the place where commodity defines our identity, but we stick around because of the fleeting moments when it's community, too. When I'm thinking about it as a means of community organizing, I'm thinking about it as a link in a larger chain, using products as tools but never the only source of visibility, never the point, never the ideal result. Maybe this is painfully optimistic of me. But when the world is burning, why wouldn't I want to hold beauty close? What else is the point of sticking around? Why wouldn't I want flowers?

June 2020. My friend sends me photos on the encrypted messaging app, Signal, of her protest kit assembly station in the East Village. There are tulips and cigarettes as the table centerpiece. Soap is in the background: Irish Spring. I can practically smell the photo.

It's a weekend, and there are at least 20 protests going on around New York City and its boroughs alone protesting police brutality and the death of George Floyd. There are protests in small towns with a population of 2,500, too. Doctors and nurses have been protesting in their scrubs, kneeling in unison; when protesters pass clinics, staff come out to clap and the protesters shout their thanks on the way past. This is what the year comes down to: one plague folded into another one, creating a springboard of rage.

I spend the afternoon going from store to store buying supplies to drop off at pickup points in my neighborhood for people going out to protest. Family Dollar is stocked with what I need, though the cleaning supplies are cleared out. I buy gauze, Band-Aids, Neosporin (store brand, $3), antacid, earplugs, burn gel, scar gel, Dramamine for vomiting, energy bars, ziplock sandwich bags to fill my tote bags. The cashier asks if the earplugs work, checking me out from behind an acrylic divider. We maintain eye contact and I nod. They're using LRAD sound cannons now. "They use these on construction sites," I offer. "I'll use them to sleep," she says. The helicopters circle, metal birds above us in the sun.

I stop by Duane Reade's beauty aisle for my last essentials: Neutrogena single-use makeup wipes, eye drops, travel-size spray bottles. I drop them off and look for flowers on the way home. The street cart florist I go to is gone.

A hair salon is boarded up. The following is spray-painted on the boards:

> Cop = 800/hr training
> Hair stylists = 1800/hr
> WHY? *SCUM*.

Over Signal, another friend asks what skincare products work against pepper spray. I explain: licorice root, ceramides, aloe vera gel. I open up Instagram and see a brand has put together a slideshow advertising this exact conversation.

When I say beauty is a means of community organizing, it is an amoral observation. Because ethics is a problem of power, not a problem of duty. Beauty as an ethical act means understanding you have the duty to use it responsibly. We are given imperfect choices. We must force better ones.

I'm losing track of time now. I work under the impression it has been Tuesday for three days straight. I am adjusted into reality by the grim task of trying to schedule the first dose of the vaccine, but after three hours of trying, every time slot gets taken before I can confirm a date. I am in Groundhog Day. I am in the Bad Place. I comfort myself by working too much on low-paying beauty articles, which isn't a comfort at all.

I spend a weekend working, on the phone with Trans Clippers Project's cofounder Klie Kliebert, NOLA to New York. They are mailing new hair clippers to trans folks across America, mostly in Southern states where the need is more visible. We talk about community organizing and action planning, how amid perpetual disaster planning the most consistent asks are often so simple, so personal: a haircut in a place they don't feel vulnerable as a trans person or exposed to a global pandemic. As social spaces become more fraught with disease and the politicized fear of it, and of the Other, people who are prescribed into that category, trans folks, are often the first to be harmed. Agoraphobia is in some ways a by-product of wanting to simply survive. The Trans Clippers Project was formed in response. On the phone, Klie says: "What we're trying to do here comes down to two things: help people feel more at home in themselves and let people know they deserve that feeling. And that other people out there care about them in this moment. We are trying to show care in a way that recognizes the whole universe's beauty and what it means to my community. That is what moves me, and that's what beauty looks like to me today. This crisis is going to increase dysphoria over time. If we know all these things, we have to plan for it."

Afterwards, I buzz my partner's hair on our terrace, following the faint ley lines of their grown-out haircut. It's sunny, and Coltrane is on the radio. Sirens weave in and out of the buzzing noise. Hair shavings fall off the balcony and stick to our feet for days. I blow on my partner's neck to make the snipped hair float off into the wind. I get hair on my lips and lick it away, a sacrament taken in the light of day, a testament to love.

The end of summer, but not the end of things.

The story of beauty is a story of survival by any means. There are riots, and there is dancing in the streets. A few blocks away from where I stand, someone taped a vat of hand sanitizer to a tree—community hygiene at a protest at Barclays Center. Across the country, Shirley Raines is handing out roses and soap. Elsewhere in Brooklyn and LA, people are boxing up crates of masks, of lip balm, of sanitizer, of cream, for total and perfect strangers. People are wrapping their tattoos in bandages and their faces in scarves and hitting the streets with water and signs and love and fear and grief. In Philly, someone takes a video of a wave of skaters holding signs against police brutality. Painters are advising protesters elsewhere that oil-based paint ruins riot shields' field of vision and sculpture artists are taking bricks planted by the police and making installations in the streets to stall police cars from kettling in protesters—a method first used in Hong Kong and shared through social media—because you can't shove people into a van if you can't get the van close enough. Herbalists are dunking handkerchiefs in lemon juice and folding them into ziplock bags to prepare people for tear gas; nail salon owners are taking in their clients' children while the parents go out to protest. Every time someone gets hurt marching or avoiding the police, there is an avalanche of people pulling them up and away. People are beheading statues and dancing on the fragments of fallen kings. There's techno in the streets, pulsating with joy and grief.

Living through this pandemic has meant a total change from the life we had before this; grief for a sense of normalcy we once had and all of the lives lost, the ones we're still losing. I see a sign at a protest near my house that quotes Jamie Anderson: "Grief is all the love you want to give, but cannot. Grief is just love with no place to go." Grief is love with no place to go, but love is an event. We're here, where the future unfolds.

But not all of us made it here. The fact that we *are* here is because so many are not. We are protesting the unjust loss of Black life, the abandonment of our communities, the brutality against people we know, and care for, and have lost too soon. And so we have to mourn our losses and try to make the losses count, to make the event of a person's absence into something everyone must attend. And when we seek to honor them, we fill their absence with flowers. Small beauties in the echo of bigger ones.

My focus on beauty in a time of plagues isn't a romanticism of the magnitude of pain. It's in direct opposition to it, while understanding how it is also often implicated. You can't move through the hurt without healing. And to make the healing sustainable we have to resist the luxury of it becoming co-opted by brand identity, by the idea that an item can protect us more than people can. Beauty is only worth keeping if it's centered on people, not things. Transformative justice of the world—and of beauty—requires what the writer Tressie McMillan Cottom describes as discursive loyalty. In her words, "It's about the only unilateral power we have." And power runs the world.

June 1, 2020. Trump declares that the military will be brought in to deal with protesters. I experience the distinct sensation of my head splitting into two. I don't believe in beauty anymore. Just the void of it, the lack of care we're experiencing.

I run a bath and hold my breath underwater for as long as I can, and then my partner comes in to join me. I wash their face, our nightly ritual on silent autopilot. We stare at each other. And there it is, immortal. Beauty again right in front of me.

August 2020. There is a meditation at the park near my house led by Black organizers. People sit in silence in the grass together, breathing into the space others can't be anymore. The only sounds are birds and sirens and dogs, the only smell is grass. The protests are still going strong, and everyone is in masks and scarves. As far as the eye can see, there are bruises on bodies, bags under eyes. Black, Brown, and Southeast Asian organizers of all ages are handing out water, masks, kits with numbers and cards in them. People hug their own knees, knowing they can't hug their friends they see across from them. Still—smiles you can feel behind the scarves. Despite everything.

By the time you read this, the beauty industry and the rest of the world may look radically different, and this could all seem antiquated and naive. But worse and far more probable: Nothing might change for the better. It could all fade into exhaustion by then, or people will have gotten bored by how much work it takes to change things. People can burn out, go broke from trying to shoulder the burden of work on their own. People can get numb from the sheer enormity of grief and mourning required to acknowledge all the change, all the loss. We can quietly abandon each other, numb. The only worthwhile point of beauty is to prevent that from happening.

I want to write to remember that. I want to preserve that, show the way that care sustains us and beauty preserves us. How caring for care changes everything.

Saidiya Hartman wrote: "Beauty is not a luxury; rather it is a way of creating possibility in the space of enclosure, a radical art of subsistence, an embrace of our terribleness, a transfiguration of the given. It is a will to adorn, a proclivity for the baroque, and the love of too much."

May we always be too much. May we always be willful. May we embrace the terrible and also its transfiguration.

7

Near Death Is the Father of Beauty

I have an interest in the wrong technology: the feminine kind, the kind that is not useful as much as it is beautiful. Beauty tools like makeup brushes and acrylic nails and micro-needling devices and jade rollers. I have spent months buried in libraries reading about the history of human tools and spent rent money on eBay on surrealist Salvador Dalí perfume bottles. Some of this comes from wanting to justify why I never became an engineer like my mother wanted and instead became, tragically, a beauty writer. I tried to apologize for my knowledge by presenting it as technical; I am an anthropologist of aesthetics, a historian of beauty. Take me seriously, please! But the real reason I am obsessed with it stems from my favorite childhood movie and my longest-standing crush: Milla Jovovich as Leeloo in *The Fifth Element*.

Leeloo was programmed with life-saving knowledge but didn't yet know how best to use it; in other words, she was a cyborg. There's a scene early on where Leeloo stumbles across a

Chanel-branded View-Master from the future. Leeloo, ignoring the hapless men around her, looks through the View-Master and emerges with fully lined eyes, mascara, shadow, and blush. I was jealous of both the View-Master for being so close to Leeloo and jealous of Leeloo for handling such technology. She didn't need to learn how to use individual tools or listen to the men around her. She indulged her curiosity and was rewarded. I wanted that for myself. I wanted that promise from the future.

Beauty technology now isn't much different from that moment of cinematic magic. A smartphone can projection-map makeup onto you from a multitude of brands and track your moves throughout a store (or protest). There are algorithm-based beauty brands that offer custom hair color, serum, acne cream, and skincare recommendations. There are AI influencers, run by teams of white men, regularly cast in global beauty and fashion campaigns. There are also skincare brands that were funded by the CIA for their ability to collect biometric information.

Leeloo wouldn't know what to do with herself.

Futurity has no single body, has no need for one person to represent it to the world. In a lot of versions of futurity, progress means perfection. I'm uninterested in flawless utopia, but I am interested in the future as surprise, as curiosity, as elaboration, as play. In his introduction to the 1986 anthology *Mirrorshades*, writer Bruce Sterling wrote that in cyberpunk, "Technology is visceral. It is not the bottled genie of remote Big Science boffins; it is pervasive, utterly intimate. Not outside us, but next to us. Under our skin." I wanted to meet the intimate, the unpolished. The punks that might deal with playing toward the future but don't have Forbes 100 profiles. I wanted to meet people deeply committed to body modification, but not *vanity*. People who worked on the line between modification and optimization—people who try to redefine the space in between.

I went to Austin, to a convention hotel.

Body hacking is a catchall term for body modifications of all kinds: Botox injections, eyelid surgery, prosthetic replacements, tattoos (ranging from stick and pokes to ink that's invisible until activated by UV light, to chemically reactive ink that monitors your blood pressure, to tattoos that claim to disappear within a year—now available in chain shops in LA and Williamsburg, actually), implants (for breast and butt augmentation, but to create Wi-Fi hotspots, too), facelifts, the list keeps growing. Those who body hack sometimes call themselves cyborgs, but not always.

The term *cyborg* is the abbreviated form of "cybernetic organism," something both part biological and part machine. The term was coined in 1960 by Manfred Clynes and Nathan Kline to describe an astronaut capable of surviving in space with artificial lungs and other modifications. But some academics assert humans have always been cyborgs because we've always incorporated our creations into our lives to extend our normal reach. A seatbelt, for example, is life-extending cyborg technology, though it's considerably less sci-fi than the idea of using stem cells to reverse the signs of aging or implanting a Wi-Fi router into your skull. Delineating the subcultures of cyborg-space is as much a philosophical debate as a technical one. Transhumanists are interested in hacking physical aspects of their bodies but are especially focused on more permanent measures like gene editing and defying death entirely. They use cyborg hybridity as a means to an end, where humanity itself—the fact of our mortality—is transformed into something eternal.

Body modification technology is one of the most profitable and omnipresent industries in the world, regardless of what tribe you fall into. You may be skeptical of being in any of the above at all, but you are if you've ever touched up your photos. Consumers are requesting surgeries to look more like the images of themselves they create with Snapchat and Instagram filters, and the photo editing application Facetune is continually one of the top-selling apps in the Apple Store. Makeup brands team up with social media companies to create filters based on their new launches, and Sephora installed virtual makeup stations at their stores years ago. Academics and military researchers spend a lot of time and money on body modification and recognition technology, coming up with "deepfakes," facsimiles of real people manipulated into saying or doing things they've never done. There is an emerging group of influencers that are *just* deepfakes—pseudo-Kylie Jenners on TikTok with more than a million followers, the China-based deepfake Elon Musk, too. There are AI influencers with Calvin Klein campaigns and deepfake influencers with designer collaborations and teeth-whitening discount codes. They are fake-people, no heartbeats, just pixels, with bigger and bigger real-life bank accounts and bigger social media platforms than you. These poltergeists from Uncanny Valley are built on the same software as your harmless and horny puppy face filter. Different edge, same sword. Beauty brands and governments are interested in seeing what technology is easiest to adopt to a larger audience, what information can be gleaned from it, and how to make it as cheap as possible. Body modification technology is extensive and shapes both your selfie lighting options and modern-day cyber-warfare. It is amoral, chaotic, dangerous, and fun.

Myths of transformation have become the basis of entire industries. Remember Hephaestus, the crippled son of the gods Zeus and Hera? He was the creator of the fire Prometheus stole and gave to mankind. He built wheeled golden tripods to help him move around.

People at BDYHAX are the first adopters of body technology, the pilot subjects of our speculative futures. The BDYHAX conference is a days-long event where body hackers, transhumanists, cyborgs, and general nerds all assimilate. It's one of many conferences of its kind, as the transhumanist movement becomes more mainstream at the behest of Silicon Valley. When I arrived, people in the hotel lobby were gathered around sources of electricity like overgrown moths. Cyborgs compared prosthetics like new handbags or tattoos, walking up and down the labyrinth of stairs between floors and waving above and below, charging their legs and arms and iPhones. An interactive sound installation tucked in the corner hummed and bellowed depending on how fast you spun the speakers, and it made mania of the room.

Governments spend serious money on the intersection of body hacking and body modification technology that this conference is meant to advertise—a member of the Department of Defense is scheduled to keynote the event. Besides that, the CIA's venture capital arm provided funding for Skincential Sciences for their skincare products that have patented DNA extraction technology. While their consumer brand Clearista makes "skin resurfacing" products for clearer, younger-looking skin, it's also a technology that could potentially permit the CIA to collect data about people's biochemistry via exfoliation. This patented technology removes a thin layer of skin to reveal unique biomarkers that can be used for a variety of diagnostic tests. It is said to be painless and supposedly requires water, a special detergent, and a few brushes against the skin. "Your biomarker profile can reflect a number of things—where you've been, what you've done, who you are," explained Russ Lebovitz, CEO of Skincential Sciences to *Fast Company*.

Elite universities are also involved in what the beauty industry calls "cosmeceuticals," this playground of ingredients that double as medical or militant products. The beauty brand Shiseido bankrolls Massachusetts's Cutaneous Biology Research Center, where MIT and Harvard researchers work on dermatology, and hosts an annual pitch event for students to contribute to the company's skincare portfolio off campus in Boston.

Many of the conference-goers in Austin met previously at Boston's International Genetically Engineered Machine (iGEM) Competition. Plenty of competitors at iGEM go on to found companies together. Edgar Andrés Ochoa Cruz, a judge at iGEM, happened to be at both. He was the first self-proclaimed biohacker in South America and opened a string of biohacking spaces all throughout Latin America. Biohacking is a more permanent approach to body hacking, focused not only on augmentation of the body but modification of your chromosomes and genetic composition. If your body is a genetic procession of AGCT in an individual sequence, biohacking is the revision process of those letters for specific and tailored ends. In layman's terms, genetic editing is akin to revising a body's capacities and health conditions through a scientist's word processor. (Due apologies for the simplicity of the metaphor to all genetic engineers.) After helping found SyntechBio, Cruz founded OneSkin, a company dedicated solely to solving aging. For the past few years, he'd been setting up public bioengineering labs for the community and sharing his knowledge with everyone who wants it. He's teaching new recruits to the biohacking scene in South America the procedures of his anti-aging work in an effort to maximize the variations of molecular markers that can be tested.

Cruz has billionaire competition in his product category: Peter Thiel, Jeff Bezos, and Elon Musk have all invested considerable amounts of money into transhumanist ventures. Google has a very secretive company called Calico that focuses on the biology of aging in mice, worms, and human cells and tissues. Both Bezos and Thiel have invested in Unity Biotechnology, a startup that aims to develop medicines that "slow, halt, or reverse age-associated diseases, while restoring human health." Thiel alone has a few anti-aging ventures in his portfolio, including Unity.

Beauty companies also visit the more commercial sister events like this because they know that customers are willing to pay thousands every year on skincare and services that makes their skin look younger and smoother while the world burns around us. They send envoys to scope out anti-aging or bioprinting technology that they can buy out or sign usage for exclusively. Bioprinting and focus on the skin microbiome has shaped the research behind now best-selling products—L'Oréal's Dermatological Beauty Division is made up of precisely this research, and it results in products from La Roche-Posay, Vichy, CeraVe,

SkinCeuticals, and Décleor. All brands I have in my vanity as I type this, products currently on my face right now.

In 2023 L'Oréal spent over 1.2 billion euros on research, and they regularly host global summits showcasing their technological discoveries. In 2016, L'Oréal announced a partnership with Poietis, a health tech company in the business of printing human hair follicles. Poietis uses a 3D laser-assisted printer and robotics to print biological tissue in multiple, customizable layers, and then L'Oréal uses that for tests. They're working toward creating a functional follicle capable of producing hair. In 2015 and 2017 Poietis also announced partnerships with the company BASF for printing skin for cosmetic testing. Printing viable hair takes three weeks; skin takes just two. The faster the technology for printing skin and hair evolves, the faster animal testing and (whole) human testing regulations can be changed. Plenty of people boycott brands that do animal testing at all. If testing on bio-printed human tissue becomes cheap and scalable enough for smaller brands to adopt, the global market changes. And when—not if—it does, it will eventually eliminate low-paying jobs for humans who get paid to be test subjects for soon-to-market skincare products. The streamlined production cycle is a capitalist's dream, and it happens to coincide with a cyborg one.

Poietis excites Cruz, who already seems like a freight train you can't stop. With access to made-to-order skin samples, OneSkin would be able to perform testing that much faster, with fewer regulatory hoops to jump through. It's a matter of finding the right collaborator in the crowd who's working on adjacent technology. If that happens and his work leads to a true discovery, he can patent and protect his molecule and end up a very wealthy man, with L'Oréal and pharmaceutical manufacturers knocking on his door. Whenever I saw him for the rest of the conference, he was in the front center of the audience, questioning every speaker about their work and to find out how they could collaborate on processes. He set up a now-defunct $10,000 award grant to entice synthetic bioengineers to work with his company for a younger, ageless future. He straddles the line between opportunist and idealist with sincerity and charm. The last thing he said to me that weekend is also on his website, evidently well rehearsed: "When you feel that you should have been born in the future, the only option is to build the future, so you can finally get to where you belong."

Anti-aging and death-freezing technology is the overarching focus of the transhumanist project. The goal is to wrest beauty from the mythical fountain of youth into a reality you and everyone else in the world would pay for. For the most influential transhumanists, which is to say the wealthiest ones, it means redefining beauty purely in terms of how it fits into capital. Laura Deming, founder of the Longevity Fund, a venture capital fund that invests specifically in anti-aging technologies, describes the "longevity market" as a "two-hundred-billion dollar plus" opportunity, and says that it "is impossible to say how big it could be, because if you cured aging you'd change medicine entirely." You would also render entire product categories in the beauty industry obsolete, which is a revolution in and of itself. More people are getting sick and dying sooner, simply put. It makes longevity research more valuable to do. Between 2019 and 2021, deaths due to COVID led to an overall decline in the average life expectancy of the average American—2.7 years shorter for the total population, with the lives of Native Americans shortened by 6.6 years overall. In other countries, particularly those with universal healthcare, life expectancy averages have rebounded.

Transhumanists assume beauty is meant for the people who can stay as young and fit as possible. Augmentations are meant to make you more powerful, help prevent you from being someone else's problem to solve. For transhumanists, to be a cyborg isn't *quite* enough. Humanity, mortality, a fallible human body—these are problems that must be solved. Transhumanist ideals aim to close the gap between life and death, because they assume that gap is a failure of our evolution. They seek immortality, but some will settle for outsmarting longevity velocity, which means that the pace of technological advancement in wellness technology would increase to the point that for every year that passes, average human life expectancy increases by more than the year. All tech along the way aiming to extend life exists because the technology for immortality isn't yet available. Now there's even something called the Rejuvenation Olympics, an online leaderboard of the top 20 age reversals "validated by phenotypically trained algorithms," and the founder, Bryan Johnson, spends close to $2 million a year on trying to win against entropy. The competition's tagline is haunting: "Where you win by never crossing the finish line." Johnson is a very fit 70-year-old man aiming to have the same body-age as his teenage son.

Donna Haraway wrote in her now-famous "Cyborg Manifesto" that for cyborgs, fathers are inessential. In this way, I am a failed cyborg. My father is deeply important to me. He is also the first cyborg of my life, having had metal inserted into his spine when I was an infant. He shot himself in the head one fall afternoon on our front porch, but he survived.

He kept the neck brace in the linen closet as I grew up. I used to try it on. It was ill fitting, the Velcro loud, the dimensions too big for my tiny body, a shell too big for my framework. His disability and his augmentation were invisible to other people but never to me or my mother. During fights with my father, my mother in a rage would bring up the fact he tried to die and leave her alone with me, a daughter she did not initially want. He kept the brace around to remind himself of what he had almost done.

The augmentation ensuring his survival became a constant object in the house. His bedroom has remained unchanged for the past decade and a half. The shelf across from his bed stocks his childhood teddy bear; old leather-bound copies of classic novels, hardly touched; guitar picks, well worn; an old Polaroid of me in high school; and his brace from the hospital. Sometimes the brace is in his closet, hidden under a pile of ties. I used to shove it to the side as I hid in the closet when my parents fought. It didn't bring me comfort then, but it did tell me that sometimes material things save us from ourselves, even if we don't want them to.

On the occasions that my mother would search for me with a baseball bat in hand, I'd crawl back into the closet and clutch the brace like a doll while my father stood sentry at the door. Then, I knew, the brace wasn't help at all.

My dad would never consider himself a transhumanist. Still, he once fit the qualifications pretty well. Transhumanists want to make their bodies inessential to their existence. They want to be redeemed through technology and be better than their organic, decaying selves. Selfhood falls away at the opportunity to be optimized into something far vaster and more eternal.

NEAR DEATH IS THE FATHER OF BEAUTY

I did ask my father about why he kept the brace. I asked him over coffee the morning he gave me my first driving lesson. He was surprised but open to talking about it. No, he didn't remember that he kept it. No, he doesn't really know why he does. No, he doesn't remember me playing with it as a child. The whole ordeal was a mistake, he said, swishing his dark coffee in the cup so aggressively that it nearly spilled. We both watched the rim in anticipation.

The head of the Biological Technologies Office at Defense Advanced Research Projects Agency (DARPA), an arm of the US Department of Defense, is the keynote speaker on the second afternoon at BDYHAX. He presents some of their projects to a rapt crowd, showcasing technology similar to a memory USB implanted into your shoulder. It's not the first time this technology has been presented to me. My last meeting with the Cyborg Foundation, some of the most well-known transhumanists and artists in the world, had dealt with this exact technology and where to get it. We'd been introduced through mutual friends over email, and they invited me to plan some projects with them over lunch. They'd been planning secretive prospective trips out of the country since an ambassador elsewhere was a fan of Neil Harbisson, the cofounder, and more inclined to coordinate a surgical rendezvous with the future. It'd been exciting then, the mysterious nature of the event, the blessing from someone in power to do something to further the capacities of the human body and human mind. To be invited by influential and smart artists to join on their project felt special to me, and I wanted to sacrifice my body as a prospective test subject—then I could write all about it, and I'd planned to. The plans never solidified enough for that to happen, but similar technology puttered along.

Seeing it again in DARPA's hands, in a clinical and militant context, reveals how it might one day be used. The presenter plays videos of people recalling a list of items with the technology and without. I think of how it could be used in interrogation rooms, to bombard you with real deaths you never witnessed but might be convinced into believing you had. Suddenly details would become all you see, a matrix of everything mattering equally because your mind can't protect you from the most painful parts. I wonder what kind of person would want to surrender imperfect, protective memory for something so binary and undeniable.

I can't bear the thought that I'd have to know my memory that well. The fact of things I know but can't *see* would drown me. I would suddenly remember too much. I would know the exact day my dad shot himself, I would perhaps know what might have been on the television at the time. I would know if there'd been music playing on the block, or children in the park behind our house, screaming their heads off at each other. I would know where he'd left me in the house, remember the routine he'd pantomimed the hours leading up to him picking up the gun. I would certainly have to remember the sound of it going off. And the sound—the sound of it—would I know if it echoed or shook the front door? Would I be able to draw the exact spray of the blood on the siding of the house, know if it reached the rosebushes he'd planted the week before? Would the blood have darkened the windows of the room I was found in? I'd know. But it's the sound that would never leave my mind, that I know would be playing on an infinite loop.

NEAR DEATH IS THE FATHER OF BEAUTY

That technology *would not* optimize me. It would completely break my heart.

Two days into the conference, people trickled into the main hall for a film screening. The hour is slated to be spent discussing disability's place in the transhumanist community. It comes in the form of a video. I realize, sitting down, that this is the only programming of the conference thus far dedicated explicitly to discussing disability and cyborgs, and there's no one even on the stage to speak on it. No disability activists were headlining the conference. They were relegated to the pre-filmed film on screen after lunch.

"Everybody loves stories about savants." Cut to a cyborg professor, who built metal legs for himself so he could return to climbing mountains. I'm reminded of what *The New Yorker* called the "three-act structure" of Silicon Valley: life hacker, rock climber, cadaver. One step more. Cut to sharp arachnid arm attachments on disabled dancers, crawling with grace on a plain black stage.

"'I don't look good enough' is also assumed to mean 'I have a disability.'" A philosophy professor reasons. Cut to a hearing aid next to a breast augmentation on a makeover show. Cut to the tearful applause, the happy families, the problems solved.

Cut to: "Why would I want to have legs just to get on your level?" Cut to a disabled woman wheeling her other disabled friend along down the street, red with laughter. Cut to a man speeding up the stairs using his arms with a bemused smile, knowing he was being gawked at by a crowd.

And then cut to this: "If my child was born with a disability, I would hang myself from a tree."

It's the idea that everyone wants to be "fixed" into a similar form or die that repulses me. The idea that disability portends doom, that people are only deserving of love and a life if they meet other people's qualifications of what a life should be composed of. The most passionate transhumanists I meet and watch operate at a deep distance from the lived life of someone who became augmented without their consent or careful planning, who lives life with a disability and who does not consider that circumstance a superhuman tale of technology transcending societal problems. They live human lives full of frustration, full of paperwork, full of budgeting and monitoring upgrades to their prosthetics; they live on a wave of credit card and medical debt in the pursuit of managing their health and life.

My father was a guitarist, once. His finger mobility was significantly damaged after he shot himself. His neck isn't as flexible as before; he can't turn it as much as he would want in order to see the chords to pluck. He *can* play, but he never does when the family is home. Every Christmas he still asks for a new guitar stand, without fail. All the guitars he owns fill up my old bedroom. I grew up surrounded by his guitars but never his music, just the promise that one day maybe he'd play a song.

Cut to: "Where's the waterproof wheelchairs, not the titanium battle suits?" Zoom out to a rapidly emptying conference room, and me running silently down the corridor.

NEAR DEATH IS THE FATHER OF BEAUTY

There's a scene in *The Fifth Element* shortly after the ViewMaster is used, where Leeloo downloads the history of war into her psyche in under two minutes. She begins to cry, overwhelmed by the destruction. She turns to the men around her, explaining her prerogative: "Life. Preserve life." She still lacks full language despite all the information in her brain—speaking to her is like watching a computer compose a poem. She's crying because she's bewildered at the prospect of her mission, knowing what she knows now. Humans are committed to killing each other. Humans are bizarre, she cries. We assume more knowledge and technology will fix us and resolve our deepest impulses. But all we seem to do is kill and survive being killed.

While the talk at the conference is about the future of these technologies and how much better lives will be—how everyone will be happier—they don't often talk about the cost of it. They instead offer visualizations of how many people die per day—an empire, a kingdom—and how the cost to save any of these lives is in effect a bargain. Their answer is a libertarian one: Make it yourself, since the institutions won't protect you, and we can't fix them. We are our only option. Wouldn't you give up a great many things to live forever? You can solve anything with enough time, right? Time is money, so infinite time is the ultimate wealth, or so it goes. People have similar conversations about beauty treatments—if I get on Ozempic, I will get thinner, and therefore be happier; if I get this nose job, I will hate myself less, and it will save me. Cosmetic surgery for so many people *is* gender-affirming care: It does save lives. You see the connections here? How body hacking and beauty services are one and the same? How the costs of them feel so dire, but the consequences of not having access to them feel just as awful for so many?

The problems for actual cyborgs is that just living costs plenty enough. Air travel becomes a gamble regarding the survival of your cyborg necessities—airlines break 29 wheelchairs every day from mishandling them, and they take weeks and months to offer restitution, rarely covering the full cost of replacing what they break. It limits the opportunities to move around for people who need their chairs to live independently. A used leg will cost you thousands of dollars, and like any other technology, they decay over time and require replacement, upgrades, modifications as you live your life. Exceptional athletes with disabilities may get their prosthetics sponsored, saving them tens of thousands of dollars in exchange for the promise that they break world records and do campaigns in between training and winning Olympic medals. That is not the lived reality of most people.

The disabled poet Cy Weise surveyed cyborg parts sellers on their stories, the cost of them, and the most joyous moments of their life. Here is an excerpt from that polling:

"Morally it is not a good price. It is a horrible price. And I feel horrible selling it. *No one* should have to pay $1,200 to walk and lead a normal life with used components."

"Ninety-nine percent of the moments I share with my daughter are the most joyous, but in relation to my amputation it would be time spent in the Gulf of Mexico. I have not been in the ocean in 18 years, I have lived within 1 mile of it for the past 8 years. I was able to finally put together parts for a water leg a year ago. My ass limped to the waterline and I went for it. I spent 3 cold hours just sitting there letting the waves hit me. Hypothermia, jelly fish, and sharks wouldn't have made me get out."

Anarchist methodology describes "temporary autonomous zones," ephemeral spaces in a suffocating reality, spaces that make other forms of reality and perception seem possible, if only for a moment. At best, maybe augmentation spaces and virtual reality technology let us create these spaces—though mostly they aren't created with such comforts in mind for the people who need them most. But being able to recognize the power of augmentation everywhere means you're prepared to understand how you might best use it to survive this world.

Latina beauty biohacker Katia Vega understands this explicitly. At BDYHAX, she presents half a dozen future-beauty technologies on stage. She shows face stickers programmed to light up phrases on a programmed monitor or operate as buttons for actions, developed in conjunction with paralyzed athletes. There's tattoo ink that changes colors on the test skin according to pH balance and glucose levels, so tattoos can be used to monitor health.

There are acrylic nails printed with QR codes, water-repellent nails programmed to transform water into an orchestra. A manicured DJ wades through a pool, and the light shifts as the current changes and the music adjusts. I have the distinct feeling of déjà vu.

In the vanity cabinet in my bedroom, there are a few ring boxes filled with leopard print acrylic nails that, when photographed, summon a school of fish into the photograph, or a galaxy of stars, or a rainbow. They're by Metaverse Nails, an augmented reality nail company based in Hong Kong, Melbourne, and Shanghai—really, firmly based in WeChat and the borderless future. The product manager Kati reached out when she was visiting New York a year before the conference in Austin.

She applied the nails onto my bare fingers in an empty bar one summer afternoon, her pink hair hovering near my own gray-dyed buzzcut. "It's hard to explain the nails to people in the tech world. They'll look at them and for some reason they assume we have never thought about what comes after this. They see us and see a door they can walk through with 'woman' on it. They see us as one-dimensional. But we've created a universe of engineering and art and business all around this idea of beauty they don't have a clue about yet. We have a vision for being able to completely make yourself over; you can look one way in the club and hold your phone over you and look completely different. We call it crystal camouflage." She sat up and ran my hand under her phone. Suddenly there were stars. A tap and they became a butterfly shooting lasers. We cackled at the quiet chaos on the cell phone screen, the world oblivious around us. She looked up and smiled, conspiratorial.

"Being able to rewrite yourself is very queer, very powerful. No?" It's not a coincidence that the company is the creation of a trans genderqueer woman and her community, or that they sought me out. It's not a coincidence that these nails are temporary, affordable, and hyperfeminine: They aren't meant for the wealthy technocrats who want beauty to mean permanence or exclusivity or to redefine humanity for everyone in the world. They're meant for the queer people who want to change on a dime, and selectively, and secretly, sometimes. Queer and otherwise marginalized people know what it means to negotiate who gets to see you for who you really are—as you define yourself. How that can be a bet you can lose. Used to being constantly both dismissed and surveilled, we have to be selective about who to show our best selves to—about who gets to see what brings us joy. We use beauty to survive the very circumstances that make our bodies the reason we're hunted down and often killed.

Vega presented hair extensions that could be programmed to the user's specifications, too. One example I loved was braiding your hair into recording a conversation or twirling it to send your GPS location to friends or the police. Using hair extensions woven with disguised circuits in the wefts, the fiber-optic strands are dyed the dimension and color of the wearer's natural style. Thinking about my friends who are too frightened to walk home alone after a bad date or a party makes me want those extensions sold in every single drugstore in America; I have more hope in these hair extensions than I do in men unlearning predatory behavior.

I wonder if they could be programmed to play music the way Vega's nails could be programmed to play the water. If I could braid my father's hair into music next time I was home. I would braid it to play the song his former band hit the charts with—or, better yet, the introduction to *Baywatch*, a TV show with an opening track he used to spin me around the living room to when I was very small.

Katia and Kati mentor people and travel the world to share their work. They're building a community of knowledge, not an industry of consumption. It's an example of what the academic Simone Browne calls "dark sousveillance," a defiance that often seems like cooperation, but is actually masked retaliation against the power structure that seeks to harm. At its best, beauty technology treats body data as something that can not only be explored but preserved, protected, and iterated on. It understands the vulnerability of the body it is meant for.

On the last day of the convention I met a cyborg named Meow-Ludo Disco Gamma Meow-Meow, who had been sued by an Australian company for implanting his transportation card chip into his hand. He'd done so because he wanted to reduce the amount of things he had to carry around to get through his day. They'd tried to deactivate the card associated with his name, only to realize he'd been using an anonymous transit card chip instead—so they got the authorities to cut it out of him. He responded with the perfect question when bringing them to court: "If you don't own your body and what's inside it, then what the hell do you own?"

What do you want the world to see about you, and what part of you would you be willing to owe in return?

Tech solutionism, the idea that tech can solve social, cultural, and structural problems, has never allowed real agency for the people who suffer most under the problems at hand. But I do think more focus and support ought to be devoted to the people who tech—and the beauty industry—often don't see or forget about, who are considered broken or too stupid to participate at all. The invisible and visibly disabled, like my father and my friends, the queer artists, who are both fetishized and reviled for who they love. The femmes and the depressed and the tired who work themselves to the bone trying to keep a roof over their heads and food on the table by juggling three different app-based jobs and still just scrape by, who go into debt in service of strangers and Silicon Valley empires. The people who cannot afford a $15,000 titanium leg or a $200 insulin shot or a $40 manicure. The people who get left behind in fantasies of future health and wealth and beauty. The people who do not get excited at the idea of genetic editing, because it would allow their family—or themselves—to be edited out of who they are. Those people make up everyone I know and love.

BDYHAX presented the arguments most people have about technology and obligation succinctly on one of the last panels of the weekend. On the white board, besides the panelists, the following eventually emerged in a frantic scrawl:

"With enough technology we can make people equal." versus "We can create a society where we treat each other equally without it."

I rewrote it in my journal to the following:

"Everyone is beautiful in an equal and good society." versus "We can create a society where beauty doesn't factor into how we treat each other after all."

When I was a teenager, I eventually wanted to dye my hair bright red, just like Leeloo. It was to be filmed and written about for my first print magazine feature, using a hair dye formula algorithmically matched to a photo I had sent in to the company. I was also filming it ostensibly to upload to YouTube. My father offered to help me bleach my roots in the kitchen and dye it in the backyard. I set up the tripod and camera and halfway through went to answer the front door.

During playback, I realized that when I was gone, my father had filmed a message for me to watch. In it, he's clumsily mixing bleach powder with a plastic take-out spoon, smiling into the camera to an audience of one. "I'm so proud of my daughter and that I can do this with her. It's only hair dye, it's only temporary. I hope if you're watching this, your parents get to help you be yourself, too. That they're supportive of whatever you decide to become. I'm so proud of you," he repeats, tapping the side of the spoon onto the tub, hearing me walk down the hall toward the camera again to finish the video. When I get back to the camera, I try to adjust it but it falls to the floor, broken but for the surviving memory card.

When I saw this clip a few days later, I made four copies and put the clip into folders on every computer in the house, every email account I had, every storage device I owned. I am terrified of losing it in the digital ether. It is the first thing I upload onto any new hard drive. My essential programming is this 30-second video of him mixing my hair color in our kitchen on a summer afternoon.

Transhumanism's focus on life extension technology is in service of a specific kind of man, but not in the preservation of the intangibles of humanity that make life remarkable. "Cyborgs" give up family for a future where everything is smooth and easy. But *life* is about who we love, and to love inherently begets loss, too.

Living cyborgs—the disabled, those with invisible disabilities as well as visible ones, the ill, the queer and trans and poor—are rarely included in visions of utopia and transhumanism because they are examples of how loss hurts. They show how transformation requires sacrifice, is not always just and programmed and planned, and is mostly a matter of survival and fighting for every scrap of joy you can find. The fantasy of optimization leaves out the intangibles that make us who we are. We keep avoiding parts of life in service of something more sterile, high gloss.

I was drawn to the transhumanist project with the hope that understanding the goal would make me more optimistic about how creative the future would be with the data farmed from our bodies. That a body digitized was still preserved as a human life, a person with family and friends and love and community. That in our obsession with the future and how to make it happen, we would make the present a little more endurable. That we'd make technology that would help keep our secrets, if we wanted; that it would share them, only if we wanted; that it would make us feel better when we're bummed out but not so much that we become addicted to a version of ourselves that we have to buy to uncover. That transhuman futures would make technology as interesting as beauty can be profane, moody, and fun.

This is now, I realize, the most utopian hope I could have fostered. None of those earlier assumptions about why I cared about transhumanism or cyborgs were even fully true. I was interested in them because I wanted to understand my father. I wanted to know what I could find for him in a world that made him think killing himself would solve any of the pain he'd had to endure or the life he tried to escape from. I wanted to know if there were other technologies that could bring us joy, and not just try to fix us. That there might be technology that didn't link beauty to improvement, or aesthetics to efficiency. Something beyond reparative correction of bodies and more about resilience and fixing the smaller and more mundane things that make the present difficult for people who can't afford endless augmentation. Who may not want to live forever, but just to live *well*. On their own terms. Able to change on a pirouette into something private for somebody they trust and love.

Recently, I visited my parents for the afternoon for the first time since we all received the COVID-19 vaccination. I hugged my father for the first time in a year and a half. We sat next to each other, sipping coffee until our mugs were empty and staining the table we painted together when I was small. He told me his memory is better than ever—that he's been writing sci-fi now, with protagonists just like Leeloo. "Don't worry," he said. "I'm going to live forever." I got up to fill his cup.

8

The House of Beauty Is Burning

I wanted the last chapter to be about love and care and leave you feeling good, and unsurprisingly it's been the hardest thing to write in this book. It's hard to feel good in the face of capitalism's devastation when you care about other people. I crawled through each paragraph with unfinished sentences scattered in a scaffolding of optimistic reason. I wanted to solve everything I discovered in previous chapters, neatly fix decades of institutional problems and generations of trauma in a smooth ten pages. In the span of my time muddling through this book's ending, waiting for it to declare itself, avoiding it, resenting it, many other things happened instead. I moved across the country, traveled to Tahiti, learned how to scuba dive, watched a whale come up from the dark below me with no boat to climb onto, biked 3,000 kilometers across multiple countries on the back of a motorcycle across endless hairpin turns, got 15? 20? manicures (some of them were even great), got my driver's license, lost dear friends. This went on for a year and a half! Lived a life—waiting, waiting, living, dallying—and then my life collapsed.

The details of the collapse don't really matter, but there was death, there was blood, there were hospital visits and breakdowns and numbness and fog. Ordinary disasters, all of them, even if they are still disasters. Body-disabling accidents, friendship-breaking life changes. Scars and surgeries and physical therapists to schedule. And on an hour-long respite from caretaking from one disaster, I was sexually assaulted by a massage therapist in my neighborhood.

It was then that the nearly finished, almost-certain final bow and neat declaration I had planned for the end, my flag in the sand: that care can save us, that beauty might be terror, but we can take care of each other when we take care of ourselves—those lessons became brutalized static in my hands.

So you think beauty matters in spite of endless cruelty, huh? So you think resilience will help us win? So you think care is the antidote to violence? Prove you can survive this: this moment where care is in fact the exact opposite. So you found beauty in the aftermath of devastation of your teenage depression, so it might have saved you. Then. Can you endure its perversion? Does your house still stand? Here's life, fate's arsonist. Survive this, bitch.

How fortunate for me I've spent so long studying care and disaster. I am crawling my way out of the rubble with very manicured hands.

So what if it hurts to care for myself in the ways I'm used to right now. A moment can feel like forever, but it isn't. I'll learn new ways. I'll sit in the sun with people I feel safe around until the old ways feel safe again. I won't let the fear win. I will list every single beautiful thing and place and memory and smell and compliment and person beauty has ever given me in the face of this until my voice cracks and my wrists hurt writing it all down. I will try every single absurd, exotic, obscure treatment or product or exercise until the familiar ones feel distant again—and then I'll claim them. I will spend hours brushing my hair in the mirror if it makes me feel pampered and safe again. I will learn how to cut my own hair. I will learn what, really, a tincture is. I'll take sound baths seriously. (Actually, I love them.) I will do all of it, in any combination and to any extent, if any of it might help me survive myself again.

I was so disassociated in the aftermath of this last assault, depersonalized from the experience, that I paid and tipped the person who violated my boundaries and my body in that massage parlor. I questioned my discomfort at what he did; I doubted my own responses. I became distrustful of my own feelings and tried to minimize them to nothingness. I didn't report it, didn't document my bruises, because I knew my experience would matter less than legal evidence. I went back into caretaking mode for everyone else but myself because that felt safer and more respected than sitting in my own body and mourning what was done to me—and the stark fact I didn't fight in the moment. That is something I have to work to forgive myself for every other minute. I know why I didn't. I know in my body that that person has likely done what he did to me to a string of other women who were looking for care the same way I was.

I can't protect any of them or myself from what we experienced, but I can try to heal my own relationship to care work, to community care, to beauty as a balm in crisis. It is all I can bear to do right now, actually. I don't have the capacity for any bigger epiphanies. Any grander schemes will have to wait until I can trust my own body and my own beliefs again: that care can still change things for the better. That we can and should trust each other with ourselves. When I experience and witness precarity, I'm still helplessly drawn to the care within the moment. I still believe in it.

The weekend after this last disaster, I booked a haircut after a year of neglect. It felt instinctual, a lesson I wrote to myself in earlier chapters: We hold trauma in our hair. I went to a Korean spa alone and took a nap in the hottest room, sweating out the disgust from my experience. I tried a new nail salon, where two queer Asian manicurists spent hours on my nails telling me about how they fell in love and built their salon—and their life together—from the ground up, from Malaysia to Beverly Hills. To have my hands held and cared for by my kin, to be safe and surrounded by queer care workers who love their work and the people they work with: That, to me, was trauma therapy. I showed them my inspiration and asked them to go wild on my hands, to have fun, to try something they hadn't done yet. "You're my person," TJ said, eyes lighting up. Building up trust in care and beauty again is a kind of therapy I can wear everywhere, an armor to me. It doesn't stop my C-PTSD from making me wake up in a cold sweat. But when I get anxious, I can stare at the jewels on my nails until I feel present again.

I was sexually assaulted in a place where I went to feel safe, in a place meant to make you feel cared for and beautiful. He told me, actually, when he was doing those things to me that I was so beautiful. You're perfect, so perfect, he said, when he held me down by the neck.

Men have only told me this when they want something from

me, and he told me this when he was taking. But people truly interested in beauty—devoted to it, like I am, give the compliment like a gift, like a prayer. Like a blessing freely given.

When the world tells you beauty is not your bounty, not your legacy, not your place, not your home, when the world tells you that you are not deserving of care: Don't believe it. Write yourself in. When it tells you that you are perfect but you feel used, when hearing that confuses you, when it makes you feel afraid: Know that you are the author of your own story, and nothing anyone may whisper will ever change that. Write past the terror, and find yourself somewhere better, somewhere safer, somewhere where you are loved and cared for, just the way you are right now. As ugly or as beautiful as you'd like to be, and worthy of love wherever you land in this made-up spectrum.

A refrain: If trauma can occur again, so, too, can recovery. I will not be defeated. I begin again, even in this ending, even in the ruins of my original plans. No happy endings here. Just more work to do. But the pleasures I find in doing it! The new friends. I have a folder of inspiration for my next nail appointment with the boys in Beverly Hills, notes to translate onto my hands. I haven't gone for another massage yet, so I do stretches in my yard. I crack my own back, clutch the grass, watch the ravens watch me back.

I am learning pressure points of my body, sitting with the ugliness of the memories of his hands, and relearning healthy pathways on top of the flashbacks. He knew how to ease pain and cause more while doing it, how to make me doubt what was happening while it happened. He was clever. I can be clever, too. He might prey on those who seek care, but this body is my kingdom and I am tired of being chased out of it. Every week, I learn a new pressure point, a new gateway of my body's meridians.

This weekend I found a nonbinary massage therapist who I might work with, who offers a sliding scale to queer people of color, because they believe care should be accessible to all. I emailed them today. I don't know when I'll be ready to have their hands on me, but I'm closer than I was yesterday, and that is progress enough.

If trauma can recur again, so, too, can recovery. If stories of getting better aren't inherently stories of staying well, so be it. I'll keep writing my way to progress, toward a final exit, and until I'm there, I will inventory every moment of beauty in the spiral toward the end, every loving distraction, every moment of glamor and comfort and tenderness. I'll build on the ashes of my burned little house something even better than before, bigger even, more hospitable, and I won't stop until I'm dead. I won't stop after it, actually—because this book exists beyond me. It's yours, too, now—ours. It's beyond me now. The ideas will win instead.

It's been a few months now since this last undoing. I'm up late, restless because I'm finally excited about something again. This weekend I applied to a cosmetology program and got in; I'll have already started it by the time you read this. What do you know—I loved this monster of an industry so much I crawled in even deeper, despite *and* because of everything I learned writing about it.

I don't know what I'll do with what I learn, just that I'd like to learn more, learn everything I can. I want there to be a future where someone comes to me for care, to set down their burdens, and they never experience the betrayal that I did. I want them to experience no doubt that they are in the right hands and that I will take care of them for who they are and leave them with beauty after.

This book was meant to be so much crueler. I thought being cruel in the face of cruelty would protect me, us. But as the world gets crueler, I found that I don't have the heart to follow the trend. I want to preserve the moments of tenderness that I reach for and cherish—moments of transformative intimacy, care work done one-on-one like secrets passed on in sleepovers. Leaning in to smell a perfume, having your hand held for hours by a stranger while they do your nails just so. A friend brushing your hair while you watch a movie together. I wanted in these pages to explore the legacies of moments in time—and I did. We traveled space and time together. And while I can't change the world and I can't undo harm done to me and others, together we can. I want to do that, and so I have committed myself to it, to beauty, all over again.

Beauty keeps teaching me how I can learn my body and my capacities differently. The industry of it taught me so many ways to surveil myself, but it also taught me so many ways to repair harm done to me, too. The history of it taught me there are so many ways we exploit each other for greed and self-interest, but it also taught me there's just as many ways we take care of each other in crisis. Sometimes the lessons haven't been pleasant. They are always surprising. I went deeper than I expected looking for the light at the end, wanting to solve something, wanting perfect, clear-cut answers to big questions, and I never got them—and that's okay. I went into this project thinking that by examining the bad guys, by understanding their origin stories, I could prevent their repetition or impact somehow. I wanted to believe empathy could stop something. That didn't prove to be true. Beauty has broken my heart and made it bigger in the wake of it.

That doesn't mean my efforts were wasted. I understand better than I did before how important undoing the systems of harm and exploitation are, and how deeply embedded we are in them. I could have sworn off care work after my undoing; instead I recommitted to it—and myself—in the wake of it. Because care is transformative, even if the exploitation of it is terrifying and terrifyingly common.

Everyone is capable of so much beauty and so much harm. They are part and parcel. It is what makes us beautiful—the constant choice, the constant surprise, the earnest efforts to avoid the long arc of disasters. To prove we're not just the worst things we've ever done or what was done to us, but that the best things can still be planned. We can always learn. We can always do better, but we have to believe it's worth the effort to try. We owe each other our lives and we owe this world everything, including our future.

It's a bigger debt than the one capitalism told us we owe it to survive. It's a bigger debt than beauty promises for power. In the end, they are the biggest and loudest stories in the room, but they're not the oldest or the most enduring. They're just what we know. But we know other things, and we know how stories infect the listeners quickly—it's how they stay alive. They convince us into their realities and keep us there until another one comes to call. The story of scarcity is infectious. Fear is infectious. But so is optimism. So is curiosity. So is care. So is love.

When I say I'm in love with you,
That means I'm not alone inside of it.
Together we talk to people
We love, separately, in one voice.
When my voice fills in love with you.
When I sing on the outside.

—YANYI, ***LEAVING THE HOUSE***

Heart Chest

This book is a journey through the beauty industry from history into present, but it is also a handbook for how we can navigate toward and cocreate a better future. There are places that use beauty to create community, remedy systemic issues, address institutional failings, and educate people about the connections between beauty, care, and crisis. Some of them offer individualized services at home and some offer more public programming. They all make efforts to use the tools and experience of beauty in a way that improves our lives. I wanted to leave you with the knowledge that there are so many people, so many organizations, working tirelessly throughout generations, that can always use and appreciate your support. Here are but a few that I know, love, and came across in putting this book together. This list is as exhaustive as I could make it at the time of writing, but organizations shift, grow, and change all the time, and it's but a reference point for your own curiosity, and so that you know you are not alone in this. So that you know that our situation is precarious, but it is a situation we are in together, and we can change it together, too. Because as Toni Morrison wrote in *Mouth Full of*

Blood: "Our past is bleak. Our future dim. But I am not reasonable. A reasonable man adjusts to his environment. An unreasonable man does not. All progress, therefore, depends on the unreasonable man. I prefer not to adjust to my environment. I refuse the prison of 'I' and choose the open spaces of 'we.'"

How to Vet an Organization or Charity 101

Utilizing ProPublica's Nonprofit Explorer is an easy way to research the financial details of nonprofits. Organizations that receive a tax exemption from the IRS and receive at least $50,000 a year must file an annual report. The Nonprofit Explorer summarizes the financial data of these reported forms. Look out for organizations that spend a lot of money on professional fundraisers and pay them a lot of the take. The more that charities spend on fundraisers, the less they dedicate to program spending. It's also a red flag if executive compensation is a large chunk *or* if they pay $0 to executives, which may indicate misreporting to the IRS. Other useful resources include Charity Navigator, GiveWell, and GuideStar.

Here's an important distinction to keep in mind: 501(c)3 organizations are for religious, charitable, scientific, and educational purposes. Donations to them are tax-deductible. These organizations can coordinate nonpartisan actions but cannot politically lobby. 501(c)4 organizations are not tax-deductible and are for social welfare groups—which means they include political action groups that can endorse candidates. So they can lobby politically toward a partisan cause and allow unlimited spending with undisclosed donors.

The organizations listed below are not exclusively tax-exempt

US-based organizations that do report their donations, and as such would not necessarily have their financials transparently available through the websites I've listed. I've included mutual aid collectives, non-US-based organizations (which adhere to different regulations), and other forms of collective organizing, too. There are many ways to organize, and a designated tax-exempt nonprofit form is just one of them. The possibility of a tax write-off for a donation is not my personal motivation toward a cause, and it is not a primary factor that influenced the following recommendations. However, I've put an asterisk (*) next to organizations that have registered tax-deductible status (or an international equivalent) to help provide you with more context to how they run. I've also quoted some of their mission statements directly as I believe their self-descriptions are more concise than I could otherwise provide.

Scent-Based Organizations

If you are interested in learning how to make your own perfume or in pursuing a more thorough fragrance education, there are many collectives and organizations around the world available to you. This list does not include institutions for professional certification in the field and is better suited to casual consumers and fragrance fans.

The Institute for Art and Olfaction (LA-based with online components)* does a lot of programming across scent. They host the podcast *Perfume on the Radio*; lead the Open Source Smell Culture, an open source project exploring and sharing strategies in the perfume industry; hold perfume classes and open lab days for the public; publish *Alabastron*, a journal exploring scent's role in society and culture; host in-person exhibitions and both online and in-person lectures; and organize Scent Fair LA. They also celebrate independent and experimental perfumes with an annual awards event, one I've been privileged to judge a category for over the years.

The Coalition of Sustainable Perfumery (online) hosts resources on sustainable perfumery practices, including an evolving list of synthetic and naturally derived alternatives to unsustainable scents, and they also host a podcast and publish a list of questions to ask essential oil providers if you're a consumer or representing a company.

The Experimental Perfume Club (England and online) helps people design their own personalized, eco-conscious fragrances. They also offer a refill service and manufacture locally in their London laboratory. They host workshops and online perfume classes, sell perfumery equipment for at home use, and offer a traditional retail experience for walk-in customers.

A Library of Olfactive Material (Scotland) is a nonprofit source "for scent education, experience, and experimentation." They offer a lending library of scents available to blend in workshops or during library hours, as well as a rare materials collection for reference and a publication archive related to scent culture. They operate primarily on a pay-what-you-can model to ensure scent education is accessible to all.

The Aroma Labs (Illinois and Michigan) offer a public scent library and workshop space, programming on how to create your own fragrances, and internship opportunities for fragrance-based apprenticeships.

The Smell Lab (Germany) is a "platform for olfactory art and interdisciplinary practices that relate to scent as a medium for expression and communication." They "coproduce, host, educate, innovate, and support artistic practices that involve the sense of smell and olfaction."

Maki Ueda's Olfactory Art Lab (Japan and online) is an "academy for olfactory artists and perfumers" from award-winning olfactory artist Maki Ueda. She offers in-person workshops, online remote education, and an online store.

Nez: The Olfactory Cultural Movement Magazine, is a print and digital publication dedicated to scent and the sense of smell. Every six months, scientists, perfumers, writers, scholars, historians, photographers, illustrators, and artists cocreate this tome. Naturally, it also comes with fragrance samples to bring the reader into the "smellscape" of the stories.

Osmotheque (France) is known as the world's "first perfume archive" as it hosts more than 3,200 perfumes, including more than 400 than are no longer available. Its purpose is to both preserve perfumes and translate knowledge about the profession of perfumery. They host perfume sessions, private appointments, and a specialized bookstore and private library.

ScenTree (online) is a collaborative platform "devoted to the classification of raw materials used in perfumery. Each time an ingredient is added to the database, a group of experts meets to classify it based on a predefined list of olfactory families and descriptors." It is an incredible resource for scent exploration no matter your fragrance expertise.

Scent Festival (online) is a digital scent festival that aims to decolonize scent and promote intersectionality in perfumery. They put together a list of perfumers, lecturers, and brands working on scent and diversity; archived magazine, books, and podcasts on scent and xenophobia; and created a database of diverse talent in fragrance and perfumery, too.

Skin, Hair, and Hygiene Services

A variety of hygiene nonprofits are scattered across the United States and around the world. Find your local one to volunteer at, donate to, or otherwise support today. If there isn't one nearby, the resources below are a good place to start to learn how to advocate for one or begin organizing for such resources to be built in your own community.

Beauty 2 The Streetz* (CA) focuses on wellness, hygiene, and direct-action services for the unhoused population on Skid Row in LA.

Beauty Banks* (UK) strives to help eliminate hygiene poverty in the UK. It works with a nationwide network of like-minded people—those within the beauty industry as well as volunteers who collect donations on our behalf to benefit their local community.

The Hygiene Bank (UK) is a grassroots charity that focuses on combating hygiene poverty through product distribution of hygiene kits to a network of community partners in the UK. They distribute donations through trusted partnerships with registered food banks, homeless shelters, NHS trusts, care leaver associations, and schools.

Showering Love (CA) is a mobile organization that offers a variety of critical services to those experiencing homelessness. Services include "providing mobile showers, new clothing, laundry, and barber services, while addressing food insecurities, hygiene, and health issues, to help restore their self-esteem and dignity while showing them the path to self-sufficiency and financial stability."

The Shower of Hope (CA) offers mobile showers, hygiene items, access to meals, and case management for the unhoused Los Angeles population.

Hair and Care (UK) is a hairstylist-founded project where volunteer hairstylists introduce blind and partially sighted women and girls to the fundamentals of self-care and hair styling and offer peer support and monthly workshops.

Hope Vibes (NC) is a mobile hygiene bus for people experiencing homelessness. They provide mobile shower and laundry services and publish research and advocacy on behalf of those they serve.

Hygiene 4 All* (OR) is a "hygiene hub for unsheltered residents in Portland, Oregon." It is a mutual aid hub with hygiene services, a bedding and clothing exchange, waste management services, and peer-to-peer mutual aid services. The employees are also local unsheltered people.

Hearts of Rescue* (TX) is a nonprofit that offers mobile showers, essential hygiene items, and spiritual support to unhoused populations in Houston and surrounding areas.

Haircuts 4 Homeless* (UK) is one of many organizations that organize hairdressers for free service to unhoused populations. It is a registered charity based in the UK, but there are similar organizations all around the world.

Nails

The Museum of Nails Foundation* (online), a nonprofit archive of the history of nail art and beauty labor, showcases nail art and oral histories of nail artists around the world, and collectivizes resources for both clients and nail professionals for art, education, and advocacy. (Disclosure: I founded this organization while revising this book.)

The California Healthy Nail Salon Collaborative (CA) is statewide grassroots organization that addresses health, environmental, reproductive justice, and other social issues faced by its low-income, female, Vietnamese immigrant, and refugee workforce.

The New York Healthy Nail Salons Coalition (NY) was founded by Adhikaar and the New York Committee for Occupational Safety and Health and joined by Workers United NY NJ Regional Joint Board. The coalition includes workers, community, occupational health, consumer, and public interest law organizations to combat wage theft, health and safety violations, and other abuses in the nail salon industry.

Michigan Healthy Nail Salon Cooperative (MI) is made up of professors, researchers, and students at the University of Michigan's School of Public Health. They investigate unsafe conditions regarding nail salon workers and employers and problem solve around solutions.

Nail Salon Workers Project (Canada) aims "to learn about and reduce the negative health impacts of working in nail salons and advocates for healthier and more just work environments for nail technicians in Toronto."

Beauty Industry–Focused Organizations

Beauty Changes Lives (US) is a nonprofit that focuses on providing scholarships, mentorships, and inspiration to people with the understanding that beauty can be a first-choice career that empowers individuals.

Glam4Good (US) provides new beauty, wellness, hygiene and care products to women, girls, and their families. They focus on creating programs, events, and initiatives to "everyday heroes" and people in need across the United States. There are four pillars to their impact: disaster recovery, child and family welfare, social equity, and mental health and well-being.

Share Your Beauty* (US) is a family-to-family project that takes in donated excess beauty products from beauty industry professionals and brands and redistributes them to women who are living in poverty or who are victims of domestic violence. They link brands to women's shelters, domestic violence shelters, and teen programs to assist with product distribution.

Support Creatives* (US) aims to provide beauty professionals with tools and education to succeed in the beauty industry and provides mentor support, grant assistance, and online live education.

Gender-Affirming Care Organizations

Point of Pride* (US) provides financial and material support to trans people in need across the United States. They have specific funds you can donate to, such at the Annual Trans Surgery Fund, HRT Access Fund, and Electrolysis Support Fund, and offer free chest binders and femme shapewear.

TransHealthCare (online) is a comprehensive database of US-based gender surgeons that has been online since 2011. You can search for surgeons by procedures, such as phalloplasty, top surgery, voice masculinization, and more.

Transgender Map (online) is an invaluable gender transition resource list and includes comprehensive info on skincare for those in transition. It offers guidance on how to pay for transition, help for young people and their families, resources for those questioning their gender identity, and ways people can be good allies to the trans community. Andrea James began it more than 25 years ago to document her own gender transition.

The Dresscode Project (online) is a global alliance of salons committed to providing gender-affirming services to LGBTQ2S+ clients.

Strands for Trans (online) is a global association of beauty organizations that pledge they are supportive of Trans communities. Their website lists registered businesses who claim to be Trans-affirming and resources to make businesses more supportive to the queer community in general.

Our Spot KC* (MO) is a hub of different kinds of resources for LGBTQ+ folks in Kansas City. Some of their resources include craft circles, biweekly social events, support groups, food resources, training and technical support, and transitional housing.

Trans Makeover (Netherlands) is a makeover and face filter–free service run by genderfluid professionals who also run Trans Academy, another institution dedicated to the art of transformation.

Chronic Illness–Related Organizations

Beautifully Loved* (TX) has a variety of programming, including a community fundraiser fashion show with free beauty services and swag bags, free wellness workshops, a Mom-to-Mom program for mothers of children with cancer diagnoses, pamper kits, in-hospital beauty care services, and Nicole's Closet—a free closet that supports families in need.

Beauty Bus* (CA) offers free pop-up salons for patients and caregivers at hospitals and service centers, and online beauty tutorials led by professional volunteers. They also collect donations of full-size products to distribute to clients.

EBeauty* (US) offers free wigs for patients with medical hair loss, and partners with Paul Mitchell schools, hospitals, and cancer centers across the US.

Lipstick Angels* (US) is a nonprofit dedicated to bringing oncology-sensitive, customized skincare, beauty, and wellness services to those affected by cancer. Their services are done at participating hospitals, clinics, or virtually from the comfort of a patient's home.

Look Good Feel Better (UK) workshops are led by trained volunteers in the beauty industry who provide advice and techniques regarding changes to beauty routines impacted by cancer treatment. It is a service dedicated to patients actively undergoing cancer treatment as a means to provide self-care support and reduce feelings of isolation.

Helen's Room (CA) offers free, private consultations for services and products for low-income, uninsured women and cancer patients. All cancer patients are welcome and will find hats, scarves, turbans, wigs, breast prostheses, mastectomy bras, community resources, support groups, and more.

Personal Ink (US), a program founded by Fuck Cancer, is dedicated to "empowering women to reclaim their bodies after mastectomies." They do so through educational programming and building a network of tattoo artists who specialized in mastectomy tattoos, so that "breast cancer never has to leave the last mark." They organize P.Ink Days, which offers free tattoos for cancer patients across North America, and created a P.Ink Fund that collects donations to artists who provide mastectomy tattoos year round.

Bodywork, Somatic Practices, and Wellness for Marginalized Communities

Black Women for Wellness (CA) focuses on increasing access to affordable health services to Black women and girls while providing mentorship and research on challenges Black women face in the health and wellness industry. They organize an annual reproductive justice conference, an environmental justice program that addresses toxic chemicals in personal products and the impacts of oil drilling, and more.

Radical Rest (OR) is an organization that began as a mutual aid pop-up of wellness providers offering free services to BIPOC communities in Portland. It has expanded to become a healing justice collective of practitioners and educators centering the needs of the BIPOC community through health events and opportunities for anti-oppressive education. They offer immersion retreats, free salons for somatic workshops, and community partnerships.

The Brave Space Alliance* (IL) is a Black-led, trans-led LGBTQ+ center on the South Side of Chicago dedicated to creating affirming and culturally competent services for the entire LGBTQ+ community of Chicago. Their Dignity Suite is a "free initiative that centers the needs of the LGBTQ+ community, the BIPOC community, and folx who have been historically othered." It consists of a makeup room, closet, den, and shop.

Project Beauty* (US) focuses on expanding personal wellness and empowerment opportunities to women and girls. They do so via manicures, styling, and makeup application, and team up with local organizations to facilitate events.

Worker Solidarity for Care Workers, Worker Collectives

The National Domestic Workers Alliance* (US) organizes domestic workers, giving them space to share information, build skills with training and resources, access benefits, get support, and organize to win rights. They develop new policies and mobilize support for solutions to improve worker conditions and economic security for domestic workers and beyond. They operate in local chapters and on a national level.

The Professional Beauty Association (US) is a national industry association that has four different charities associated with it and offers education, advocacy, special programming, and discounts for members for professional perks.

Red Canary Song (NY) is a grassroots massage worker coalition in the US. They offer a language exchange, mobile health van, oral history projects, mutual aid, fundraising, art shows, and more.

Adhikaar (NY) is dedicated to improving the lives of the Nepali-speaking community and provides direct services to low-income workers across industries, including the nail and care industries.

Kailash Satyarthi Children's Foundation* (India) addresses child labor and exploitation in the mica regions of Bihar and Jharkhand and envisions a child-labor free mica industry.

Terre des Hommes* (Switzerland) advocates for children's rights to health, hygiene, education, security, and justice and monitors child labor exploitation in the mica industry.

Climate Justice

Indigenous Climate Resilience Network* (US and online) is an Indigenous-led organization from communities and religions across the country. They gather to discuss threats to Indigenous ways of life and formulate "mitigation strategies, dialogues, and educational programs that build Indigenous capacities to address climate related issues." They host all kinds of resources and programs on their website and help parse climate change on an individual, tribal, and global scale.

International Work Group for Indigenous Affairs is a "global human rights organization dedicated to promoting, protecting, and defending Indigenous Peoples' rights."

Imagine Water Works (Louisiana) focuses on climate justice, land stewardship, and disaster readiness and response. They've stewarded the Trans Clippers Project, the Mutual Aid Response Network, an Anonymous Storm Prep Q&A, the Queer/Trans Guide to Hurricane System, the Little Library of Water, and more.

Organizations for Beauty Entrepreneurs and Industry Education

Beauty Backed Trust (UK) began as a fundraising initiative in 2020 to support beauty entrepreneurs who were impacted by COVID-19. It now aims to assist everyone and anyone who works or wants to work in the beauty industry.

Beauty Inside Out * (NY) is a working group of WE ACT for Environmental Justice. Past work done by the group includes a survey on chemical relaxers among femme-identifying people of color in NYC, a webinar on colorism in the beauty industry, educational booklets for free and public distribution, and panel discussions around toxic chemicals in beauty products that target the queer community.

B Beauty Navigator (online) is a working database to help beauty shoppers and companies understand how to make more sustainably centered choices and educates them on packaging, logistics, and ingredient options available to them.

Hair and Beauty Charity * (UK) provides practical and financial support to beauty industry professionals and their families who have fallen on hard times.

MASCED (UK) was developed by national skincare cancer charity Skcin and is an online training program for beauty professionals to teach them signs of how to spot skin cancer.

Pact Collective (US and Canada) offers educational resources for both consumers and brands, including a packaging drop-off guide, collection guidelines, and instructions on how to clean your products for recycling. They also offer a recycling program on a membership model for corporate partners.

The Sustainable Beauty Coalition (UK) was formed by the British Beauty Council and is made up of industry experts, brand owners, and industry body representatives across the beauty sector. They seek to create stronger frameworks and policies with sustainability and green credentials as a central focus.

Women's Voices for the Earth * (CO) "envisions a world free from the impacts of toxic chemicals, one where our planet and communities are thriving, one where our gender, race, sexuality, zip code, income level, or job does not determine our health incomes." They target a multitude of issues: safer cleaning and wellness products, safer salons, period health and reproductive justice, fragrance sustainability, and worker's rights.

ACKNOWLEDGMENTS

This part of the book is something I fantasized about writing for years—I can't thank everybody enough. There have been so many places and communities that have given me time, space, and camaraderie. I have to thank the Parisian bookstore Shakespeare and Company and the Whitman family for that beautiful time and the privilege of editing with a view of Notre Dame. My friend Tiffany Godoy housed me in Paris and bullied me into being way cooler than I am naturally inclined to be, and wrote the first book to make me fall into fashion. Thank you for opening the door and always celebrating me. Closer to home, there have been so many artist communities that have supported me over the course of writing this book the past eight years. Thank you to Wildacres Retreat in North Carolina for the cabin and congeniality. I'm grateful to SPACE on Ryder Farm for every time they've opened their doors and set the table for me, for both the snacks and paying my rent that one time during the pandemic when I had no other options. I owe large stretches of this book to the time I spent in the Rose Garden at Yaddo, chasing ghosts, who were very friendly and good listeners. Gratitude also extends to the MacDowell Fellowship for the privilege to be able to be in residence with my partner during a long stretch of revisions in

ACKNOWLEDGMENTS

2022, and Hedgebrook for giving me time to complete the next round of revisions among the trees. I have also been the recipient of several funding initiatives, which have supported me through the research and writing process for this book: Queer Writers of Color Relief Fund, the PEN America Emergency Fund, the Montclair State University Pandemic Reporting Initiative, and Substack's Artist scholarships and health insurance stipend, too. Thank you very much for your support.

    To all my transient translators on the ground during my travels, the readers who volunteered in Paris, in Florence, in Venice, the bartender in Berlin—thank you for consoling me on a truly terrible research misadventure and making sure my drink was topped up when I returned shell-shocked from personal disaster. I owe every single librarian who has ever answered my emails, and I can't even list you all, but I appreciate every cell of you that has ever existed and that ever will. Specific gratitude is extended to the team at the New York Public Library for graciously providing a research seat and answering my frantic emails. I'm also grateful to the librarians at the National Archives in the UK and the Parisian archivists at Bibliothèque Nationale for their work preserving and digitizing their WWII-era archives. To my readers, who have over the years sent me letters of encouragement and books for research, and shown up to the events I've organized and have shown beauty matters because care does—thank you for proving my heart right, every single time. Thank you to every single person who ever tipped me on Tumblr. You bought me groceries and bodega chips and you paid my library fines. You helped keep me alive when I bet on myself, over and over again, for weeks that turned into months that turned into years. I am lucky it worked out, and you are my luck. We have shaped

ACKNOWLEDGMENTS

each other's lives. I know this intimately. Some of you may never find me again and may never read this. I love you so much anyway.

First readers and friends: Obehi Janice, Jenna Wortham, Darian Symone, Larissa Pham, Stephen Alain Ko, Jeanna Kadlac, Tyler Ford, Eric Thurm, Addie Wagenknecht, Charlotte Palermino, and Fariha Roisin. Zeba Blay and Mary HK Choi for their affirmations and synchronized spirals and wisdom and lunch dates, especially in the early years of this book. For paying for my groceries when magazines didn't pay on time and for never saving our voice notes. Thank you to every coffee shop employee who ever put up with me. The brilliant academics Simone Browne and Mimi Thi Nguyen for their scholarship, community, and commiseration. Other incredible scholars whose work I have cited throughout this book: Tiffany Gill, A'Lelia Bundles, Ayana Byrd and Lori Tharps, Shirley Anne Tate, Susan Schweik, Saidiya Hartman, adrienne maree brown, Tyrone McKingley Freeman, and Susannah Walker. The Stanford Railroad Workers Project has been an invaluable archive of history. Thank you to Leanne, head organizer of the New York Healthy Nail Salons Coalition, for always welcoming my curiosity—and for all the work you do. Your commitment inspires me. Thank you to Ocean Vuong for the early-stage pep talks on what this work had to be. Jia Tolentino for the affirming conversations. Alexander Chee and Sheila Heti for the writing classes that prepared my brain. Thank you to Yanyi, the Shipman Agency, Kundiman, and the Asian American Writers' Workshop for fostering spaces for writers like me to connect in, to be vulnerable in, and to find solace in. Thank you to the Institute for Art and Olfaction, particularly Saskia Wilson-Brown and Minetta Rogers, for much of

ACKNOWLEDGMENTS

the same. I am so grateful to be in community with you and the people you bring into smellscapes. Your commitment to beauty helps us all dream.

Editors and places that have helped me get here, through assignments that aided the core reporting: the Racked team turned Vox—Meredith, Julia, and Cheryl, for setting an example on what beauty reporting can look like. I owe a great deal to many of the people who have been on the masthead at *Teen Vogue* and *Allure*, fact-checkers and editors alike, people I now gladly call friends as much as accomplices in this disintegrating hellscape we call media. Gratitude to Phillip Picardi and Elaine Welteroth for my beauty internship and then years of camaraderie and support throughout my career. And especially thank you to *Rookie*, for being my first writing (and feminist) family. I am *so* grateful to have grown up with you. Thank you for bringing us together, Tavi.

My research assistants Alina Kim and Rhiannon McGavin were vital, and especially Karolyn Gehrig, my work wife for many years through beauty and terror and, thankfully, failed kidnappings. Deep gratitude extends also to my therapist, Karen, and the Asian Mental Health Collective (AMHC) for their mental health scholarships for Asian American journalists. Their care has held me close during difficult times in life and writing. I could not have finished dozens of drafts of these pages without your support. Knowing what to keep and what to let go of is heavy work best not done alone. Your support has helped heal so much of me and carried me through the hardest parts of living. Thank you for holding space for me.

Finally, thank you to my agent, Marya Spence, Clare Mao, my editor, Melanie Tortoroli, and the entire Norton team who

ACKNOWLEDGMENTS

put their faith in me and a future that would have me. Kadal Jesuthasan, my multilingual fact-checker—you saved me endlessly throughout these pages—thank you for putting up with me. Maxwell Neely-Cohen, my best friend and Apocalypse Captain. I would not have started without you daring me to begin. Thank you for being my family.

I wrote this book while falling in love with my partner. To W: I know you design buildings, but I can too, see? I wrote the house in which we live.

NOTES

The research process for this book was a multiyear, international undertaking. In the process of researching, writing, and publishing, some of the materials may have moved databases, media companies may have folded, and internet links invariably decay. I've tried to include the most relevant information for you to peruse on your own time, with all of that in mind.

INTRODUCTION

4 **"the very lifestyle of the holders of power":** Bourdieu, Pierre. *The Logic of Practice.* Stanford University Press, 1990, p. 139.

5 **"Caring for myself is not self-indulgence":** Lorde, Audre. *A Burst of Lights.* Sheba, 1988.

7 **"an ax you break down doors with":** Solnit, Rebecca. *Hope in the Dark.* Canongate Books, 2016.

CHOOSE YOUR OWN DISASTER

10 **70 percent of beauty products in the world:** Lim, Amanda. "Sustainable Personal Care: Moving Away from Palm Oil Is 'Not the Solution'—Croda." Cosmetics Design Asia, 5 Aug. 2019.

12 **Your day begins in a cave:** Cavazuti, Lisa, et al. "'Zone Rouge': An Army of Children Toils in African Mines." *NBC News*, 18 Nov. 2019.

12 **in thousands of years:** Hedrick, J. B. "Mineral Resource of the Month: Mica." *USGS Publications Warehouse*, 1 Jan. 2008

NOTES

13 **splits open like a coconut:** Bhalla, Nita, et al. "Blood Mica: Deaths of Child Workers in India's Mica 'Ghost' Mines Covered Up to Keep Industry Alive." Reuters, 8 Aug. 2016.

13 **Children's Village:** "Interventions." *ChildLabourFreeMica*. Accessed 11 Sept. 2024.

14 **ten deaths each and every month:** van der Wal, San, and SOMO. *SOMO Report: Child Labour in Madagascar's Mica Sector*. SOMO, Nov. 2019, p. 68.

14 **back to school:** Bhalla, "Blood Mica." Pooja, 13, shows off the school she attends since leaving mining.

14 **no one takes your work:** Cavazuti, "'Zone Rouge.'" "If I left here overnight, people would steal the mica."

16 **from electronics to cars:** van der Wal, *SOMO Report*.

16 **the mica belt:** van der Wal, *SOMO Report*. Later field research in 2022 counts at least 22,000 children in an area that did not cover even *half* of the mica belt. See: "India: Investigation Finds Significantly More Illegal Mica Mines than Suspected; Child Labour a Concern in Informal Sector." Business & Human Rights Resource Centre.

18 **Pratap:** Bhalla, "Blood Mica."

18 **100,000 rupees:** equivalent to roughly US $1,500.

19 **call him Bakti:** see: 3:00 of the video in Cavazuti, "'Zone Rouge.'"

19 **education to do so:** "Behind the Glitter: Mica and Child Mining in India." 101 East, *Al Jazeera*, 12 June 2020.

20 **public record:** *Trade-Related Illicit Financial Flows in 135 Developing Countries: 2008–2017*. Global Financial Integrity, 3 Mar. 2020.

20 **100,000 tons:** "Behind the Glitter."

20 **18,500 tons:** Renaud, Karine M. *2013 Minerals Yearbook*. U.S Department of the Interior, Nov. 2016, p. 22.

20 **127,629 tons:** Bhalla, "Blood Mica." Figures from India's Bureau of Mines show the country produced 19,000 tons of mica in 2013–14. But the same data shows exports were 128,000 tons, with more than half, or 62 percent, going to China, followed by Japan, the United States, the Netherlands, and France.

21 **no signs of it going down:** Olick, Diana. "Shipping Industry Could Lose $10 Billion a Year Battling Climate Change by 2050." CNBC, 30 Oct. 2023.

22 **100,000 ships at sea carrying the products we use to live:** Stalker, Peter, editor. *The Review of Maritime Transport 2022*. United Nations, 2022.

NOTES

22 **more than halfway around the planet:** George, Rose. *Deep Sea and Foreign Going: Inside Shipping*. Faber & Faber, 2014.

22 **"chance of being drowned":** "'Being in a Ship Is Being in a Jail, with the Chance of Being Drowned.'" *Lapham's Quarterly*. Archived 23 Nov. 2017.

22 **2,200 nautical miles long:** George, *Deep Sea*, p. 112.

22 **safe and sound:** "CTF 151: Counter-Piracy." *Combined Maritime Forces*, 17 Sept. 2010. See also: Chibelushi, Wedaeli. "Somalia Piracy: Are We Witnessing Its Return off the Country's Coast?" *BBC World*, 3 Feb. 2024.

24 **will pop up:** Refinery29. "How ColourPop Eyeshadow Is Made | How Stuff Is Made | Refinery29." YouTube, 4 June 2016.

24 **men killed over:** Finlay, Victoria. *Color: A Natural History of the Palette*. Random House, 2004.

26 **a fortunate poet:** My favorite lipstick packaging is high luxury, Guerlain or Chanel, because the packaging feels decadent in the hand. Both click decisively, like a gun. It took them maybe 15 tries to get it right, the right clicking sound when you press down on the bullet. I forget the real number but not the ritualized devotion, like burlesque in reverse: how to make you want to put it on.

26 **a formula is perfected:** Tungate, Mark. *Branded Beauty: How Marketing Changed the Way We Look*. Kogan Page, 2011, pp. 151–54.

27 **L'Oréal's Women of Color Lab:** Segran, Elizabeth. "The L'Oréal Chemist Who's Changing the Face of Makeup." *Fast Company*, 1 Oct. 2015.

27 **aquamarine blue:** Hyman, Vicki. "Jersey Chemist at L'Oréal Liberates Cosmetic Palette." NJ.com, 7 July 2016.

28 **lipstick stolen or trash-picked:** Fleck, Ella. "Beauty Dumpster Divers Are the Underdogs of the YouTube Haul Vlog Clan." *Dazed*, 8 Jan. 2019.

29 **ships slowing down:** Chambers, Sam. "Container Ships Moving at All-Time Low Speeds." Splash247.com, 29 May 2023.

29 **had never fallen in love with the ocean:** George, *Deep Sea*, p. 116.

30 **$50 billion industry:** Voora, Vivek, et al. *Global Market Report: Palm Oil Prices and Sustainability*. International Institute for Sustainable Development, June 2023, p. 46.

30 **would-be investor he doesn't know is a reporter:** "Sarawak's Way of Evading Tax and Shareholding Rules." *Malaysiakini News*, 19 Mar. 2013.

30 **"king, in the land of the blind":** "Inside Malaysia's Shadow State:

NOTES

Backroom Deals Driving the Destruction of Sarawak." Global Witness, Mar. 2013, p. 7.

30 **Malaysia and Indonesia are the primary exporters of palm oil:** Zion Market Research. "Global Report: Palm Oil Market Size and Share Estimated to Touch the Value of USD 92.84 Billion in 2021." Globe Newswire, 30 July 2019.

30 **further deals along:** "Corruption in Malaysia's Forest Industry." Global Witness, 19 Mar. 2013. Cramb, Rob, and John F. McCarthy, editors. *The Oil Palm Complex: Smallholders, Agribusiness and the State in Indonesia and Malaysia*. NUS Press, 2016. See also: Hunt, Luke. "Global Witness Video Exposes Alleged Corruption in Sarawak." *Diplomat*, 21 Mar. 2013.

32 **Dr. Biruté Galdikas:** Shoumatoff, Alex. *The Wasting of Borneo: Dispatches from a Vanishing World*. Beacon Press, 2016.

32 **the *gaip*:** For the Uut Dunum people, ancestors take the form of invisible people, transformed without death, their corpses never found. See: *Ngaju Gaip Myths*, collected by Schärer, 1966.

32 **acreage you denied them:** The logging companies persist endlessly, unless the license is nullified by proof that the concession is in customary Indigenous territory. Shoumatoff, *The Wasting of Borneo*, p. 123.

33 **community plots are razed:** Dhandapani, Selvakumar, and Stephanie Evers. "Oil Palm 'Slash-and-Burn' Practice Increases Post-Fire Greenhouse Gas Emissions and Nutrient Concentrations in Burnt Regions of an Agricultural Tropical Peatland." *Science of the Total Environment*, vol. 742, Nov. 2020.

33 **"slash and burn" technique:** Bell, Loren. "What Is Peat Swamp, and Why Should I Care?" *Mongabay Environmental News*, 20 July 2014.

33 **climate change:** Shoumatoff, *The Wasting of Borneo*, p. 87.

33 **seen from space:** "Nasa's Latest Satellite Photo Draws Similarities to 2015 Haze Crisis—TODAY." *Malay Mail*, World, 19 Sept. 2019.

33 **little compensation for this:** Jiwan, Norman. "The Political Ecology of the Indonesian Palm Oil Industry: A Critical Analysis," in Pye, Oliver, and Jayati Bhattacharya. *The Palm Oil Controversy in Southeast Asia: A Transnational Perspective*, ISEAS Publishing 2012, p. 68.

33 **thousands a hectare:** Cramb, *The Oil Palm Complex*.

33 **courtesy of the government:** "Native Customary Rights in Sarawak." *Cultural Survival,* 19 Feb. 2010. See also: "More Missing Millions,

NOTES

More Broken Promises to Sarawak Native Landowners." *Sarawak Report*. 18 Mar. 2021.

34 **the forest is burned:** see: Jiwan, "The Political Ecology of the Indonesian Palm Oil Industry," p. 69.

35 **in beauty products:** "The Role Of Palm Oil in Cosmetics Products." Malaysian Palm Oil Council (MPOC). Archived 22 June 2021.

35 **only 2 percent of the global palm oil production:** RSPO cosmetics industry factsheet, emailed by Firdaus Tarmizi.

35 **found in 70 percent of beauty products:** Chin, S. C. "Palm Ingredients in Cosmetic and Personal Care Products." *Malaysiakini*, 21 Aug. 2019.

35 **than other oil plants:** Cheah, Wai Yan, et al. "Circular Bioeconomy in Palm Oil Industry: Current Practices and Future Perspectives." *Environmental Technology & Innovation*, vol. 30, May 2023.

35 **than alternative plant options:** "Half the Products in Stores Have Palm Oil. Worker Exploitation Gets Them There." Associated Press, World, 24 Sept. 2020.

36 **importing European countries:** Byerlee, Derek, et al. *The Tropical Oil Crop Revolution: Food, Feed, Fuel, and Forests*. Oxford University Press, 2017. See also: "The Political Ecology of the Indonesian Palm Oil Industry."

37 **gloveless most days:** Maftuchan, Ah, and Irvan T. Harja. *The Fulfillment of Palm Oil Workers' Rights: One of the Pillars of Sustainable Plantations*. English Version, 29, PRAKARSA Initiative for Better Societies, Dec. 2021, p. 4.

39 ***patronize* for support:** Yunus, Mohammad. "Governance Reform Essential to Reducing Palm Oil Deforestation." *East Asia Forum*, 6 Mar. 2024.

39 **every 25 years:** see: Cramb, *The Oil Palm Complex*.

40 **packaging supergiant Uline:** Hakim, Danny. "The Most Powerful Conservative Couple You've Never Heard Of." *New York Times,* 7 June 2018.

41 **puzzle fanatic, a fisherman, and a bird-watcher:** Zuckerman, Jocelyn C. "Oil Crisis." *Men's Journal*, Feb. 2019, pp. 87–93.

41 **armed with air guns:** Beech, Hannah. "One Casualty of the Palm Oil Industry: An Orangutan Mother, Shot 74 Times." *New York Times*, 29 June 2019.

41 **"people of the forest":** see: Beech, "One Casualty of the Palm Oil Industry."

NOTES

41 **banished for blaspheming:** see: Shoumatoff, *The Wasting of Borneo*, p. 90.

42 **cascade of small apocalypses:** Nursamsu, Eyes on the Forest Coordinator, et al. "Eyes on the Forest: No One is Safe." *Google Earth Outreach*. 2012.

44 **"The answer is no":** Bhasin, Kim, and Gerald Porter, Jr. "Estée Lauder Workers Demand Heir Ouster Over Trump Support." *Bloomberg Business*, 2 Mar. 2024.

44 **"then politics will run your business":** Lipton, Eric, and Rachel Abrams. "Their Hair Fell Out. Should the F.D.A. Have the Power to Act?" *New York Times*, 15 Aug. 2016.

45 **the chaos of a city and its sounds:** "Honduras: Killing of Human Rights Lawyer Exposes Dire Need for Action." *Amnesty International*, 25 Sept. 2012.

45 **his tongue:** Miller, Richard. *On the Art of Singing*. Oxford University Press, 1996.

46 **into his gut:** "Oil Palm Plantations in the Bajo Agúan, Honduras." *Global Atlas of Environmental Justice*, 26 June 2023.

46 **palm oil region in Honduras:** Lakhani, Nina. "Honduras and the Dirty War Fueled by the West's Drive for Clean Energy." *Guardian*, 7 Jan. 2014.

46 **the thing between a business and the land they want:** "Honduras: No Justice for Wave of Killings Over Land." Human Rights Watch. 12 Feb. 2014.

47 **you're a cleansing agent and an emollient:** George, Neethu Mary, and Amruthavalli Potlapati. "Shampoo, Conditioner and Hair Washing." *International Journal of Research in Dermatology*, vol. 8, no. 1, Dec. 2021, p. 185.

48 **cutting them in half with a knife:** Star, Jeffree. "Glowing 1000 Degree Knife vs. Chanel Bag + Makeup." YouTube, 10 Jan. 2017.

48 **trying to dye their hair in someone else's kayak:** Slime, Yeon. "Destroying & Mixing Eyeshadow into Slime! Satisfying Slime Video #1." YouTube, 29 Sept. 2019.

48 **quartz and mica minerals:** DKRK279. "Mica Quarry to California Brandywine Creek State Park, DE." YouTube, 6 May 2020.

48 **180 miles outside of Cape Town, South Africa:** Henshilwood, Christopher S., et al. "A 100,000-Year-Old Ochre-Processing Workshop at Blombos Cave, South Africa." *Science*, vol. 334, no. 6053, Oct. 2011, pp. 219–22.

49 **melted ochre:** Wadley, Lyn, et al. "Implications for Complex

Cognition from the Hafting of Tools with Compound Adhesives in the Middle Stone Age, South Africa." *Proceedings of the National Academy of Sciences*, vol. 106, no. 24, June 2009, pp. 9590–94.

49 **glittered quartz:** Joyce, Christopher. "In African Cave, An Early Human Paint Shop." NPR, 14 Oct. 2011.

49 **a beauty workshop:** Wadley, Lyn. "Those Marvellous Millennia: The Middle Stone Age of Southern Africa." *Azania: Archaeological Research in Africa*, vol. 50, no. 2, Apr. 2015, pp. 155–226.

LE MONSTRE

50 **more than $19 billion:** Sibun, Jonathan, and Jessica Reid. "Chanel Limited Financial Results for the Year Ended 31 December 2023." Chanel, 21 May 2024.

50 **no small part to the perfume:** Danziger, Pamela. "Chanel Holds as Luxury's Number Two Brand, but Hermès Is Gaining Ground." *Forbes*, 29 May 2024.

50 **how well they're getting on:** Wattles, Jackie. "Chanel Reveals Earnings for the First Time in 108-Year History." CNN Business, 22 June 2018.

50 **one of the first perfumes that ever used synthetic ingredients:** Jicky by Guerlain can claim to be the first modern perfume, thanks to Guerlain's use of synthetic ingredients. See: Isaac-Goizé, Tina. "The Icon: Jicky, by Guerlain." *New York Times*, 1 Dec. 2017. Contrary to legend, aldehydes first made their fragrant debut in 1905 in a scent called Rêve d'Or (Golden Dream), by Armingeat. They also feature in Houbigant's Quelques Fleurs (created in 1912) and Lanvin's Arpège.

51 **high-ranking officers:** Mazzeo, Tilar J. *The Hotel on Place Vendôme: Life, Death, and Betrayal at the Hotel Ritz in Paris.* HarperCollins, 2015.

52 **when Coco was eleven:** Picardie, Justine. *Coco Chanel.* HarperCollins, 2009.

52 **Catholic nuns:** Vaughan, Hal. *Sleeping with the Enemy.* Knopf Doubleday, 2011.

52 **"Death to the Jew!":** Nix, Elizabeth. "What Was the Dreyfus Affair?" *History*, 1 June 2023.

53 **Étienne Balsan:** see: Picardie, p. 37.

53 **back of the Hôtel Ritz:** "31 rue Cambon: Une Histoire Derrière la Façade." Chanel, 23 Feb. 2011.

53 **"the name of Chanel is on the lips of every buyer":** "The Gadabout." *Harper's Bazaar*, Feb. 1915, pp. 52–53, 84.

NOTES

54 **come crashing down:** Roberts, Richard. "The Great Financial Crisis of 1914 | Alchemist." LBMA, no. 73.

54 **Not so for Coco:** Virginia Tech. "The End of Optimism? The Great Depression in Europe." European History: The Digital History Reader.

54 **one of the wealthiest men in the world:** see: Vaughan and Madsen.

54 **the Link, an anti-Semitic group:** Griffiths, Richard. *Fellow Travellers of the Right: British Enthusiasts for Nazi Germany: 1933–9.* Oxford University Press, 1980.

54 **"She is very agreeable, a strong being fit to rule a man or an empire":** see: Vaughan, p. 67; Picardie, p. 111.

55 **Karlie Kloss married Joshua Kushner:** Kushner is a founder and managing partner of Thrive Capital, a VC firm whose portfolio also contains Grailed, ClassPass, Instacart, Patreon, Instagram, and Warby Parker. In the interest of full disclosure, I have been a customer of ClassPass, Instacart, Patreon, and Warby Parker, an ancient user of Instagram, and have worked with Glossier as well as received commission for recommending products from the company over the years on my blog. "Josh Kushner." *Forbes.*

55 **when Weiss worked at *Vogue*:** O'Dell, Amy. "Inside the Rise of Emily Weiss's Glossier." Back Row.

56 **still a new synthetic discovery:** Doré, Jeanne, ed. *The Big Book of Perfume—for an Olfactory Culture.* Nez Editions, 2020. Though, so be precise, he wasn't the *first* perfumer to use it: The process of producing aliphatic aldehydes was discovered by August Darzens in 1903, and the more stable aldehydes from that process were used by perfumer Robert Bienaimé for Houbigant in 1912. In 1921 Beaux did use specific aldehydes first at an industrial and high-quality scale, however, through his work with the Givaudan-Lavirotte factory in Lyon. This particular note of aldehydes C-10, C-11, and C-12, which smell like candle wax and orange with metallic characteristics, became very popular across cosmetic products outside of Chanel No. 5—it is also used in Elnett hairspray.

56 **no worse sin:** Wilson, Bee. "Why Are You So Fat?" *London Review of Books*, vol. 32, no. 01, 7 Jan. 2010.

56 **"Perhaps a natural perfume must be created artificially":** see: Masden, p. 133.

56 **when the lakes smelled fresh and clean and quiet:** "At what period did I create it [Chanel No. 5]? In exactly 1920. Upon my return from the war. I had been led on campaign to the northern part of Europe

NOTES

beyond the Arctic Circle at the time of the midnight sun, when the lakes and rivers release a perfume of extreme freshness. I retained that note and replicated it, not without some difficulty, as the first aldehydes I could find were unstable and of an irregular production." Victoria. "Perfumers on Perfume: Ernest Beaux on Fragrance Masterpieces." *Bois de Jasmin*, 2 Dec. 2013.

56 **more than eighty ingredients:** Kraft, Philip, et al. "From Rallet No. 1 to Chanel No. 5 versus Mademoiselle Chanel No. 1." *Perfumer & Flavorist+*, vol. 32, October 2007, 36–47.

56 **glass flacons distinguished only by numbers:** Beaux, Ernest. "Souvenirs d'un parfumeur." *Industrie de la Parfumerie*, 1.7. Oct. 1946, pp. 228–31.

57 **discreetly sprayed it as her would-be customers walked by:** see: Madsen, p. 135.

57 **luxury fumes curling out the windows of the shop doors:** "1920s." Chanel.

58 **profits of tie-making:** Abescat, Bruno, and Yves Stavridès. "Derrière l'empire Chanel . . . La fabuleuse histoire des Wertheimer." *L'Express*, 2005.

58 **They refuse to sit in the front row at the shows of the brands they own:** Thomas, Dana. "The Power Behind the Cologne." *New York Times Magazine*, 24 Feb. 2002.

58 **plane manufacturer Félix Amiot:** Lecarpentier, Justin. *Félix Amiot*. OREP Editions, 2020.

59 **Théophile Bader:** see: Vaughan, p. 48.

59 **the Wertheimers acquired 70 percent of Chanel Perfumes:** see: Madsen, p. 129. See also: Galante, p. 146.

59 **for beauty products:** see: *L'Express*.

60 **enfleurage:** Enfleurage is an old-school perfumery technique that requires you to layer freshly wilted flowers on solid fat, press it but not submerge it, remove the flowers after a few days, and renew them repeatedly, until the level of fragrance you need is achieved. This may take more than 40 rounds. The fat is then washed in alcohol to obtain an absolute. Other versions require heating and stirring the flowers in oil in a temperature-controlled bath. Both techniques are manual and offer an incredibly low yield. For my favorite tutorial on the process, I suggest the film of the novel, *Perfume: Story of a Murderer*, which is a bacchanalian feast of murder and enfleurage techniques. Enfleurage is not used much anymore. Since the 1930s, it's been mostly replaced by the extraction method.

60 **at the mercy of large conglomerates:** Vulser, Nicole. "Perfume

NOTES

Manufacturers Must Cope with the Scarcity of Precious Supplies." *Guardian*, 4 Mar. 2014.

61 **South African Coast:** Yeld, John. "Couple's Stinking-Rich Find." Independent Online, 11 Mar. 2013.

61 **whale vomit:** It is not literally whale vomit. According to Christopher Kempt, the author of *Floating Gold: A Natural (and Unnatural) History of Ambergris*, it's more like squid beak that's been hardened and shat out by a sperm whale. But don't get too caught up in the semantics of shit, OK?

61 **smuggling of sandalwood and other precious fragrance materials:** This has been going on for decades, and there's a task force dedicated to stopping it in India and Kenya, with murder sprees related to the trees in 2015. It was suspected that the police were behind the murders. For an academic analysis on the interconnection between colonization, violence, and sandalwood, consider reading Rashkow, Ezra, D. "Perfumed the Axe That Laid It Low: The Endangerment of Sandalwood in Southern India." *Sage* vol. 51, no. 1, 10 Mar. 2014. On the task forces and alleged police smugglers, see: AFP. "India Police Charged with Murder of 20 Suspected Sandalwood Smugglers." *Guardian*, 15 Apr. 2015.

62 **regulated, licensed, and guarded:** "What Requirements Must Natural Ingredients for Cosmetics Comply with to Be Allowed on the European Market?" CBI Ministry of Foreign Affairs, 7 May 2024.

62 **Global warming can and does consistently destroy crops:** Godin, Mélissa. "Climate Crisis Brings Whiff of Danger to French Perfume Capital." *Guardian*, 18 Feb. 2023.

62 **2010 earthquake:** "Haitian Vetiver: Uprooted?" *Perfumer & Flavorist*, 9 Apr. 2010.

62 **petunias so far:** Cna'Ani, Alon, et al. "*Petunia* × *hybrida* Floral Scent Production Is Negatively Affected by High-Temperature Growth Conditions." *Plant, Cell & Environment*, vol. 38, no. 7, July 2015, pp. 1333–46.

62 **to stay afloat:** Laudamiel, Christophe. "Christophe Laudamiel on Perfumery's State of Affairs." *Beauty Matter*, 26 June 2022.

63 **"Chanel's anti-Semitism was not only verbal, but passionate.":** see: Vaughan, p. 20.

63 *the Jews more than the Chinese*: see: Vaughan, p. 20.

63 **one of the most prominent collaborators of the next world war:** see: "Black List." *Life*, 24 Aug. 1942.

64 **"that bandit who screwed me":** see: Madesen, p. 138.

NOTES

65 **"four and a half million dollars"**: Flanner, Janet. "31, Rue Cambon." *The New Yorker*, 13 Mar. 1931.

67 **an apartment nearby just for entertaining**: see: Hotchner, A. E. "As the Paris Ritz Shutters, Remembering Its Mysteries, Misbehaviors, and Unhurried Luxuries." *Vanity Fair*, 21 June 2012.

67 **potato rationing inspired riots**: see: Smith, Meredith. "The Civilian Experience in German Occupied France, 1940–1944." History Honors Papers, 2010.

67 **wines were sent to Germany under the Reich's orders**: Monaco, Emily. "How French Winemakers Outwitted the Nazis." BBC, 6 June 2024.

67 **More people died of starvation during World War II than from being killed in combat**: Sova, Chase, and Eilish Zembilci. "Dangerously Hungry: The Link between Food Insecurity and Conflict." CSIS.org, Apr. 2023.

69 **13,000 Jews to be sent to death camps**: see: "The Vel' d'Hiv Roundup." World Holocaust Remembrance Center.

72 *Never react to an evil in such a way as to augment it*: Weil, Simone. *First and Last Notebooks*. Translated by Richard Rees. Wipf and Stock, 2015.

72 **"supreme and exceptional place among the hotels requisitioned"**: Mazzeo, p. 27.

73 **shuttled to camps by the thousands**: Webster, Paul. "World Wars: The Vichy Policy on Jewish Deportation." BBC, 17 Feb. 2011.

73 **"I have sent to you by registered air mail"**: see: Abescat, Bruno, and Yves Stavridès, p. 12.

74 **questioned by the Germans**: see: Mazzeo, p. 151, and Abescat, Bruno, and Yves Stavridès, p. 13.

74 *still a Jewish company*: see: Abescat, Bruno, and Yves Stavridès, p. 13.

74 **"must be given up or given to Aryans"**: see: Abescat, Bruno, and Yves Stavridès, p. 13.

75 **Arendt was Jewish**: Arendt was forced to leave Germany in 1933 and lived in Paris for the next eight years, working for several Jewish refugee organizations. See: Tömmel, Tatjana, and Maurizio Passerin d'Entreves. "Hannah Arendt." *The Stanford Encyclopedia of Philosophy*, edited by Edward N. Zalta and Uri Nodelman, Fall 2024, Metaphysics Research Lab, Stanford University, 2024.

75 **"guilt implies the consciousness of guilt"**: Arendt, Hannah. "Organized Guilt and Universal Responsibility," originally appeared

NOTES

in *Jewish Frontier* (1948). Found in *Collective Responsibility: Five Decades of Debate in Theoretical and Applied Ethics*, edited by Larry May and Stacey Hoffman, Rowman & Littlefield, 1992, p. 278.

76 **What have I done?:** see: Arendt, Hannah. *The Portable Hannah Arendt.* Edited by Peter Baehr, Penguin Books, 2003.

76 **vice president of the Bourjois Company in New York:** see: "Studies Cosmetic Needs; Thomas Flies to Europe for Data on Essential Oils, Etc." *New York Times*, 18 Aug. 1940.

76 **without anyone finding out:** see: Vaughan, p. 178.

77 **Chanel's competitor, Guerlain:** see: "H. Gregory Thomas, Chanel Executive, 82." *New York Times*, 10 Oct. 1990.

77 **700 pounds of jasmine to keep production up:** see: Updike, John. "Qui Qu'a Vu Coco?" *The New Yorker*, 21 Sept. 1998, p. 132.

77 **production going through World War II:** see: Vaughan, p. 288.

77 **OSS:** The OSS was the predecessor agency to the Central Intelligence Agency. It was the wartime intelligence agency for the USA during World War II and ceased operations in 1945. We can confirm that Thomas was part of the OSS thanks to declassified personnel files in the National Archives. NARA, OSS Personnel Name File, Thomas, Entry 168A, Box 2.

77 **"four or five thousand dollars in 1941":** see: Vaughan, p. 288.

78 **"The feats accomplished by Gregory Thomas are out of a James Bond movie":** see: Vaughan, p. 181.

78 **Aryanization laws:** The Nazi German state encouraged Jewish business owners to sell their businesses at radically reduced prices, often for only 20 percent of the actual business value. After Kristallnacht, they began forcing transfers by assigning non-Jewish trustees to oversee forced sales. These were required services, and the cost of the sales were also forcibly paid for by the former Jewish owners. Some of the profits of these sales also went to the office of the Four Year Plan, headed by Nazi official Hermann Göring. These fees were directly used for Nazi logistics during World War II.

79 **"They produced it in *Hoboken*":** see: Vaughan, p. 178.

79 **the steamship tickets:** see: Lehrer, Steven. *Wartime Sites in Paris: 1939–1945.* SF Tafel, 2013.

79 **code name WESTMINSTER:** see: Vaughan, p. 168.

80 *France got what she deserved:* see: Vaughan, p. 186.

80 **"to be assassinated":** *Life*, Aug. 1942.

81 **sleeping with the enemy:** see: Picardie, p. 195, and Vaughan, p. 16.

83 **paid for all her life expenses until the end:** see: Thomas.

NOTES

AN EMPIRE OF HAIR

87 **Forced haircuts:** see: Onion, Rebecca. "The Infamous Government Order Mandating Forced Haircuts for Native Americans." *Slate*, 20 Aug. 2013.

87 **Corporate:** see: Halley, Catherine. "How Natural Black Hair at Work Became a Civil Rights Issue." *JSTOR Daily*, 3 July 2019.

87 **military codes of conduct:** "Updated Hair Policies for Navy Women." *All Hands*. https://www.dodreads.com/wp-content/uploads/2019/06/Military-Haircut-Standards-Navy-Female-FemaleRegsPrint.pdf.

87 **children are sent home with their braids cut:** Germano, Beth. "Mother Says 11-Year-Old's Braid Cut Off in Melrose School: 'It Was Racially Targeted.'" CBS News, Local, 31 May 2024.

87 **their Afros cut:** Reid Bradford, Rayna. "Minnesota Teacher Cuts Black Boy's Hair Without Permission." *Essence*, 20 Apr. 2022.

87 **myriad things:** Griffith, Janelle. "When Hair Breaks Rules: Some Black Children Are Getting in Trouble for Natural Hairstyles." NBC News, 23 Feb. 2019.

88 **Gómez Ortigoza in 2022:** Gómez Ortigoza, Danié. "Not Just a Hairstyle, Braids Can Be a Powerful Connection to Mexican Culture." *Oprah Daily*, 28 Sept. 2022.

89 ***Hair Story:*** see: Byrd, Ayana, and Lori Tharps. *Hair Story: Untangling the Roots of Black Hair in America*. St. Martin's Griffin, 2014.

89 **before they hit the ground:** Oldstone-Moore, Christopher. "Why Alexander the Great Told His Army to Shave Off Their Beards." *Atlantic*, 15 Dec. 2020.

89 **they stole them away from their families:** "Boarding Schools—Native Words, Native Warriors." National Museum of the American Indian.

89 **braided into the hair of the enslaved:** Gege. "Cornrows and the TransAtlantic Slave Trade." The Afro Curly Hair Coach, 25 Oct. 2022.

89 **"tied into buns on the top":** Brown, DeNeen. "Afro-Colombian Women Braid Messages of Freedom in Hairstyles." *Washington Post*, 2 May 2024.

90 **by cutting it:** "Filial Piety (孝) in Chinese Culture." *Greater China Journal*, 14 Mar. 2016.

90 **the Chinese Revolution in 1911:** Hall, Nicholas Sean. "WASP: Racism and Satire in the 19th Century." *FoundSF*.

93 **Toussaint L'Ouverture:** Sontag, Deborah. "Canonizing a Slave: Saint or Uncle Tom?" *New York Times*, 23 Feb. 1992.

NOTES

93 **no longer permitted to assemble at night:** Everett, Donald E. "Free Persons of Color in Colonial Louisiana." *Louisiana History: The Journal of the Louisiana Historical Association*, vol. 7, no. 1, 1966, pp. 21–50.

94 **"from habits and feelings could be distinct from the Negroes":** "Legacies of Chinese Indenture Aboard the Empire Windrush in 1948." *National Archives Blog*, 31 May 2023.

94 **We weren't slaves, we were *indentured*:** Chinese Indentured Laborers in Cuba Collection (MS 2117). Manuscripts and Archives, Yale University Library.

95 **Asians in Chinatowns, being chased through the streets, lynched:** Dowd, Katie. "140 Years Ago, San Francisco Was Set Ablaze During the City's Deadliest Race Riots." *SFGate*, 23 July 2017.

95 **Stabbed on the corner across the street from my favorite dumplings:** O'Kane, Caitlin. "Christina Yuna Lee Followed into Chinatown Apartment and Stabbed to Death." CBS News, Crime, 15 Feb. 2022.

95 **where many Asians first stepped foot in America:** *Ancestors in the Americas*. PBS, 2001.

95 **"for having abandoned the control of his old master":** "Sacramento Delta Blues: Chinese Workers and the Building of the California Levees, 1860–1880." Undated, Series 2, Box: 14, Folder: 9, The Leo Deaner Radical Left-Wing Publications collection, LAC0011, Special Collections Research Center, The George Washington University.

95 **to keep the wages down:** M. Cronin, Mary. "When the Chinese Came to Massachusetts: Representations of Race, Labor, Religion, and Citizenship in the 1870 Press." *Historical Journal of Massachusetts*, vol. 46, no. 2, Summer 2018, pp. 72–105.

95 **"made foremen of them":** see: Charles Crocker. "Testimony before Congress." Report of the Joint Special Committee to Investigate Chinese Immigration, Senate Report No. 689, 44th Congress, 2nd sess., 1876–1877.

96 **for the same job:** "Geography of Chinese Workers Building the Transcontinental Railroad." Chinese Railroad Workers in North America Project at Stanford University.

96 **their deaths were never recorded formally:** Shao, Elena. "Remembering the Chinese Railroad Workers That Built Stanford's Fortune." *Stanford Daily*, 23 May 2019. See also: Chinese Railroad Workers in North America Project at Stanford University. See also: Hollington, Debbie. "Teacher's Guide: Chinese Railroad Worker's Experience Exhibit." California State Railroad Museum Interpretation and Education, California State Parks & California State Railroad Museum.

NOTES

96 **their names never acknowledged in any way:** Kennedy, Lesley. "Building the Transcontinental Railroad: How 20,000 Chinese Immigrants Made It Happen." *History*, 23 Apr. 2024.

96 **"Negro Alley":** Wallace, Kelly. "Forgotten Los Angeles History: The Chinese Massacre of 1871." *Los Angeles Public Library Blog*, 19 May 2018. See also: Shyong, Frank. "The 1871 Los Angeles Chinese Massacre Still Resonates Today." *Los Angeles Times*, 24 Oct. 2021.

97 **Pigtail Ordinance of 1878:** see: "Pigtail Ordinance, 1878." National Archives Records of Rights.

97 **those requirements demanded:** "The Chinese Experience in 19th Century America." University of Illinois Teaching Resources, 2006.

98 **wore them on a daily basis:** Derby, Cecil. "Lure of the Human Hair Net." *New York Times*, 23 Oct. 1921.

98 **180 million human-hair nets from China that year:** Tarlo, Emma. *Entanglement: The Secret Lives of Hair*. Oneworld Publications, 2016.

98 **denied citizenship or immigration to Chinese:** Department of State National Archives and Records Administration. Office of the Federal Register. "An Act to Execute Certain Treaty Stipulations Relating to Chinese." US National Archives Research Catalog.

98 **were prohibited from buying land:** "How States Used Land Laws to Exclude and Displace Asian Americans." *Governing*, 23 Nov. 2022.

99 **banned from immigrating:** An act to execute certain treaty stipulations relating to the Chinese, May 6, 1882; Enrolled Acts and Resolutions of Congress, 1789–1996; General Records of the United States Government; Record Group 11; National Archives.

100 **in Louisiana:** McKinley Freeman, Tyron. *Madam C. J. Walker's Gospel of Giving: Black Women's Philanthropy during Jim Crow*. University of Illinois Press, 2020.

100 **a hair institute:** see: Byrd.

100 **the first Black codes in December 1865:** Pixon, Sara. *The Law Library of Louisiana: History of the Codes of Louisiana: References*.

101 **the 13th Amendment:** Hassett-Walker, Connie. "How You Start Is How You Finish? The Slave Patrol and Jim Crow Origins of Policing." *Human Rights Magazine*, vol. 46, no. 2, 11 Jan. 2021.

101 **they kidnapped free Black people and sent them back into slavery:** Wells, Jonathan Daniel. "The So-Called 'Kidnapping Club' Featured Cops Selling Free Black New Yorkers Into Slavery." *Smithsonian*, 14 Oct. 2020.

101 **less intergenerational wealth than their white counterparts:** Blackwelder, Julia Kirk. *Styling Jim Crow: African American Beauty*

NOTES

Training during Segregation. Texas A & M University Press, 2003. p. 15.

102 **In spite of it:** Walker, Susannah. *Style & Status: Selling Beauty to African American Women, 1920–1975.* University Press of Kentucky, 2007.

105 **"that kind of hapless freedom":** St. Felix, Doreen. "When God Came to the Washerwoman." *Wags Revue,* no. 20, Fall 2015.

105 **while working for a wig manufacturer:** Crowhurst, Anna-Marie. "Remembering Christina Jenkins, the Woman Who Invented the Weave." *Stylist UK.* See also: Tsatalis, John. "Christina M. Jenkins: Weaving the History of Artificial Hair Extensions." *SKIN Journal of Cutaneous Medicine,* vol. 4, no. 3, May 2020, p. 302.

105 **the Vietnam War:** Petrulis, Jason. "'A Country of Hair': A Global Story of South Korean Wigs, Korean American Entrepreneurs, African American Hairstyles, and Cold War Industrialization." *Enterprise & Society,* vol. 22, no. 2, 2021, pp. 368–408.

107 **"wigs were used to address employment":** Greaves, Kayla. "Black Women's Deep Relationship With Wigs Isn't What You Think It Is." *InStyle,* 1 June 2024.

107 **the main consumers of synthetic wigs are Black American women:** Chang, Felix B. "Ethnically Segmented Markets: Korean-Owned Black Hair Stores." *Indiana Law Journal,* vol. 97, no. 2, article 2, 2022.

108 **"I don't want others to feel the same way":** Harvin, Darian Symone. "Brooklyn's Very Own 16-Year-Old Beauty Supply Store Owner." *Studio Symone,* 8 Oct. 2020.

108 **nontoxic alternative to synthetic hair:** Taylor, Savannah M. "Sustainability Power Player: Ciara Imani May, Founder of Rebundle Hair, Believes Extensions Shouldn't Be Toxic." *Ebony,* 14 Apr. 2023.

108 **One in two Black women experience hair loss in their lifetime:** Gathers, Raechele Cochran, and Meredith Grace Mahan. "African American Women, Hair Care, and Health Barriers." *Journal of Clinical and Aesthetic Dermatology,* vol. 7, no. 9, 2014, pp. 26–9.

109 **in California in 2019:** Wayt, Lindsy. "California Becomes First State to Outlaw Hair Discrimination." *GovDocs,* 25 July 2019.

110 **growing hair for a while:** Vreeman, Rachel C., and Aaron E. Carroll. "Medical Myths." *British Medical Journal,* vol. 335, no. 7633, Dec. 2007, pp. 1288–89.

NOTES

NAILING THE LANDING

112 **the "Forgotten War" by the generations old enough to remember it:** Stack, Liam. "Korean War, a 'Forgotten' Conflict That Shaped the Modern World." *New York Times*, 1 Jan. 2018.

112 **sanctions still in place to this day:** A sanction is a punishment imposed on a country by another, taking the form of tariffs, asset freezes, embargos, and quotas. Who would have thought a book on beauty would explain political policy! For an expanded history on these sanctions, see: National Committee on North Korea. *Timeline: U.S. Sanctions and Treasury Departments Actions against the DPRK*. Jan. 2008.

113 **cut its teeth:** see: Seth, Michael J. "South Korea's Economic Development, 1948–1996." *Oxford Research Encyclopedia of Asian History*, Oxford University Press, 2017. South Korea was able to use political and military relations with the Americans for economic development purposes. South Korean President Park Chung-hee sent 300,000 troops to support the Americans in Vietnam; in exchange, South Korean firms were to be given lucrative contracts to supply goods and services to the South Vietnamese, American, and allied military forces. South Korean firms such as Hyundai gained valuable experience in completing construction and transportation projects for the United States in Vietnam, experience that they applied to win contracts in the Middle East and elsewhere.

113 **"This is our offspring. We cannot abandon it":** see: Papers of John F. Kennedy. Pre-Presidential Papers. Senate Files, Box 895, "America's Stake in Vietnam, American Friends of Vietnam, Washington, DC, 1 June 1956." John F. Kennedy Presidential Library.

113 **Agent Orange:** Agent Orange was an herbicide mixture used by the US military during the Vietnam War. Much of it contained a dangerous chemical contaminant called dioxin. Production of Agent Orange ended in the 1970s and it is no longer in use. The dioxin contaminant, however, continues to have harmful impact today. See: "What Is Agent Orange?" *The Aspen Institute*. https://www.aspeninstitute.org/programs/agent-orange-in-vietnam-program/what-is-agent-orange/.

113 **millions of people fled their country:** see: "How the End of the Vietnam War Led to a Refugee Crisis." *History*, 29 Aug. 2023.

114 **Ngày Quốc Hận:** see: Flanagan, Jake. "How Vietnamese-Americans Reintroduced the US to Vietnam." *Quartz*, 30 Apr. 2015.

NOTES

114 **the country imploded into flames:** see: "First Days Story Project." *Voices of the Vietnamese Refugee Experience*, PBS.

114 **130,000 Vietnamese began entering the United States:** "Indochina Migration and Refugee Assistance Act (1975)." Immigration History Provided by the University of Texas at Austin Department of History.

114 **near Sacramento:** see: Morris, Regan. "How Tippi Hedren Made Vietnamese Refugees into Nail Salon Magnates." *BBC News*, 2 May 2015.

114 **tuberculosis treatment center:** "Ex-Vietnamese Refugees Reunite with, Thank Those Who Helped Them 40 Years Ago." *Orange County Register*, 29 July 2015.

114 **Adele Pham:** see: *Nailed It*. Directed by Adele Pham, 2019.

115 **in their own neighborhoods:** see: West, Z., Weaver, R., and Wagner, K.C. "Unvarnished: Precarity and Poor Working Conditions for Nail Salon Workers in New York State." Cornell University, ILR School, The Worker Institute.

116 **to their white peers:** see: West et al., above.

116 **"To be or not to be. That is the question. A question, yes, but not always a choice":** see: Vuong, Ocean. *On Earth We're Briefly Gorgeous*. Penguin, 2019.

117 **"victims of persecution by the Nazi government":** Displaced Persons Act of 1948, Pub. L. No. 80–774, 62 Stat. 1009, June 1948.

117 **"rejected communist-occupied areas of Europe":** see: US Statutes at Large, Public Law 203, Ch. 336, pp. 400–7.

118 **in nonwhite neighborhoods:** see: Sharma, P., et al. "Nail File: A Study of Nail Salon Workers and Industry in the United States." UCLA Labor Center and California Healthy Nail Salon Collaborative.

118 **Olivett Robinson and a Vietnamese refugee named Charlie Vo:** see: Driver, Krista Beth. "I Am Living Proof of the American Dream: "If You Believe You Can Achieve Something, That Is Half the Battle." *Authority Magazine*, 30 Jan. 2020.

120 **part-time as a nail technician in a salon:** see: Drummey, Cyndy. "Flo Jo Has It All." *Nails*, 1 Feb. 1993.

120 **Redlining:** see: Jackson, Candace. "What Is Redlining?" *New York Times*, 17 Aug. 2021.

121 **minority-owned businesses in America for decades:** The most recent census data shows that 30.8 percent of franchise businesses are minority owned, compared to just 18.8 percent of nonfranchised businesses.

NOTES

122 **franchise models and Black America:** see: Chatelain, Marcia. *Franchise: The Golden Arches in Black America*. Liveright, 2021.

122 **80 percent more than the general market on beauty products:** see: Smith, Stephanie D. "Essence Panel Explores Beauty Purchasing." *WWD*, BeautyInc, 19 May 2009.

123 **Editorial nail artists:** These manicurists have a clientele primarily consisting of movie stars, models, and musicians. They do work for magazine spreads, advertising, runway, film, and red carpet and do not typically make the bulk of their income from salons.

124 **Mimi Thi Nguyen:** Nguyen, Mimi Thi. *The Gift of Freedom: War, Debt, and Other Refugee Passages*. Duke University Press, 2012.

126 ***Minor Feelings***: see: Hong, Cathy Park. *Minor Feelings: An Asian American Reckoning*. One World, 2021.

127 **"It is 'both/and' rather than 'either/or'":** see: Kim, Elaine H. "'At Least You're Not Black': Asian Americans in US Race Relations." *Social Justice*, vol. 25, no. 3 (1998), pp. 3–12.

128 **the rest had wages withheld:** Among the more than 100 workers interviewed by the *Times*, only about a quarter said they were paid an amount that was the equivalent of New York State's minimum hourly wage. All but three workers, however, had wages withheld in other ways that would be considered illegal, such as never getting overtime. See: Maslin Nir, Sarah. "The Price of Nice Nails." *New York Times*, 17 May 2015.

129 **$2 million in damages to 652 employees:** see: "New York Orders Nail Salons to Pay $2 Million in Unpaid Wages, Damages." Reuters, 9 May 2016.

129 **risking all their future jobs:** see: Chang, Sophia, et al. "Majority of NYC Nail Salon Workers Still Face Wage Theft, New Report Finds." *Gothamist*, 18 Feb. 2020.

129 **New York Nail Salon Workers Association:** see: *Healthy Nail Salons—NYCOSH*.

129 **healthy salon core requirements:** California Healthy Nail Salon Recognition Program, AB 2125, from California Department of Toxic Substances Control. *Healthy Nail Salon Recognition Program Guidelines*. 2018.

129 **beauty service licensing applications:** *Nail Salon Bill of Rights from New York Department of Labor*. Accessed 12 Sept. 2024.

130 **VietLEAD in Philadelphia:** Huỳnh, Trân B., et al. "A Participatory Approach to Designing and Implementing an Occupational Health Intervention for the Nail Salon Community in the Greater

NOTES

Philadelphia Region." *Occupational and Environmental Health*, 13 June 2023.

130 **Michigan Healthy Nail Salon Cooperative:** see: "What We Do." Michigan Healthy Nail Salon Cooperative, 19 Feb. 2017.

130 **Women's Voices for the Earth in Montana:** see: *Protecting Nail & Salon Workers Health—Women's Voices for the Earth*.

130 **Healthy Nail Salon Network in Toronto:** see: "Detail on Nail Salon Workers Project." Parkdale Queen West Community Health Centre.

130 **Manitoba Federation of Labour Occupational Health Centre in Winnipeg:** see: OHC—MFL Occupational Health Centre.

130 **how to protect yourself in a pandemic:** Le, Aurora. "U-M Partnership with Michigan Nail Salons Promotes Better Environment for Workers." University of Michigan School of Public Health.

130 **Mutual aid funds as part of a salon environment aren't unusual:** see: Yen Liu, Yvonne. "For Asian Immigrants, Cooperatives Came From the Home Country." *Yes!*, 22 May 2018. See also: Oh, Joong-Hwan. "Economic Incentive, Embeddedness, and Social Support: A Study of Korean-Owned Nail Salon Workers' Rotating Credit Associations." *International Migration Review*, vol. 41, no. 3, 2007, pp. 623–55.

131 **Kesang:** Kesang Gurung is a Cambodian nail artist based in Queens, New York. You can book her here: kesangthenailartist.com. Tip her well!

IN CASE OF EMERGENCY

136 **Power grids are already failing:** "The World's Power Grids Are Failing as the Planet Warms." *Bloomberg*, 15 July 2024.

136 **gas prices are soaring:** Tumala, Mohammed M., et al. "Climate Change and Fossil Fuel Prices: A GARCH-MIDAS Analysis." *Energy Economics*, vol. 124, Aug. 2023, p. 106792.

136 **droughts are common:** "Droughts in Northern Hemisphere Made 20 Times More Likely by Climate Change." *Imperial News*, 6 Oct. 2022.

136 **your skin's microbiome out of balance:** Mousavi, Sayed Esmaeil, et al. "Air Pollution and Endocrine Disruptors Induce Human Microbiome Imbalances: A Systematic Review of Recent Evidence and Possible Biological Mechanisms." *Science of the Total Environment*, vol. 816, Apr. 2022, p. 151654.

136 **disrupts your skin barrier:** Mancebo, S. E., and S. Q. Wang. "Recognizing the Impact of Ambient Air Pollution on Skin Health." *Journal

NOTES

of the European Academy of Dermatology and Venereology, vol. 29, no. 12, Dec. 2015, pp. 2326–32.

136 **itchy skin from poor air quality:** Huang, Chao-Hsin, et al. "Detrimental Correlation Between Air Pollution with Skin Aging in Taiwan Population." *Medicine*, vol. 101, no. 31, Aug. 2022.

136 **quaint or even comical:** Hassan Bhat, Tavoos, et al. "Air Pollution Health Risk Assessment (AP-HRA), Principles and Applications." *International Journal of Environmental Research and Public Health*, vol. 18, no. 4, 4 Jan. 2021, p. 1935.

137 **climate change exists:** "2023 Poll: Americans' Views on Climate Change and Policy in 10 Charts." *EPIC*.

137 **fewer resources:** Foster, Nina, and Simon Retallack. "Greenhouse Gloss: Is the Beauty Industry's Commitment to Tackling Climate Change More than Skin Deep?" Carbon Trust. 18 Jan. 2023.

137 **sister organizations internationally:** Vysniauskaite, Justina. "What Does Clean Beauty Mean?" NUORI.

137 **"hypoallergenic":** Office of the Commissioner, US FDA. "'Hypoallergenic' Cosmetics." Aug. 2024.

138 **"the doubt creates a bigger psychological problem":** author interview with Nicole Loher, 10 Sept. 2024.

139 **"this is an emergency":** "60 Seconds on Earth with Xiye Bastida." *Atmos*, 24 Sept. 2013.

139 **degrees of recyclability:** Gatt, Isaac Jordan, and Paul Refalo. "Reusability and Recyclability of Plastic Cosmetic Packaging: A Life Cycle Assessment." *Resources, Conservation & Recycling Advances*, vol. 15, Nov. 2022.

139 **Only 9 percent of all plastic has ever been recycled:** Min, Douglas. "Think That Your Plastic Is Being Recycled? Think Again." *MIT Technology Review*, 12 Oct. 2023.

139 **2-day rush order:** L'Haridon, J., et al. "SPOT: A Strategic Life-Cycle-Assessment-Based Methodology and Tool for Cosmetic Product Eco-Design." *Sustainability*, vol. 15, 2023, p. 14321.

140 **"chemophobia":** Kilikita, Jacqueline. "The Truth About Chemicals in Skincare Products." *Refinery29*, 3 July 2022.

141 **by-products of fossil fuels:** Waldeck, Sabine. "Petrochemical Alternatives Abound amid Heightened Scrutiny from Consumers and Regulators." *Personal Care Insights*, 9 Apr. 2024.

141 **safe for skin:** Anderson, Elizabeth, and Joe Zagorski. "Trending—Petroleum Jelly." Center for Research on Ingredient Safety, Michigan State University, 20 Feb. 2023.

NOTES

141 **faster than it would otherwise:** Lin, Tzu-Kai, et al. "Anti-Inflammatory and Skin Barrier Repair Effects of Topical Application of Some Plant Oils." *International Journal of Molecular Sciences*, vol. 19, no. 1, Dec. 2017, p. 70.

141 **reduce scarring:** Kamrani, Payvand, et al. "Petroleum Jelly: A Comprehensive Review of Its History, Uses, and Safety." *Journal of the American Academy of Dermatology*, vol. 90, no. 4, Apr. 2024, pp. 807–13.

141 **"the petrochemical industry sells ingredients into the beauty industry":** Brown, Rachel. "Amyris CEO John Melo's Views On Why 'Everything Is Chemicals' Is an Oversimplification and Clean Beauty Is the Future." *Beauty Independent*, 7 July 2021

143 **"Killing humanity? Killing the world?":** author interview with Nicole Loher, 10 Sept. 2024.

143 **the liberation of Palestine launched:** "Palestinian BDS National Committee." *BDS Movement*, 9 May 2016.

144 **prone to flood, drought, and frost:** Klein, Naomi. "Let Them Drown." *London Review of Books*, 2 June 2016.

144 **the violence of climate crisis:** "Social Dimensions of Climate Change." World Bank. See also: Islam, S. Nazrul, and John Winkel. "Climate Change and Social Inequality." UN Department of Economic and Social Affairs, 2017.

144 **a crucial role in fighting global warming:** Frechette, Alain, et al. *A Global Baseline of Carbon Storage in Collective Lands: Indigenous and Local Community Contributions to Climate Change Mitigation.* Indigenous Peoples Alliance of the Archipelago, Mesoamerican Alliance of Indigenous Peoples and Forests, and the Coordinators of the Indigenous Organizations of the Amazon Basin, Sept. 2018, p. 12.

144 **Eighty percent of the planet's biodiversity survives in their keeping:** "Indigenous Peoples Defend Earth's Biodiversity—but They're in Danger." *National Geographic*, 16 Nov. 2018.

144 **the combined emissions of North America:** Goldtooth, Dallas, and Alberto Saldamando. *Indigenous Resistance Against Carbon*. Indigenous Environmental Network, Aug. 2021, p. 20.

144 **to Ohio:** "Climate Change Is Causing Extreme Weather in Ohio, Sen. Brown Wants to Protect Workers from It." *WYSO*, directed by Welter, 21 July 2022.

144 **over 100 degrees Fahrenheit in the shade:** "Climate Change Is Already Happening in Bangladesh." *Labour Behind the Label*.

NOTES

145 **American cosmetics:** "US and EU Cosmetics Regulation." *Personal Care Products Council.*

145 **powder on her face:** Drew-Bear, Annette. "Cosmetics and Attitudes Towards Women in the Seventeenth Century." *Journal of Popular Culture*, vol. 9, no. 1, Summer 1975, p. 31.

145 **Radioactive chin straps:** *Cosmetics and Skin: Radioactive Cosmetics.*

146 **expect people to not cause harm:** One particularly egregious example is the history of Johnson & Johnson's testing of talc powder on incarcerated Black people in the 1950s. University of Pennsylvania dermatologist Albert Kligman experimented on hundreds of inmates at Massachusetts's Holmesburg Prison and injected inmates with asbestos to compare its effect on the skin with talc. His clients for these experiments ranged from Johnson & Johnson to Dow Chemical to the US government. Participants reported all sorts of side effects. Since 2013, J&J has paid out $3.5 billion in talcum-related settlements. See: Vinluan, Frank. "Bloomberg: Court Docs Reveal J&J's Role in Prison Tests Comparing Talc to Asbestos." *MedCity News*, Pharma, 7 Mar. 2022.

146 **won't kill you:** Mandell, Janna. "Why Paraben-Free Might Not Be Better." *Washington Post*, 15 Feb. 2022.

147 **will kill something later on:** DuFault, Amy. "Ditching Microbeads: The Search for Sustainable Skincare." *Guardian*, 5 May 2014.

147 **FDA for health-related claims:** "Is It a Cosmetic, a Drug, or Both? (Or Is It Soap?)." Office of the Commissioner, US FDA, Sept. 2024.

148 **less wasteful than travel-size and sample packaging:** "Plastic Waste: 980 Tonnes of Travel-Sized Products Are Dumped Every Year." *Direct Line Group Corporate Website*, 29 July 2018.

148 **"It's on manufacturers to use less plastic, period":** "Allure Won't Call Plastic Packaging 'Recyclable' Anymore." *Allure*, 22 Apr. 2021.

149 **"in a significant way":** Taddonio, Patrice. "Plastics Industry Insiders Reveal the Truth About Recycling." *Frontline*, PBS, 31 Mar. 2020.

149 **to save their bottom line:** Allen, Davis, et al. *The Fraud of Plastic Recycling.* Center for Climate Integrity, Feb. 2024.

150 **midrange luxury brands:** "How Mycelium Packaging Could Help Solve the Beauty Industry's Waste Problem." *Vogue*, 14 Aug. 2020.

151 **asthma:** "Air Pollution." *Asthma & Allergy Foundation of America.*

151 **lung cancer:** "How Can Air Pollution Cause Cancer? Lung Cancer and Air Pollution." *Cancer Research UK.*

151 **central nervous system dysfunctions:** Armas, Frances Vivienne, and Amedeo D'Angiulli. "Neuroinflammation and Neurodegeneration of

NOTES

the Central Nervous System from Air Pollutants: A Scoping Review." *Toxics*, vol. 10, no. 11, Nov. 2022, p. 666.

151 **stroke:** Verhoeven, Jamie I., et al. "Ambient Air Pollution and the Risk of Ischaemic and Haemorrhagic Stroke." *Lancet Planetary Health*, vol. 5, no. 8, Aug. 2021, pp. e542–52.

151 **diabetes:** "Air Pollution Linked to Type 2 Diabetes." *CIEH*.

151 **resource materials from:** *Anti-Pollution Skincare: Protecting Skin in Urban Environments.*

152 **zip codes, countries:** Hill, Elaine L., and Lala Ma. "Drinking Water, Fracking, and Infant Health." *Journal of Health Economics*, vol. 82, Mar. 2022, p. 102595.

153 **Amazon drop-off location:** Neela-Stock, Siobhan, and Chase DiBenedetto. "How to Recycle Amazon Packaging (Yes, All of It)." *Mashable*, 22 Apr. 2023.

153 **landfills or the natural environment:** "China Quits Recycling US Trash as Sustainable Start-Up Makes Strides." *Forbes*, 20 Jan. 2021.

154 **than plastic to produce:** Gujba, Haruna, and Adisa Azapagic. "Carbon Footprint of Beverage Packaging in the United Kingdom." *Towards Life Cycle Sustainability Management*, edited by Matthias Finkbeiner, Springer Netherlands, 2011, pp. 381–90.

154 **stickers on it or not:** *Stickers—San Jose Recycles.*

154 **their products as a result:** Jégou, Pierrick, et al. *Communication on Our Sustainability Progress.* Guerlain, p. 38.

155 **production of what you're looking at:** "Carbon Neutral, Net Zero, and Zero Emissions: What's the Difference?," WorkforClimate, 22 June 2023.

156 **terrible success rate preventing deforestation:** Morton, Adam. "Australia's Carbon Credit Scheme 'Largely a Sham' Says Whistleblower Who Tried to Rein It In." *Guardian*, 23 Mar. 2022.

156 **climate colonialism:** Wang, Jess. "Carbon Offsets, a New Form of Neocolonialism." Columbia Climate School, 3 May 2021.

156 **"the lands will be logged anyway":** Jackson, Elizabeth J. "Changing Seasons of Resistance: Impacts of Settle Colonialism and Climate Change in Indigenous Worlds." Humboldt State University, 2020.

156 **time and time again, to be true:** Sena, Kanyinke. "Carbon Credit Schemes and Indigenous Peoples in Kenya: A Commentary." *Arizona Journal of International and Comparative Law*, vol. 32, 2015, p. 257.

156 **the first deal of its kind:** "How Diamonds and a Bitter Feud Led to the Destruction of an Amazon Reserve." *Guardian*, 27 Sept. 2017.

NOTES

158 **doesn't have to be:** "What Is a 501(c)(3) Organization: Types and Requirements." *Azeus Convene*, 11 Jul. 2024.

158 **"single-handedly tilted the playing field for his party":** "Ronald Lauder: New York's Billionaire Political Disrupter." *New York Times*, 6 Nov. 2022.

160 **more than $491,000 in 2020 alone from his coal company holdings:** Cannon, Matt. "Joe Manchin, Biden's Climate Nemesis, Makes $492K a Year From Coal." *Newsweek*, 18 Oct. 2021.

162 **"L'Oréal starts thinking about it, too":** Geyman, Maria. "How Mycelium Packaging Could Help Solve the Beauty Industry's Waste Problem." *Vogue*, 14 Aug. 2020.

162 **The world's five richest men:** Luhby, Tami. "The Wealth of the World's Five Richest Men More Than Doubled Since 2020." *CNN*, 14 Jan. 2024.

163 **"The more I learned about the industry, the worse I felt.":** Russell, Cameron. "Dear Fossil Fuel Executives." *All We Can Save: Truth, Courage, and Solutions for the Climate Crisis*. One World, 2020, p. 205.

164 **$3,342 a year on cosmetics and beauty services:** "Global Wellness Institute Ranks 145 Countries by Wellness Market Size." Global Wellness Institute, 30 Jan. 2024.

165 **COVID-19 pandemic did not change our consumer habits for the better of the planet:** *The Consumer Demand Recovery and Lasting Effects of COVID-19*. McKinsey, 17 Mar. 2021.

165 **carbon output:** Bhanumati, P., et al. "Greenhouse Emissions Rise to Record, Erasing Drop During Pandemic." *IMF*, 30 June 2022.

165 **despite a recession:** "The Beauty Market in 2023: New Industry Trends," *McKinsey*, 22 May 2023.

HOW BEAUTY SURVIVES A PLAGUE

167 **every nail salon, hair salon, spa, tattoo parlor, and beauty supply store:** Steinbuch, Yaron. "Cuomo: Hair Salons, Barbershops, Tattoo Parlors to Close amid Coronavirus." *New York Post*, 20 Mar. 2020.

167 **no more beds in the ICU:** Rothfeld, Michael, et al. "13 Deaths in a Day: An 'Apocalyptic' Coronavirus Surge at an NYC Hospital." *New York Times*, 25 Mar. 2020.

167 **or the morgue:** Alsharif, Mina, and Rachel Sanchez. "COVID-19 Victims Still Stored in Refrigerated Trucks in New York City." *CNN*, 7 May 2021.

NOTES

167 **the epicenter of COVID-19:** Liveris, Anna, et al. "When New York City Was the COVID-19 Pandemic Epicenter: The Impact on Trauma Care." *Journal of Trauma and Acute Care Surgery,* vol. 93, no. 2, 2022, pp. 247–55.

167 **won't reopen at all:** "Reasons We've Loved New York: A Send-off to the Many Places, Big and Small, That Closed During 2020 COVID-19 Pandemic." Curbed, 7 Dec. 2020.

168 **can damage their respiratory system for life:** Sirayder, Ukbe, et al. "Long-Term Characteristics of Severe COVID-19: Respiratory Function, Functional Capacity, and Quality of Life." *International Journal of Environmental Research and Public Health*, vol. 19, no. 10, May 2022, p. 6304.

168 **rarely enforced by the government:** *Health Hazards in Nail Salons—Chemical Hazards.* Occupational Safety and Health Administration.

168 **do not provide gloves to their technicians:** Maslin Nir, Sarah. "Perfect Nails, Poisoned Workers." *New York Times,* 8 May 2015.

168 **have donated them to hospitals:** "Nail Salons and Spas around the Country Are Donating Masks, Gloves to Hospitals." Today.com, 25 Mar. 2020.

168 **masks to frontline workers:** Cascone, Sarah. "Galleries, Auction Houses, and Museums Are Joining Growing Efforts to Donate Their Protective Medical Gear to Hospitals." *Artnet,* 31 Mar. 2020.

168 **Tattoo parlors and hair salons have done the same:** Preston, Devon. "Tattoo Artists Are Donating Their Supplies to Help Medical Professionals." *Inked,* 24 Mar. 2020.

168 **L'Oréal:** "L'Oréal Takes Part: Our Response to COVID-19." https://www.loreal.com/en/articles/group/our-response-to-covid/.

169 **Georgia salons:** Mull, Amanda. "Georgia's Experiment in Human Sacrifice." *Atlantic,* 29 Apr. 2020.

169 **severely underresourced:** The Staffs of KFF Health News and *The Guardian.* "Lost on the Frontline." *KFF Health News,* 11 Aug. 2020.

170 **get haircuts:** Wilson, Jason. "US Lockdown Protests May Have Spread Virus Widely, Cellphone Data Suggests." *Guardian,* 18 May 2020.

170 **cage mask:** Da Costa, Cassie. "White Anti-Quarantine Protesters Have Cruelly Co-Opted a Black 18th-Century Slave." *Daily Beast,* 22 May 2020.

170 **cutting hair:** Censky, Abigail. "Barbers Cut Hair on the Michigan Capitol Lawn to Protest Anti-Coronavirus Shutdown." NPR, 20 May 2020.

NOTES

170 **citywide curfew in LA:** Gupta, Saumya. "Curfew Enacted across Entirety of Los Angeles County to Promote Public Safety." *Daily Bruin*, 31 May 2020.

170 **New York City:** "New York City's Curfew: What You Need to Know." *New York Times*, 30 June 2020.

170 **Chicago:** Nolen, Jermaine, and Ben Pope. "Mayor Lifts Citywide Curfew Effective Immediately." *Chicago Sun-Times*, 7 June 2020.

170 **Atlanta:** Taylor, La'Raven. "Atlanta Curfew Extended For Next 5 Days Amid Protests." Georgia Public Broadcasting, 5 June 2020.

170 **after the killing of George Floyd:** "Associated Press Tally Shows at Least 9,300 People Arrested in Protests since Killing of George Floyd," AP News, 2 June 2020.

170 **partially blinded:** "Police Partially Blind Eight People at Protests." *Berkeley Human Rights Center*, 2020.

170 **June 4, 2020:** Rose, Jacqueline. "Martin Gugino: 75-Year-Old Buffalo Protester Has a Fractured Skull and Cannot Walk." CNN, 16 June 2020.

171 **Soap saves lives:** Pradhan, Deepak, et al. "A Review of Current Interventions for COVID-19 Prevention." *Archives of Medical Research*, vol. 51, no. 5, July 2020, pp. 363–74.

171 ***"We're Left for Dead":*** Ransom, Jan, and Alan Feuer. "'We're Left for Dead': Fears of Virus Catastrophe at Rikers Jail." *New York Times*, 30 Mar. 2020.

172 **most infectious place in the entire world:** "Coronavirus Update: Rikers Island Rate of Infection 7 Times Higher Than Citywide, Legal Aid Says." CBS New York, 26 Mar. 2020.

172 **running out of soap:** Bryant, Miranda. "Coronavirus Spread at Rikers Is a 'Public Health Disaster', Says Jail's Top Doctor." *Guardian*, 1 Apr. 2020.

172 **with their commissary funds:** Pinto, Nick. "Coronavirus Has Arrived at Rikers Island: Inside New York City Jails, Where the Pandemic Is Set to Explode." *Intercept*, 18 Mar. 2020.

172 **Illinois commissary:** Weill-Greenberg, Elizabeth, and Ethan Corey. "Locked In, Priced Out: How Prison Commissary Price-Gouging Preys on the Incarcerated." *Appeal*, 17 Apr. 2024.

172 **$947 per year:** Raher, Stephen. "The Company Store." Prison Policy Initiative, May 2018.

172 **$762 alone:** Bureau of Labor Statistics. *Consumer Expenditures in 2017.* Apr. 2019.

NOTES

173 **Black and Pink Boston's $33K fundraiser:** Fundraiser by Katie Omberg: Mutual Aid for MA Prisoners during COVID-19.

173 **20 percent transaction fee:** Deutsch, Kevin. "Captive Market: Companies Earn Millions in Fees From NYC Prisoners' Families, Despite Law Limiting Surcharges." *Bronx Justice News*, 19 July 2019.

173 **the Texas prison system has spent more than $1.1 million in legal fees:** Bostock, Bill. "Texas Spent $1.1 Million Fighting a Lawsuit from Prisoners Who Asked for Soap, Hand Sanitizer, and Social-Distancing Measures, Documents Say." *Business Insider*, 28 May 2021.

173 **did get COVID:** McCullough, Jolie. "Texas Prison Lawsuit about Coronavirus Weighed by Federal Appeals Court." *Texas Tribune*, 28 May 2020.

174 **deaths among prisoners in any state in the United States:** "New Report Reveals the Devastating Toll of COVID-19 in Texas Prisons and Jails." LBJ School of Public Affairs, 9 Nov. 2020.

174 **letters in black or blue pen:** "Find out the Prison Mail Rules before Starting a Prison Correspondence." *Wire of Hope*.

175 **via a conference call:** Ciment, Shoshy. "A Sephora Employee Describes the Devastating Moment She and Others in Her District Were Suddenly Fired via a Conference Call." *Business Insider India*, 31 Mar. 2020

176 **worth over $500 billion:** "The 13 Largest Luxury Companies in the World." Quartr.com, 5 Feb. 2025.

176 **more than $190 billion:** "Bernard Arnault and Family." https://www.forbes.com/profile/bernard-arnault/.

176 **did not do the same:** "LVMH Unit Announces Layoffs." Happi, 30 June 2020.

176 **"brand building opportunity":** Sherman, Lauren. "Why Luxury Came to the Rescue." Business of Fashion, 18 May 2020.

177 **how they could do better:** Rosenstein, Jenna. "Uoma Beauty Founder Launches #PullUpOrShutUp to Raise Awareness About the Lack of Black Beauty Executives." *Harper's Bazaar*, 4 June 2020.

177 **other beauty editors:** Mau, Dhani. "Fashion and Beauty Editors Are Using Their Brand Contacts to Get Product to Frontline Workers." *Fashionista*, 16 Apr. 2020.

177 **April 6, 2020:** Valenti, Lauren. "Shirley Raines on Helping the Homeless of Skid Row During COVID-19." *Vogue*, 6 Apr. 2020.

178 **store-bought boxed hair color:** Lebsack, Lexy. "What Beauty Is Like for Homeless Women on the Streets." *Refinery29*, 3 Dec. 2019.

NOTES

179 **80 percent over the last eight years:** Smith, Doug, and Ruben Vines. "Homelessness Grows 10% in the City of Los Angeles." *Los Angeles Times*, 29 June 2023.

179 **5,000 people on Skid Row alone:** CVillacorte. "More Housing and Services in Skid Row." *Homeless Initiative*, 16 June 2023.

181 **kneeling in unison:** Williams, David. "Health Care Workers Are Taking a Knee for George Floyd." CNN, 5 June 2020.

181 **LRAD sound cannons:** Earplugs don't actually protect from RFID—you have to run very fast in the opposite direction or risk permanent hearing damage. Earplugs are for the general noise you might deal with before then. Wear earplugs anyway and consider that an RFID blaster can't work if it's broken or there is a plastic shield to bounce the sound off of. See: Moynihan, Collin. "NYPD to Limit Use of 'Sound Cannon' on Crowds After Protesters' Lawsuit." *New York Times*, 19 Apr. 2021.

182 **trans folks across America:** Trans Clippers Project. Imagine Water Works.

183 **total and perfect strangers:** Bed-Stuy Strong.

184 **taking bricks planted by the police:** Dupuy, Beatrice. "Bricks Become Fodder for False Claims around Protests." AP News, 5 June 2020.

185 **"the only unilateral power we have":** Cottom, Tressie McMillan. *Thick: And Other Essays*. New Press, 2019.

185 **military will be brought in to deal with protestors:** Cohn, Lindsay. "Trump Appears Likely to Call Military Force into US Cities. Can He Do That?" *Washington Post*, 20 June 2020.

187 **"the love of too much":** Hartman, Saidiya. *Wayward Lives, Beautiful Experiments*. W. W. Norton, 2019.

NEAR DEATH IS THE FATHER OF BEAUTY

189 **throughout a store:** Miyazaki, Mizuho. "Japan's Kose Develops Projection Mapping Simulator for Makeup." *Nikkei Asia*, 29 Jan. 2023.

189 **skincare recommendations:** Ferrer, Benjamin. "Smart Beauty: Brands Advance AI-Driven Platforms for Personalized Hair and Skin Analysis." Personal Care Insights, 19 Jan. 2023.

189 **biometric information:** Fang, Lee. "CIA's Venture Capital Arm Is Funding Skin Care Products That Collect DNA." *Intercept*, 8 Apr. 2016.

189 **"Under our skin":** Rutledge, Amelia. "Defining Cyberpunk."

George Mason University, 17 Jan. 2005. See also: Sterling, Bruce. Preface to *Mirrorshades*. Arbor House, 1986.

190 **a convention hotel:** BDYHAX. BodyHackingCon.com/Austin.

190 **ink that monitors your blood pressure:** Olsen, Karen. "Temporary 'Tattoos' That Measure Blood Pressure." National Institute of Biomedical Imaging and Bioengineering, 28 Nov. 2022.

190 **tattoos that claim to disappear within a year:** "How Ephemeral Ink Works." *Ephemeral Tattoo*. I will say that most of the people I know who have tried these tattoos still have them, more than a year later, and have required multiple tattoo sessions to remove them entirely. Not very ephemeral!

190 **to create Wi-Fi hotspots, too:** van Hooijdonk, Richard. "How the Internet of Bodies Is Redefining Human Connection." *Richard van Hooijdonk Blog*, 1 June 2024.

190 **artificial lungs and other modifications:** Madrigal, Alexis. "The Man Who First Said 'Cyborg,' 50 Years Later." *Atlantic*, 30 Sep. 2010.

190 **extend our normal reach:** Schussler, Aura Elena. Review of *We Have Always Been Cyborgs. Digital Data, Gene Technologies, and an Ethics of Transhumanism* by Stefan Lorenz Sorgner. Bristol University Press, 2022.

191 **gene editing:** Ranisch, Robert. "When CRISPR Meets Fantasy: Transhumanism and the Military in the Age of Gene Editing." *Transhumanism: The Proper Guide to a Posthuman Condition or a Dangerous Idea?*, edited by Wolfgang Hofkirchner and Hans-Jörg Kreowski. Springer International, 2021, pp. 111–20.

191 **Academics:** Kent, Chloe. "From Grinders to Biohackers: Where Medical Technology Meets Body Modification." Medical Technology, Issue 23, Jan. 2020.

191 **military researchers:** Bhuiyan, Johana. "Ukraine Uses Facial Recognition Software to Identify Russian Soldiers Killed in Combat." *Guardian*, 24 Mar. 2022.

191 **"deepfakes":** Deepfakes are a portmanteau of "deep learning" and "fake," and the victims include Donald Trump, Emma Watson, and now anyone who uses the Chinese-built Instagram app called ZAO. It allows you to superimpose any photo you choose onto scenes from famous movies, but ultimately it can be used on any kind of video.

192 **to help him move around:** "The Automatic Tripods of Hephaestus." Museum of the Ancient Greek Technology.

192 **CIA's venture capital arm:** It is not the first time the CIA has invested in DNA harvesting. They ran a fake hepatitis vaccination program

in Pakistan to collect DNA to hunt Osama bin Laden. Fake vaccination campaigns had been so rampant that the Taliban refused to let healthcare workers into Pakistan to vaccinate until drone strikes stopped. It worked, for a few years—and when polio cases rose again and the Taliban rescinded the threat, the drone strikes continued, and the killing of healthcare workers presumed to be spies resumed, too. See: Boone, Jon. "Taliban Leader Bans Polio Vaccinations in Protest at Drone Strikes." *Guardian*, 26 June 2012. See also: "How The CIA's Hunt For Bin Laden Impacted Public Health Campaigns in Pakistan." NPR. 6 Sept. 2021.

193 **Fast Company:** Raphael, Rina. "Why Clearista Is the CIA's Favorite Skin Care Product." *Fast Company*, 4 July 2016.

193 **"cosmeceuticals":** Technically the FDA does not recognize the term "cosmeceuticals," and states that any cosmetic that claims to provide qualities that cure anything will be regulated like a drug. Some products meet the definitions of both cosmetics and drugs, like an anti-dandruff shampoo. For products in this category, they'd have to meet the requirements for both categories to be FDA approved. See: Office of the Commissioner. FDA. "Cosmeceutical." Aug. 2024.

194 **transhumanist ventures:** Sample, Ian. "If They Could Turn Back Time: How Tech Billionaires Are Trying to Reverse the Ageing Process." *Guardian*, 17 Feb. 2022.

194 **Unity:** see: Sample, above.

194 **precisely this research:** Woldt, Jeffrey. "L'Oréal ACD's Fair Explores Skin Care Opportunities." *Chain Drug Review*, vol. 44, no. 3, 6 Feb. 2022, p. 12.

195 **1.2 billion euros on research:** "L'Oréal Annual Report—Beauty Born from Science." L'Oréal Finance, 2023.

195 **technological discoveries:** Janderson. "L'Oréal Paris Summit Reveals the Other Side of Product Science." Cosmetic Executive Women, 17 Jan. 2022.

195 **printing skin for cosmetic testing:** "BASF and Poietis Sign New Agreement on 3D Bioprinting Technology." BASF Press Release, 25 Oct. 2017.

196 **transhumanist project:** Regalado, Antonio. "The Transhumanists Who Want to Live Forever." *MIT Technology Review*, 16 Aug. 2019.

197 **6.6 years overall:** "Recent Widening of Racial Disparities in US Life Expectancy Was Largely Driven by COVID-19 Mortality." *KFF*, 23 May 2023.

NOTES

197 **life expectancy averages have rebounded:** "How Does US Life Expectancy Compare to Other Countries?" *KFF*, 30 Jan. 2024.

197 **fathers are inessential:** Haraway, Donna. "A Cyborg Manifesto: Science, Technology, and Socialist-Feminism in the Late 20th Century." *The International Handbook of Virtual Learning Environments*, edited by Joel Weiss et al., Springer Netherlands, 2006, pp. 117–58.

199 **transhumanists and artists in the world:** Jeffries, Stuart. "Neil Harbisson: The World's First Cyborg Artist." *Guardian*, 6 May 2014.

201 **life hacker, rock climber, cadaver:** Friend, Tad. "Silicon Valley's Quest to Live Forever." *The New Yorker*, 3 Apr. 2017.

204 **airlines break 29 wheelchairs every day:** Morris, John. "Checking in on Wheelchair Damage: How Airlines Are Doing." *Wheelchair Travel*, 25 Oct. 2023.

204 **Olympic medals:** Bushwick, Sophie. "How Paralympic Wheelchairs and Prostheses Are Optimized for Speed and Performance." *Scientific American*, 31 Aug. 2021.

205 **"sharks wouldn't have made me get out":** Weise, Cy. "Common Cyborg" *Granta*, 24 Sep. 2018.

205 **"temporary autonomous zones":** Bey, Hakim. "T.A.Z.: The Temporary Autonomous Zone, Ontological Anarchy, Poetic Terrorism." The Anarchist Library, 1985.

205 **Katia Vega:** Criado, Lula. "Katia Vega: Proposing New Ways of Interacting with the World." *Clot*, 20 Oct. 2016.

208 **"dark sousveillance":** Browne, Simone. *Dark Matters: On the Surveillance of Blackness*. Duke University Press, 2015.

208 **chip into his hand:** Griffiths, Meredith. "Biohacker Meow-Ludo Disco Gamma Meow-Meow Who Implanted Opal Card into Hand Escapes Conviction." ABC News, 17 June 2018.

208 **problems at hand:** Byrum, G., and Benjamin, R. Disrupting the Gospel of Tech Solutionism to Build Tech Justice. *Stanford Social Innovation Review*, 2022.

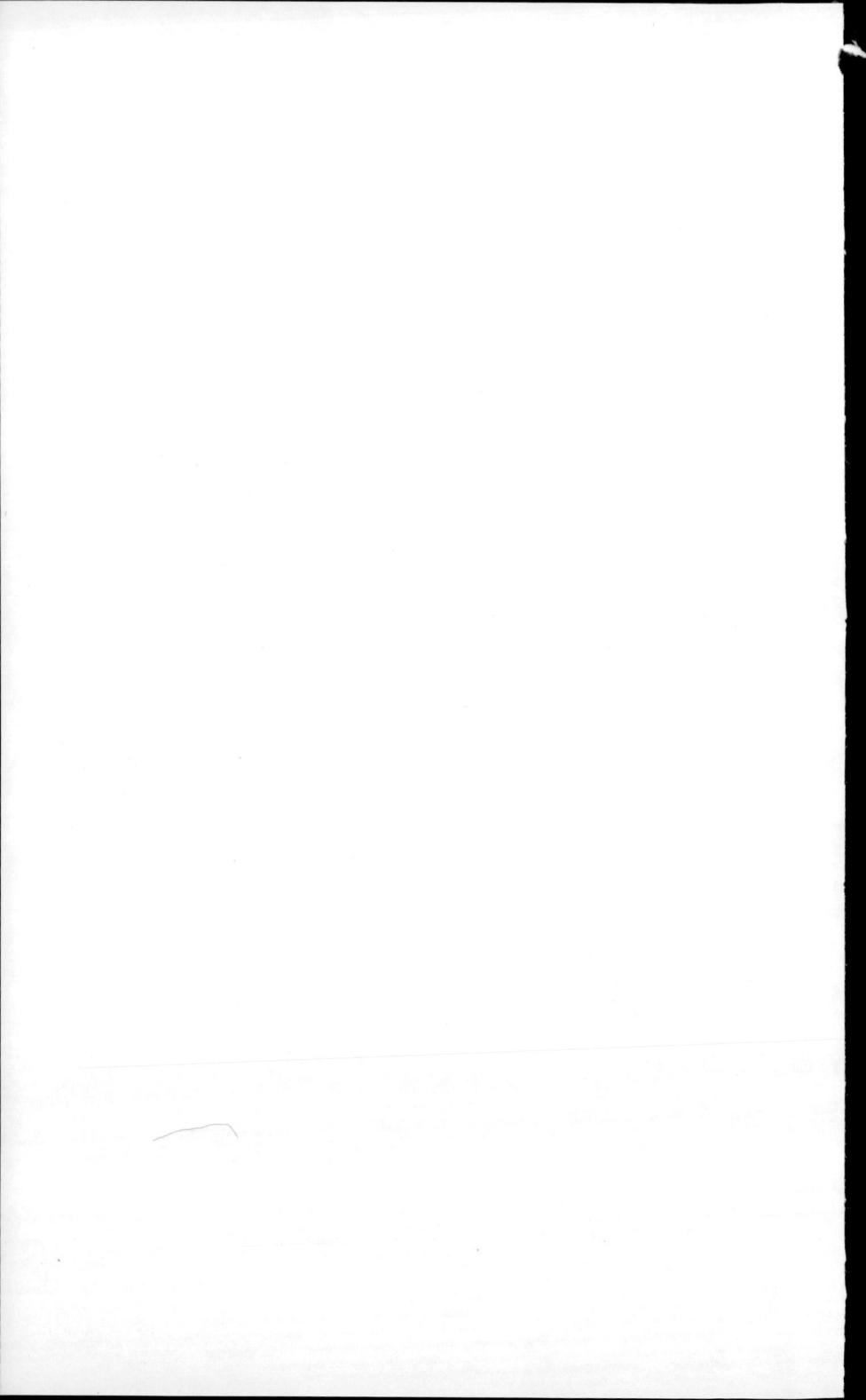